THE RELIGIOUS LIVES OF OLDER LAYWOMEN

The Religious Lives of Older Laywomen

The Last Active Anglican Generation

ABBY DAY

OXFORD
UNIVERSITY PRESS

OXFORD
UNIVERSITY PRESS

Great Clarendon Street, Oxford, OX2 6DP,
United Kingdom

Oxford University Press is a department of the University of Oxford.
It furthers the University's objective of excellence in research, scholarship,
and education by publishing worldwide. Oxford is a registered trade mark of
Oxford University Press in the UK and in certain other countries

First Edition published in 2017

Impression: 1

Published in the United States of America by Oxford University Press
198 Madison Avenue, New York, NY 10016, United States of America

British Library Cataloguing in Publication Data

Data available

Library of Congress Control Number: 2016949770

ISBN 978-0-19-873958-6

Printed in Great Britain by
Clays Ltd, St Ives plc

For my mother

Preface

This book has been several years in the making, from the time in 2009 that I first proposed it for funding, through to the fieldwork on which it is based, and the many talks, presentations, and work-in-progress publications. During that time I have received helpful encouragement and constructive feedback from an enormous variety of people, not least the women I studied. There have been colleagues, conference delegates, editors, friends, family (and thanks to my children, Jake and Alex, for their patience in being dragged around churches wherever we happened to be!), and often complete strangers who happened to hear about my work and wanted to talk about it. The wonderful response I received from them kept me energized and enthusiastic. Like me, they realized that there was no in-depth record of this unusual and yet taken-for-granted generation, often known as 'the backbone of the church' or 'the silver ladies' or 'the tea-makers' or the 'brass polishers'.

To begin to thank everyone is a daunting task, as even the small comment or two at a conference, or the telling anecdote at a social event, have all enriched my understanding. I will limit myself to only a handful of people, and apologize to anyone I have not included by name.

First, to Simon Coleman who encouraged me from the beginning, and reassured me, at the end, that there often is no end because all research based on people is ultimately about relationality; and to Grace Davie, whose enthusiasm and interest never wavered and who understood about the complexity of research relationships, also gave me a good piece of advice: be careful not to lose the detail of the ethnography in the act of creating theory. I hope I have accomplished that. Jay Demerath cheered me on, and offered advice and wisdom. Matthew Engelke helped me shape the project by advising me to keep it focused on a single institution. That was excellent advice as I had been tempted to spread the theme across other religions, as I know similar dynamics occur there, but the work would have lost in depth what it gained in breadth. Gordon Lynch, whose advice and direction throughout helped me focus and not lose my nerve, was also instrumental in helping me pull together a fine group of scholars at our symposium in Canterbury.

I am grateful to the many professional staff in churches and at Church House who provided key resources, background briefings, and advice, particularly Anne Richards and Bev Botting. Paul Bramadat and colleagues at the Center for Studies in Religion and Society at the University of Victoria in Canada provided a warm place and a creative, stimulating environment for me to visit as a Research Fellow in the summer of 2014. And, thanks to Simon Blundell for advice on historical aspects and resources.

Other colleagues I would like to thank for their time and advice include those who formed the initial advisory group to help frame the project and its method and were available for advice and ideas as it began: Eileen Barker, Fenella Cannell, Sylvia Collins-Mayo, Helen Cameron, Kirk Hadaway, Tim Ling, Charles Kadushin, Ariela Keysar, Sarah Lloyd, Penny Marler, Linda Woodhead, and David Voas. Partway through the project Gordon Lynch and I organized a two-day symposium to discuss the Anglican Communion, including its women, and those who attended provided fascinating papers and also feedback on my own work. Several people who could not attend later contributed chapters to our edited collection. For all their contributions that help me put my study in the context of the Anglican Communion and the wider social context I would like to thank Anna Strhan, Gemma Penny, Michael Kennan, Diane Rees, Adrian Stringer, Anderson H. M. Jeremiah, Joanne McKenzie, Andrew McKinnon, Nancy Nason-Clark, Leslie Francis, Catherine Holtmann, Martyn Percy, Callum Brown, and Bev Skeggs.

In 2010, several close colleagues joined me on a panel I organized at the annual conference of the Society for the Social Scientific Study of Religion (SSSR), under the title 'Exploring the Gender Gap: Why Women May Be More Religious/Spiritual Than Men'. That was the first time I tried out some of my arguments concerning the apparent imbalance of religiosity, particularly concerning risk theory. I am grateful to the SSSR for funding, and to my dear friends and colleagues for participating with me as we moved against the flow: Charles Kadushin, Ariela Keysar, Adam Klin-Oron, and Bethamie Horowitz.

I thank the Economic and Social Research Council for funding the project, and its anonymous reviewers for providing constructive and generous feedback. To Oxford University Press, and particularly Commissioning Editor Tom Perridge and Assistant Commissioning Editor Karen Raith: thank you for the opportunity to work with you again and for the close care and attention that is paid to the review, editorial, production, and marketing processes. The anonymous reviewers who provided detailed comment have helped make this, I hope, a strong publication.

To the many Generation A women who shared their time, opinions, stories, and skills, I can't thank you enough or even, as we agreed, name you or your churches publicly. All names and several markers of identity have been changed, but you know who you are.

Finally, and most importantly, I dedicate this book to my mother, Gwen Day, a consummate woman of Generation A. Like most women of my age, I have not met the high religious standards of her generation, but I thank her for believing in me anyway.

Contents

Section I

Roots and Branches

The first two chapters are designed to show how the women studied here are located both spatially and temporally. The Anglican Communion is the international body to which most of the churches discussed here belong, and the time period the women share of post-war challenges and possibilities have shaped them as a 'generation'.

1

Introduction

The Anglican Church was conceived through the love for a woman. Since then, women have formed the heart and soul, but not the head, of the Church throughout its history; from the moment King Henry VIII fell in love with Anne Boleyn to contemporary schisms over women priests and bishops. Hervé Picton (2015, 1) notes that the English Church's final break with the Church of Rome in 1534 was not only about Henry's love life:

> Indeed, the Church in England had long been estranged from the papacy when King Henry ascended the throne. Long before the 16th century it had acquired a distinct national character partly due to its insularity.

And yet, despite their prominence in church politics and power struggles, in-depth knowledge about the everyday experiences of laywomen remain remarkably absent from the record.[1] As Prelinger remarked (1992, 3) 'Oddly, few so far have addressed the situation of women in the mainline or asked what it may have to tell us about the mainline's widely analyzed "decline".'

One reason for the gap in knowledge about women is methodological. The Church of England, in common with other national churches, has never collected statistics about gender. Large-scale data about women in the Anglican Communion and, more generally, Christianity is therefore limited to inferences based on other surveys. The churches I studied were all part of the worldwide Anglican Communion and the women were the laywomen I call Generation

---

[1] Earlier drafts of portions of this chapter and book have been discussed at conferences such as the ISSR 2011, Socrel 2012, and through publication in Day 2015a, 2015b; Day and Lövheim 2015.

A: the predecessors, and often the mothers, of the post-war generation, the 'baby-boomers', and many were grandmothers and great-
grandmothers of the so-called generations X, Y, and Z.
They belong to the Church of England, the core institution at the focus of this
work, part of the international, colonial-era inspired loose network of
churches created in 1867, where three-quarters are in former colonies. Colonialism still marks the religious landscapes of the Global
South, as Jeremiah (2015, 191) described:

> Nevertheless, the complex socio-cultural make-up of South Asia offers a
> challenging context to situate the life and work of the Anglican Church.
> India, Pakistan and Sri Lanka are characterised by complicated socio-
> religious landscape, with overwhelming religious majority and minority
> communities, compounded by ethnic, linguistic and regional differ-
> ences. These differences are often corroborated and shaped by the
> region's colonial history, be it the ethnic conflict between Sinhalese
> and Tamils in Sri Lanka or Caste-based social discrimination in the
> Indian subcontinent.

The worldwide Anglican Communion thus provides a background
international story for Generation A, sometimes speaking to issues of
mission, power, sexuality, and gender. The Communion also has
particular significance for the women being studied, as I will discuss
in detail in the next chapter when I consider their shared generational
imaginary.

In their book *Why are Women more Religious than Men?*
Trzebiatowska and Bruce (2012, 3) begin by noting that evidence
on national churches is scant and therefore their evidence will be
based on statistical evidence from secondary data (surveys and censuses) and statistics gained from Nonconformist and other sects. The
omission from the record of the two UK national churches, the
Church of England and Church of Scotland is glaring: there is not
even mention of those churches in the index. Their chapters explore
gender through non-mainstream movements such as new religions,
spirituality, and Pentecostalism.

As the American research centre Pew presented in March 2016, the
question of greater female than male participation in religion only
applies to Christianity in the West. The Pew report explains:[2]

---

[2] <http://www.pewresearch.org/fact-tank/2016/03/24/a-religious-gender-gap-for-
christians-but-not-for-muslims/>, last accessed 5.4.2016.

One of the most striking findings in a new Pew Research Center analysis of survey and census data on gender and religion is that while Christian women are on the whole more religious than Christian men, Muslim women and Muslim men have similar levels of religious commitment. And when it comes to attendance at worship services, Muslim men are more active than Muslim women.

That same point was made by Walter and Davie (1998) nearly two decades earlier, when they wrote their formative paper about women and religiosity in 1998 which specifically focused on 'why women belong in large numbers to mainline, patriarchal religion' (Walter and Davie 1998, 641). And yet church officials and academics have known for decades that first-hand, primary research on gender in the national churches was lacking. For example, an edited collection about the Anglican Communion did not include any chapters about laywomen (Wingate et al. 1998). One chapter titled 'Five Years In: Where are the Women in the Church of England' tells only the story of women priests (Pemberton and Rees 1998, 22–6). A report commissioned by the think-tank Respublica, in 2013,[3] showed that the majority of voluntary church activities consisted of 'Promoting Church, e.g. Coffee Mornings'. No further detail was given in the report about those activities or, significantly, the people who organized them. As I will show in this book, the 'people' are women of Generation A. The neglect of that cohort fits a general pattern.

As Davie wrote in 1990 and again in 1994 about religion in general, although there were large data sets available, and some small studies about the 'exotic edges' of religion in Britain, 'the picture in the middle remains alarmingly blurred', with very little known about 'the beliefs of ordinary British people in everyday life' (Davie 1994, 6). As national churches and academics have not collected statistics about gender, one wonders if they only count what counts? In the next chapter I will review in more detail the explanations academics have given about reasons for the apparent gender disparity, and offer some thoughts about how those explanations reify essentialist notions of women and religiosity.

My work here, in contrast, attempts to make visible the invisible by focusing on a particular cohort known to be the most active in mainstream Christianity. It is not a study of 'ageing' but of a certain

[3] <http://www.respublica.org.uk/our-work/publications/holistic-mission-social-action-church-england/>, last accessed 30.1.2016.

generation generally described as 'the backbone of the church'; a generation that is dying, that has not been researched in depth, and will not, I argue, be replaced. The gender/age component is therefore critically important in terms of the mainstream churches' decline. Writing about the UK religious landscape in 1994, Davie (1994, 2) made two statements that caught my imagination when I conducted my doctoral research nearly a decade later:

> The churches attract an audience which is disproportionately elderly, female and conservative [. . .] the nature of family life, including the traditional codes of morality, are altering rapidly [. . .] Changes in gender roles have for better or for worse, penetrated the churches and influenced theological thinking.

The women of Generation A were in their sixties when she wrote this, and were then witnessing the kinds of changes she was writing about. Davie's source was primarily the European Values Survey, a large quantitative data set. The problem with those data and related methods lay, as she noted, in a preference for that which was easily defined and measured. As McGuire (2008, 5) commented when describing her preferred approach to studying lived religion, quantitative data on their own are of dubious value.

The most common reason for church decline is the demographic profile. When elderly churchgoers die, they are not being replaced by the next generation, and nor are they attracting or retaining children or teenagers. A consultancy project commissioned by the Church of England and carried out during the same period as my research was tasked to identify factors affecting church growth and to make recommendations for increasing it. They concluded that:[4]

> In nearly half of our churches there are fewer than five under 16s. On the positive side, the research highlights that churches where there is a high ratio of children to adults are twice as likely to be growing; There is an urgent need to focus on children, young people and their parents and a challenge to identify how the church can best invest in people, programmes and strategies which will encourage young people actively to continue exploring faith.

While that recommendation is unsurprising, and reflects the general advice I have heard in every church I have studied, it is implausible.

---

[4] <http://www.churchgrowthresearch.org.uk/UserFiles/File/Reports/FromAnecdote ToEvidence1.0.pdf>, 26, last accessed 1.10.15.

It contradicts generally accepted social theory (Voas and Crockett 2005): religious activity is stable,[5] closely tied to generational effects, and every contemporary generation in the UK is less religious than the one before. I will argue that social and cultural shifts, combined with the Church's intransigence on significant moral issues, resulted in alienating the sons and daughters of Generation A—the baby-boomers, born in the late 1940s. The Church lost that middle generation and, consequentially, their children, the X, Y, and Millennials. And so, I contend, it ends. Children are unlikely to arrive at a church door on their own. Further, the Church alienated women in particular, a dangerous move considering that most research also shows that mothers are more important than fathers for religious transmission.

In November 2015, launching a programme to reverse church decline, the Church of England's director of finance, John Spence, said that the evidence for decline was 'indisputable':[6]

> Twenty years ago the demographics matched the population as a whole. Now we're 20 years older than the population. Unless we do something, the church will face a real crisis.

While I agree that the evidence is clear, I will be less optimistic that the church can reverse such a trend. In the chapters to follow, the picture I create is one of an institution not simply divided by an age gap, but by significant values and practices. Again, the importance of those differences has not, I will argue, been fully researched or appreciated. For example, Picton (2015, vii) situates his detailed history book in the realm of hierarchal and institutional power and admits that, while 'One might also regret the scant treatment of clergy and parish life', the historical record is necessary to understand current trends and issues. His summary of the issues focuses on the now-familiar list (2015, 2):

> the ordination of female bishops, homosexuality, and other ethical or societal issues. More generally, its role in an increasingly secular society is being questioned.

---

[5] I will return to this point in Chapter 9, as the stability of religious identity (see, in particular, Wink and Dillon 2003 for longitudinal evidence) makes it unlikely that the church will recruit otherwise non-religious converts.

[6] <http://www.theguardian.com/world/2015/nov/21/justin-welby-church-england-new-synod>, last accessed 8.9.2016.

Some, inside and outside the Church, have even called for its disestab-lishment, arguing that it is no longer a national Church.

Those issues are, I will argue, symptoms rather than causes of what is an inevitable, irreversible, decline embedded more in 'parish life' than peer politics. A closer inspection of parish life reveals important characteristics, which is why this book draws on ethnographic field-work, cross-cultural comparisons, and relevant theories exploring the beliefs, identities, and practices of the women I refer to as 'Generation A'. Although many religious organisations share the same age profile, I have chosen to focus specifically on Anglican laywoman born in the 1920s and early 1930s, now in their eighties and nineties, often described as the 'backbone' of the Church, and likely, I will argue, to be its last active generation. The prevalence of laywomen in mainstream Christian congregations is a widely accepted phenom-enon that will cause little surprise amongst the research community or Christian adherents. What is surprising is that we know so little about them, and therefore about how their beliefs, behaviours, and patterns of religiosity can inform us about the character and changing nature of contemporary and future religion. This is the generation that has sometimes been seen to lead a parallel church. They attend the mainstream churches every Sunday, polish the brasses, organise fund-raisers, keep the church open on weekdays, bake cakes, and visit vulnerable people in their homes. Their often invisible labour not only populates the physical space of the church but helps ensure its continuity and enriches surrounding communities.

For the purpose of this book I will describe the women I studied as 'Anglican', following Livingstone (1977, 21): those belonging to churches which are 'in communion with, and recognising the lead-ership of, the see of Canterbury'. For many Generation A women, the Anglican term meant almost literally 'English', with all its historical and symbolic meanings, and warm associations with the ultimate woman of their generation, Queen Elizabeth II. I will review that relationship in more depth in the Chapter 2.

The development and decline of the worldwide Anglican Commu-nion followed the course of the development and decline of British colonies, particularly understood according to Mann's (2012, 91) analysis of power, where he argued that power is not a resource, but should be analysed in terms of overlapping networks. Resources might emerge as a means to attaining and maintaining power, he argued, defined as the capacity to organize and control people through organization, control, logistics, and communication. His four types of social power can be related directly both to the decline of the British Empire and the worldwide Anglican Communion: ideological, economic, military, political relationships.

Generation A's contribution to the continuation of the worldwide Anglican Communion was to sustain its ideology through participating in the services and prayers that explicitly named and bonded its members and through supporting mission and exchange. As the main fundraisers, they often supported members of the Communion and their communities through direct economic contributions. In the chapters that follow, I will describe in detail how they did that, and why successive generations are not, and likely will not, follow their example. First, I will turn to the means by which I produced my data and interpretations.

METHOD

Thanks to funding from the Economic and Research Council, I was able to enrich the story of those women through a study carried out, half-time, over two years. My objective was to begin by immersing myself in the daily routines of one mainstream Anglican church in southern England, where I would identify key themes. I would then broaden and interrogate those themes by comparing them through study visits to other UK and international churches. In total, I attended sixty-four services and visited eighteen churches. In my 'host' church I was also involved throughout the week in non-service events, of which my regular participation in twenty-five 'church watch/opening' duties were the most regular.

Every researcher makes choices about method. Ideally, these choices should be provoked by the research question. As Davie, mentioned earlier (1994, 6), pointed out, 'the picture in the middle remains remarkably blurred' with little known about 'ordinary British people'. Writing more than twenty years before my study was to begin, Davie pointed out that although there were large data sets available, and some small studies about the 'exotic edges' of religion in Britain, 'the picture in the middle remains alarmingly blurred' with very little known about 'the beliefs of ordinary British people in everyday life' (Davie 1994, 6).

It was that single phrase that drove my research questions then as now: what do ordinary people believe in everyday life, and how do we find out? The question was fraught with difficulty: what is meant by ordinary and everyday? Who does this include and exclude? Describing my research as 'everyday' and fitting within a broader method of 'anthropology at home' does not excuse me from casting my research informants as 'other'. The 1980s' critique in anthropology about the propensity to study the 'other' as simply, if implicitly, constituted as distant and primitive (encapsulated by Trouillot (1991) as 'the savage slot') sparked new moves to study anthropology closer to 'home'. George Marcus (1995) provoked researchers to think about multi-sited ethnography as a technique to break the fetishization of the far-away field, focusing not on territorial place but on an ethnographic theme or topic that often transcended place. This observation informed my own research design, a dialectic between 'home-place' peopled by a few handfuls of informants I came to know well, and several other sites created through purposive sampling according to emerging themes. The challenges of studying people in one's immediate society is aptly described by Buch and Staller (2014, 112) as an attempt by 'Native' ethnographers to 'denaturalize taken-for-granted aspects of their own social worlds'. The subjective sense of what is taken for granted therefore depends on ethnographers' ability to use themselves as instruments of knowledge-gathering, staying attuned to 'their own culturally conditioned common sense' (Buch and Staller 2014, 108).[7]

During the course of my research, I was to reflect often on the realization that I did not have to travel far to experience the 'other'. Most of the people I met during my daily research encounters were different from me in outlook, age, and national history. Further, it helped me realize the effect of locality and how any one church is a contextualized social institution that to some extent reflects its surroundings. Knowing, over time, who belonged, who did not, and who perhaps nearly did helped me realize that the congregation both

---

[7] One of the most distinctive qualities of feminist ethnography is the emphasis on long-term relationships in the research, they say (2014, 108). While this certainly chimes with my own experience, I think it is fair to point out that long-term research practice is also a feature of the classic anthropological method.

encourages and filters out strangers. In reviewing Trouillot's contribution to anthropology, Robbins (2013, 449) said that the shift in place reflected a more general acknowledgement of:

> transformations in this broader symbolic organization that defines the West and the savage, transformations by which the narratives of development and progress that had driven Western history were beginning to lose their power to organize our understanding of the world.

Robbins claims (2013, 450) that a new 'other' has emerged in anthropology, that of the 'suffering subject', and calls for a new kind of anthropology that focuses both on the vulnerability that all we as humans share, and considers how the people we study 'organize their personal and collective lives in order to foster what they think of as good, and to study what it is like to live at least some of the time in light of such a project' (Robbins 2013, 455). It gradually became evident to me that my enquiry was not focusing so much on the theologies of the women, but on my growing fascination with how they constructed their lives to do what they perceived to be good.

In my earlier research, when I wanted to find out how people described their beliefs and why they self-identified as Christian on the UK decennial census, it was appropriate to ask them in such a way that would not skew the conversation immediately to religious categories. My critique of surveys thus far had concluded that forming the research around pre-existing religious definitions only helped to funnel the responses into predetermined routes. My task then was to design a method, and questions, that did not select people on the basis of their adherence to or rejection of religion, or to ask them using vocabulary that rested on assumptions about what religion, belief, or Christianity meant to people. It was inappropriate to do so through a formal, closed-question survey because the vocabulary itself was unknown and untested. Researching religion without asking religious questions was the challenge, and one to which I responded in various ways, which are described in detail elsewhere (Day 2009b, 2011 [2013]).

The research questions concerning my study described here were not about why the women would self-identify as Christian on a census, nor about how they would describe their religious beliefs. Rather, I wanted to find out more about who they were in the context of their occupation of an unusual set of church-attending women, what they did, how they did it, and what difference it might make when they disappeared. What did they know about being regular church-attending women? What kinds of knowing were important to the richness of their experience and those in the congregation and, perhaps, the wider community? What were their habits and techniques of acquiring and performing that knowledge, and how, if at all, had that knowledge been transferred to future generations? The kind of knowledge they had would be, I assumed, situated, relational, everyday, lived, and embodied. From my previous work on belief I was aware that just as there were different forms of belief, there would also be different forms of knowledge. Having already made the case for multidimensional, felt, embodied belief along with forms of propositional or creedal belief (Day 2013f), it was likely that I would find belief and knowledge embedded together, rather than produced in a parallel sequence or in some kind of conflict. Such research would depend on the ethnographic method, set in the context of everyday, lived religion. The effect of using such a method to create fine-grained studies will, I hope, be seen to be particularly useful for researchers in the sociology of religion, ageing and religion, and feminist research into older women's religious lives.

Being There

The American Anthropology Association (AAA) describes ethnography as 'the researcher's study of human behaviour in the natural settings in which people live'.[8] I therefore chose to observe women in their 'natural setting' of their church. Further, the AAA definition describes ethnography as producing a 'description of cultural systems or an aspect of culture based on fieldwork in which the investigator is immersed in the ongoing everyday activities of the designated community'.

Bielo (2015) explores how religious ethnography poses distinctive issues. He asks how we manage the intense relationships we forge through fieldwork alongside our scholarly research goals. What does it mean to do participant observation, a hallmark of ethnography, in religious settings where the stakes of participation can be especially

---

[8] <http://research.fiu.edu/documents/irb/documents/ethnographyReview.pdf>, last accessed 2.2.2016.

high? What, if anything, is compromised or gained when a researcher finds personal value in the religion that they are in the field to learn about? What is the proper place, if any place at all, for notions such as 'objectivity' or 'bias' in doing religious ethnography? (Bielo 2015, 30). He succinctly describes ethnography as 'being there, wherever there is' (Bielo 2015, 31).

Brewer (2000, 6) picks up the same themes, describing ethnography as:

> the study of people in naturally occurring settings or 'fields' by methods of data collection which capture their social meanings and ordinary activities, involving the researcher participating directly in the setting, if not also the activities, in order to collect data in a systematic manner but without meaning being imposed on them externally.

Those intentions have met, over time, with significant critiques whether from a 'positivist' or natural science quarter (for an extensive review, see Hammersley and Atkinson 1995, 1–26) summarized by Brewer (2000, 20):

> Ethnography also breaches dearly held principles in science concerning the nature of data. The natural science model of social research seeks to describe and measure social phenomena, but both description and measurement are achieved by assigning numbers to the phenomena. In short, it deals with quantity and collects numerate data. Ethnography also describes and measures, but it does so by means of extracts of natural language (long quotations from interviews, extracts from field notes, snippets from personal documents) and deals with quality and meaning [...]

Not only can ethnographers become 'too subjective', but they can recognize themselves as an important tool of data collection—possibly, I will argue, as important as a notebook or recorder. As Brewer points out (2000, 20):

> The natural science model of research does not permit the researcher to become a variable in the experiment, yet ethnographers are not detached from the research but, depending on the degree of involvement in the setting, are themselves part of the study or by their obtrusive presence come to influence the field.

I would also add to his observation that ethnographers do not visit a field; they create it. Ethnographic fieldwork is often said to be the *sine qua non* of anthropology, and what distinguishes it from other disciplines such as sociology or human geography. As anthropologists Gupta and Ferguson described it (1997, 1):

> The single most significant factor determining whether a piece of research will be accepted as (that magical word) 'anthropological' is the extent to which it depends on experience 'in the field'.

Anthropologists have also recognized that one site or location would not be a self-sufficient, bounded container of cultural knowledge and practice that can be studied in isolation. As Coleman and Collins point out (2006, 5), the 'field' is not a place waiting to be discovered, but a construction where researchers map:

> certain understandings of culture and theoretical concern on to regions, thus naturalizing their subsequent 'discovery' or elucidation by the ethnographer. Such processes of cultural cartography have reflected and reinforced the colonial legacies of the discipline.

Not being unique to anthropology, fieldwork became progressively something fiercely protected by the discipline, they suggest, creating increasingly more difficult and remote excursions to exotic locations generally inaccessible to those from competing disciplines of, say, human geography, and marking the anthropologist as someone different from, and implicitly superior to, even the most intrepid tourist. In their process of deconstructing such terms as field and place, Coleman and Collins remind us that the spatial metaphors and related language we use reveals much about our implicit assumptions. 'Field', of course, is easily construed as a physical place bounded by a fence, neatly described in maps, set apart from other 'fields', and properly inhabited by non-roaming entities such as sheep and, presumably, people. If people do leave such fields they inhabit another bounded place called 'diaspora', itself another metaphor presuming a distant and fragmented movement from the original, intact, 'field'.

Being Where?

Conventionally, anthropologists have often created more than one field site for the purpose of comparisons, but Marcus (1995, 102) suggested a multi-sited ethnography would go beyond simple comparison by referring to:

> an emergent object of study whose contours, sites, and relationships are not known beforehand, but are themselves a contribution of making an

account that has different, complexly connected real-world sites of investigation. The object of study is ultimately mobile and multiply situated, so any ethnography of such an object will have a comparative dimension.

He therefore suggests (Marcus 1995, 105) that such a method needs to be:

designed around chains, paths, threads, conjunctions, or juxtapositions of locations in which the ethnographer establishes some form of literal, physical presence, with an explicit, posited logic of association or connection among sites that in fact defines the argument of the ethnography.

In the case to be presented here of Generation A, I began with the assumption that there were physical places where Generation A religious laywomen would be studied, and that their presence there would be explicitly linked to wider connections within the Anglican Communion. That assumption provided one of the logics of the design and the foundational argument: here was a generation linked by time and places in a particular form of religiosity: Anglicanism. As I followed the threads of their practices and relationships through the UK and elsewhere, I realized more than I had anticipated the importance of 'nation' for these women in Anderson's (1991) sense of an imagined community, and the lack of importance, apart from competitor concerns, of nearby churches. That awareness reinforced for me the notion that beyond a fixed 'place' there is 'space', a realm of both materiality and immateriality, produced by social relationships (Lefebrve 1991; Massey 2005).

As ethnography involves studying the natural settings in which people live, it was important for me to choose a host church that could be accessed frequently so that I could observe the women's activities as unobtrusively as possible. I also wanted to study a church that was more mainstream than evangelical. After a few weeks browsing local churches, I found one that seemed ideal. It had a typically sized congregation of thirty to forty regulars, the age profile matched what seemed to be the norm for Anglican churches—mostly over fifty and with a concentration of elderly women. Once I had decided to study it, I introduced myself to the priest and explained what I wanted: an opportunity to attend services regularly and become a working member of the congregation. Given the research ethics that govern contemporary research, I also needed the congregation as a whole to understand what I was doing, so that I was not conducting covert research. We agreed that at the next Sunday service he would introduce me as a researcher and I would make a brief statement about my intentions. I would leave sheets of paper at the rear of the church with a summary of my research intentions, my contact details, and a section of the form where they could explicitly request that they opted out. On the appointed day, we did as planned and I stayed after the service to mingle with the congregation over refreshments and discuss my role and work. No one opted out, and my practice of staying behind every Sunday to discuss with people my role as a researcher was important to ensure that I maintained a practice of informed consent. Over time, as I will discuss in the following chapters, my requests to be involved in various roles and 'duties' at that church and others were met with good grace and, even, enthusiasm. Immersion in their community thus developed over the two years of my project, making it rich in depth and difficult to leave.

Living Every Day

Being immersed in the women's church life required an orientation to the 'every day', partly literal, partly symbolic, and partly hermeneutic. Most of the women's involvement happens on every day but on a Sunday, and yet it is 'Sunday' that usually captures the attention of statisticians and clergy. Once again, I will suggest we may have different views of what counts. The symbolic meaning of 'everyday' signals the deeply embodied, habituated, routine experience of being a Generation A laywoman. Ammerman (2007, 5) developed the idea of the 'everyday' as a way of privileging the experience of laypeople, the 'nonexperts, the people who do not make a living being religious or thinking and writing about religious ideas'. This was an important sociological move, not because scholars had neglected researching everyday religion; anthropology has historically always done so.[9] Further, the 'everyday' offers a hermeneutic, a way to interpret and analyse social worlds.

---

[9] Stephen Hunt (2014, 160) mentions in his review of Schielke and Debevec's edited collection that 'there is a tendency (although this is not the case with all the chapters), also evident in similar books, that in claiming to break new ground authors often neglect to engage with older anthropological themes and the well-established relevant literature'.

In the Editors' Introduction to 'Sociologies of Everyday Life', a special issue of *Sociology*, Neal and Murji (2015, 813) write that it is through the micro study of the 'everyday' that researchers become aware of how:

> the micro, the slight, the most mundane and the banally ordinary practices, emotions, social relationships and interactions also reflect convergences with and manifestations of wider social factors, forces, structures and divisions.

Writing in the same issue, Back (2015, 820) suggests that 'the value of thinking about the everyday is that it signals the routine and unfolding aspects of social life'. The lived, everyday experience of doing ethnography was performed through three technologies: participant observation, conversation, and reflexivity. As Ortner observed (1995, 173), 'minimally (ethnography) has always meant the attempt to understand another life world using the self—as much of it as possible—as the instrument of knowing'.

The method for that research therefore needed to be one that allowed me close observation of the women and myself, and close conversation. Few of those conversations corresponded to what might generally be understood as an 'interview' as they tended to be long conversations conducted as we carried out our tasks of, for example, cleaning or serving. I had assumed I would conduct formal, recorded interviews with all my informants; in practice this was unachievable. They largely resisted that format, preferring to chat as we worked together, and the few opportunities that arose then were complicated by my own participation as vegetable peeler, dishwasher, and kettle-boiler. All the formal interviews I created were in the second stage of the research, when core themes had been identified, and I directly approached women in other churches. In total I conducted sixty-two structured or semi-structured 'conversations' of which nineteen were formal 'interviews'. These do not include the informal, casual conversations that continued throughout the project.

Reflecting on how social scientific knowledge about interviews has changed over time, Gubrium and Holstein (2003, 3), describe how interviews were once seen as neutral events amongst strangers where distance and structure were maintained. Mirroring postmodern sensibilities, however, they note that:

> Standardized representation has given way to representational invention, where the dividing line between fact and fiction is blurred to

encourage richer understanding. Reflexivity, poetics, and power [italics theirs] are the watchwords as the interview process is refracted though the lenses of language, knowledge, culture and difference.

In their chapter on revisiting the relationship between participant observation and interviewing, Atkinson and Coffey argue (2003, 110) that participant observation and interviewing should not be seen as occupying different spheres: 'Social life is performed and narrated, and we need to recognize the performative qualities of social life and talk.' The talk of an interview is a kind of action and itself performative, as I argued in previous work (Day 2011 [2013]) about how people brought certain kinds of identity and relationships into being through talking about it.

Probably the best-known critique mounted against the conventional practice of interviewing was Oakley's (1981) exploration of the practice in the context of her interviews with pregnant women. What she found, as suggested in her book's subtitle, was a 'contradiction in terms'. The main problem, she argued, is that interviewing arose from a masculinist viewpoint that privileges such notions of objectivity and distance. Further, the mystification of interviewing again reflects a masculinist orientation in contrast, she argues, to a feminist philosophy of openness and collaboration: 'Very few sociologists who employ interview data actually bother to describe in detail the process of interviewing itself' (Oakley 1981, 31). Oakley was concerned with the ethics and power of interviewing, noting that what is good for the interviewer is not necessarily good for the person being interviewed.

Nearly forty years later, Oakley (2016) and a team of researchers created a research project to reconnect with the women who had been interviewed. That project gave Oakley an opportunity to reflect both on the academic reaction to her original work and the women's recollection of it (Oakley 2016, 196). One of her reflections most relevant for my work was that she had originally underestimated the power and nuances of the friendships that were created and sometimes sustained as a result of her research. As I discuss throughout this book, a sense of genuine warmth and friendship that emerged both from me and the women I studied complicated and also enriched the study. Oakley also considers the notion of the 'gift', following Mauss (1954), as an act, she argues, of unconditionality, to which I will add through my reading of Mauss, implied reciprocity.

In her wide-ranging study of religion and spirituality in the contemporary United States, Ammerman (2014, 13) proposed that researchers must:

> go beyond questions that presume an existing range of responses and questions that ask for conceptual and categorical answers—all the more so when religious and spiritual categories are being culturally redefined.

Her methods were designed to get to the stories and practices that had spiritual significance for research participants. A life-story interview was only the first step in more detailed explorations of people's lives. Participants were given a camera to capture scenes they thought of as significant, and asked to keep a diary noting significant moments and events. Members of the research team accompanied the participants in a variety of settings. Ammerman notes that this method did not represent ethnography in its classic, immersed sense, but allowed important insights into the participants' worlds. She explains that (Ammerman 2014, 15) 'One cannot study the practices of everyday life without paying attention to the places in which those practices are entangled'. In trying to capture people's stories without imposing preconceived categories or terminologies, Ammerman and her researchers followed a method similar to the one I created in my own research (Day, 2009a) to research religion and belief without asking religious questions. She did not avoid the terms of religious, spiritual, or sacred, but rather asked participants to use them in their own ways while telling their stories. When the terms arose, researchers later analysed those sections as 'sacred stories'.

There has been a shift away from the notion that objectivity was impossible in social science to the realization that subjectivity is not only inevitable but desirable in all stages of the research process. This is now a well-rehearsed discussion which I do not intend to repeat here, apart from signalling that when my ethnographic writing reflects on my own responses and perceptions, this is not a lapse but an intentional device.

Analysing emotional responses recognizes their weight combined with the body and mind as data gatherer and analyst. It helped me sense my reaction to strangers, recognize the impact of speech acts, and feel the pain of leaving the group. All groups maintain boundaries to entry. Ethnography permits the researcher to sense, both by the first stage of being a stranger, and by observing from the perspective of one who gradually becomes more intimate, the subtle ways in which insiders and outsiders are recognized and boundaries maintained, filtering out the strangers. The process of ethnography is, implicitly at least, predicated on a process of belonging. The stages I experienced and later theorized in this book were:

1. Recognition
2. Social intimacy
3. Integration
4. Routinization
5. Obligation
6. Ritualization
7. Internalization

The real benefit of ethnography, however, comes with time. By spending time with the same people, in the same place, doing what they do with them, the ethnographer can acquire a number of sensitivities, particularly in relation to who belongs (and how insiders filter out those who do not), what and why some things change, what people regularly talk about, and therefore what really matters to them, the relevance of the initial research questions, the role of the body and emotion as equivalent to the mind as data gatherer and interpreter, and, finally, the tension between participant observer and non-observing participant.

ISSUES OF REPRESENTATION

It was an important phase of this project to test the rigour of the method and descriptions of the women by visiting other churches, addressing gatherings both of church-based Christians and wider audiences, presenting to academics, and gauging wider responses through popular media coverage.

I strongly agree with Fetterman's (2010, 11) criterion that the:

> success or failure of either report or full-blown ethnography depends on the degree to which it rings true to natives and colleagues in the field. These readers may disagree with the researchers' interpretations and conclusions, but they should recognize the detail of the description as accurate.

During my research period I attended a variety of events at Church House and Lambeth Palace, the residence of the Archbishop of

Canterbury in London, where I tested my emerging findings though presentations and discussions with laywomen, clergy, bishops, and senior management. Through my association with Generation A women involved in my study, I became a regular speaker at a local Women's Institute, and was able then to explore similar themes with other Generation A women. At the conclusion of the project I presented my main findings to my host church congregation. During a discussion then and afterwards over refreshments, they agreed that my observations rang true in both capturing their characteristics and highlighting the problems and potentials.

As part of the project I organized a two-day research symposium in September 2013 in Canterbury composed of international researchers specializing in the Anglican Communion. My findings were presented there and benefited from detailed discussions amongst colleagues. The symposium resulted in an edited collection, *Contemporary Issues in the Worldwide Anglican Communion: Powers and Pieties*, published in 2015 by Ashgate. The symposium and its linked published collection's objectives were to explore what the academic research community, Anglican clergy, and laypeople were suggesting were the critical issues facing the Anglican communion as, particularly, power and authority relations are shifting spatially and temporally. Generation A is part of that changing landscape, influencing and being influenced by changes in gender roles, family structures, the challenges of an ageing population, the demands and opportunities generated by young people, mobility, and changes of worship communities, contested degrees of conformity to policies concerning sexual orientation, impact of social class and income differences, variable patterns of congregational growth and decline, global power and growth shifts from north to south.

Further international perspectives were gained through church visits and interviews in Sri Lanka, the United States, and Canada, including a Visiting Research Fellowship in the Center for the Studies in Religion and Society at the University of Victoria in August 2015, where findings were discussed with other scholars and at a public lecture I delivered to more than sixty members of local churches, who generally agreed that my interpretation of Generation A was accurate, if my prognosis too pessimistic for their liking.

During the project I presented emerging findings to three international conferences, which helped strengthen the focus and detail of the themes and argument. Emerging publications confirmed the record: a peer-reviewed and suitably revised paper outlining preliminary findings and my method was published in *Modern Believing* (Day 2015b), following the annual conference of *Modern Church* where clergy and laypeople heard my paper. At the end of the paper I asked the more than one hundred people present to give a show of hands if they recognized the women, the issues, and my main observations. There were no dissenting votes. The weekly Anglican newspaper *Church Times* published my short article describing my research (Day 2014a), later reproduced as a chapter in an edited collection (Day 2014c). In December 2015, the daily newspaper the *Telegraph* featured my research in a prominent article on p. 6,[10] under the headline 'How the passing of the coronation chicken era spells the end for the Church of England'.

The above events and publications, however, only tested preliminary thoughts and methodological reflections. The more deeply embedded findings and conclusions elucidated in this book will, I hope, resonate with many, although not everyone will agree.

OVERVIEW OF BOOK

This book is timely as the female Christian Generation A is on the cusp of a catastrophic decline in mainstream Christianity that accelerated during the 'post-war' (post-1945) age. The age profile of mainstream Christianity represents an increasingly ageing pattern, with Generation A not being replaced by their children or grandchildren—the baby-boomers and generations X, Y, and Z. More detail about this generational decline is found in Chapter 2.

Generation A laywomen have remained largely invisible in previous work on institutional religion in European and American countries, particularly as the focus on religion and gender has turned to youth, sexuality, and priesthood. I will discuss further in Chapter 2 the wider problems of women's invisibility in organized religion. Studying these women now is particularly important, as the record will end with their passing. Women are not filling the spaces this current generation is leaving open: for reasons to be explored in this book, the core attraction of the Church of England is not being felt by

---

[10] <http://www.telegraph.co.uk/news/religion/12046913/How-the-passing-of-the-coronation-chicken-era-spells-the-end-for-Church-England.html>, last accessed 15.1.16.

younger people. That observation is not particularly original: the pattern of decline in the Church of England and its equivalents in the Anglican Communion has been told elsewhere. What is original, I will suggest, is my claim that the pattern is irreversible; the women of the generation I study here are the last active generation in the church. Their unique disposition towards their lay roles is not being, and will not be, replicated. The purpose of this book is to explain why they are unique and what difference their passing will make to the Church and wider society.

The book's objective is fourfold: (1) to provide a detailed record of a vanishing people in the form of documentary evidence collected through ethnographic fieldwork situated historically and socially;[11] (2) to offer insights and theory into why the women engage in a particular mode of religious practice; (3) to reflect on the consequences of their loss in both religious and secular domains; and (4) to test, revise, and introduce theories related to religiosity, women, and generations.

My claim that Generation A is the last active Anglican generation will be substantiated throughout the book and brought to a conclusion in Chapter 9. The rest of this book is structured to reveal the above by describing and analysing their activities and ideas, principally gathered around themes of being women of a certain generation (Chapter 2), maintaining open churches (Chapter 3), cleaning and otherwise 'purifying' the church (Chapter 4), practising and interpreting theology (Chapter 5), attending and in other ways sanctifying Sundays (Chapter 6), raising and nurturing their biological and wider church family (Chapter 7), having fun and maintaining community through social events (Chapter 8), and reflecting on their role as probably the last active Anglican generation (Chapter 9).

[11] In order to protect anonymity all names of people and churches have been changed, along with any identifying detail.

2

Gendering Generation

One November Sunday morning, six months into my fieldwork, I was sitting and watching the preparations before the service. Just in front of me was the sacristan, a woman, who was slipping into her pew; her job was done. She had prepared the cup for the wine and the plate for the bread to be used for communion. She had washed and pressed the cloths now spread on the altar and the vestments worn by the priest, servers, and choir. She would be counting the communicants to give that number to the priest for the weekly record. I glanced behind me and saw a woman finalizing the preparation for the post-service refreshments table with cups and saucers and—oh joy!—a plate of freshly baked cookies. As the women took their places in the pews I saw the male priest begin to lead the male servers who would stand with him at the front of the church and help conduct the service. And as I carefully counted the number of congregants by gender and (roughly estimating) by age, I found what I had found every week in this church and the others I had visited: most people in the pews were over sixty and women; most people at the altar were slightly younger and male. Suddenly, in what struck me so strongly that I described it later as an epiphany, I realized that the men and women in that building, known as a church, within the social institution known as religion, were behaving in exactly the same manner as they behave outside that building, in other social institutions. Women populate in greater numbers the low status, less visible, low paid, or unpaid jobs, often in service roles, while the men populate the higher status, more visible, better paid positions. In the social institution known as the family, the women more often than men prepare the food and drink, wash and iron the clothes, and lay the table. In schools and universities, most primary school teachers are women, with male numbers increasing at the top end of professorial and senior administrative positions. If all I was observing was gendered behaviour within one social institution in a society that is already structured along gender lines, what else but this would I expect to find? I had to stifle a laugh. A quarter of the way into my research project and one of my key questions had just collapsed: why do women more than men participate in the ordinary, pew-based form of religiosity? Because, I was concluding, that is how men and women behave in all social institutions. Further, I was exploring gender, which is socially constructed, not 'sex', which refers to biology. Being a social construct, gendered performances will vary in different places and times, no matter how common-sense and fixed they may appear. An apparently 'natural' scheme of gender relations can be supported through what Walby (1990, 20) describes as 'discursive patriarchy', being 'a system of social structures and practices in which men dominate, oppress, and exploit women'. Her analysis focuses on how patriarchy can be understood best through exploring structures of production, paid work, the state, male violence, sexuality, and cultural institutions, to which I add religion and the family.

Watching the performances in front of me that Sunday, I began to question the odd way that arguments about women being more religious than men are formed. What does 'more religious' mean? The observation that many religious men prohibit women from attending gender-mixed services, and most actively and fiercely prevent them from taking senior roles, appears only fleetingly in most work, if at all. Put another way, why have religious men in most religions everywhere prevented women from performing certain key religious acts, such as attending gender-mixed services, or from becoming priests, rabbis, popes, monks, imams, and so on? While the possibility that women are more religious than men has spawned many research projects, there seems little, if any, focus on the propensity of men to claim and maintain, at almost any cost, their religious power. That observation could have provoked an equally popular question: why is religion so much more important to men than women, if we take 'importance' as a measure of specific behaviours relating to power and hierarchy? Buchanan (1992, 312), reflecting on how men have increasingly turned away from institutionalized religion, quoted an unnamed official of a major seminary who remarked: 'pay scales go down, prestige goes down and the men get out'. She refers to Wuthnow's (1998, 160) work showing that between 1950 and 1970 male clergy as a proportion of professionals halved from 4.2 to 2.2 per cent of professionals. As the numbers of college-educated people of both genders increased, their involvement in religion decreased, but the male decline was more dramatic than the female. She explains this by saying (Buchanan 1992, 315):

> More specifically, in both laity and clergy the pronounced decline being experienced by the Episcopal church is the decline of men, particularly young men. It is this decline that is especially acutely perceived because symbolically and institutionally it represents within the denomination a decline not simply of male status but of authority itself.

I decided, that Sunday morning, to trace more closely the genealogy of theories proposing that women are more religious than men, and to discuss more frequently that claim with the women I was studying.

GENEALOGIES OF GENDER

There are several important theories that seek to make sense of women's religiosity, usually framed in opposition to men, trying to explain why women seem to be more religious than men. Although generally accepted, there have been a few dissenters. Cornwall (2009) found some differences in her study of men and women, but the differences were so small she suggested that general acceptance of the apparent phenomenon exaggerates it. Sullins (2006) compared gender by religion and found that men in Islam and Judaism are more religious than women, adding that a problem in research on this topic is compounded by the different ways in which scholars choose to measure religiosity. He also points out (Sullins 2006, 849) that surveys show that the largest gender differences are related to affective (prayer, feelings of closeness to God) rather than active (attendance, volunteering) forms of religiosity.

For those who support the notion that women are more religious than men, the apparent disparity tends to be expressed in simple terms: 'It is obvious that women are more religious on every criterion' claimed Argyle and Beit-Hallahmi (1975, 71). A recent book that exhaustively presents primarily quantitative data about the gender gap (Trzebiatowska and Bruce 2012) is unequivocal in its finding that data everywhere, on every religious measure, support the claim that women are more religious than men. That apparent disposition is explained through six main ways: biology, deprivation, guilt, risk, social structure, and socialization. Importantly for this study, Trzebiatowska and Bruce note that the data on national Churches (such as the Church of England) are scarce. Nevertheless, the data they present on other Churches and other religions are robust enough to support their claims according to the criteria set by the various surveys they quote. Two findings are, they report, most significant (Trzebiatowska and Bruce 2012, 3–4): first, the more salient the measure, the more significant the gap. Regular church attendance is, for example, more likely to be gendered. Second, the largest gap is in a private realm, where women are much more likely than men to report that they pray frequently. Other private issues are also significant, such as commitment to certain creedal assents, belief in God and to the importance of self-identifying as a religious person. These differences appear, the authors report, everywhere, showing the same gender differences exist in different places and in different religions. It appears according to some surveys that the gender ratio is reversed when comparing Muslims to Christians, they note; but as women are prohibited from attending religious services in certain forms of Islam and Judaism, attendance is not a useful way to measure women's commitment to their religion. Using other surveys measuring religion in terms of personal commitment and adherence, the authors conclude that: 'In no tradition are men more likely than women to describe themselves as observant' (Trzebiatowska and Bruce 2012, 11).

Theories about a gender imbalance were reviewed in a seminal paper by Tony Walter and Grace Davie (1998), which formed the basis of my teaching and conversations during my research project. The Walter and Davie paper was carefully framed as 'The Religiosity of Women in the Modern West' about women and religiosity, marking out the territory: 'Women in the Modern West' in the title, and 'Christianity' in the text. More specifically, they centred on 'why women belong in large numbers to mainline, patriarchal religion' (Walter and Davie 1998, 641). Their delimitation was important to ensure they avoid sweeping statements about how, perhaps, women are and always have been religious everywhere. Davie makes a similar point later (Davie 2013, 236–7), saying that as gender balances will feature differently in different parts of the world and in different faiths, attempts at comparisons should be avoided without the requisite sociological and theological knowledge. Walter and Davie summarized studies showing how, on the usual measures of church

attendance and belief in God, women consistently show higher frequencies and intensities. What is notable so far is Walter and Davie's
unmarked assumptions of what is meant as religious. Most striking,
as with Trzebiatowska and Bruce (2012), is their observation that the
biggest gender difference relates to private religious practice, such as
prayer and Bible reading. Moreover, as with Trzebiatowska and Bruce
(2012), they point out that in Islam and Judaism, men are more
publicly involved than women. To explain the gender differential in
private practice, they suggest that perhaps men succumb more to
social pressure and therefore do not practise privately, or that in pre-
industrial eras men attended more as a public duty. As I observed
with Trzebiatowska and Bruce (2012), the consistent finding that men
often exclude women from religious practices, particularly linked to
public performances and power, remains virtually untouched.

Most significantly, for Davie's own work, is the possibility that
women are private believers, just as, she argued in separate works
(Davie 1990, 1994), the UK as a whole tends to 'believe without
belonging'. Unexplored is the possibility that women were inflating
their reported frequencies in order to conform to the expectations of
the surveyor, or, probably more likely and more significantly, that the
practices of prayer and Bible reading are understood differently by
men and women.

Walter and Davie consider how the apparent gender bias towards
women and religion has generated a number of explanatory theories.
One such theory is that of social vulnerability, which proposes that
women compensate for various forms of inequality, material, and
social deprivation by turning to churches for assistance and, to some
extent, empowerment, status, and fellowship. Walter and Davie suggest such theories present women as 'cultural dupes' (Walter and
Davie 1998, 645) and ignore the social life and community built up in
the church. They also point out that, particularly in the British
context, women attenders tend to be white and middle class, and
materially deprived men of working-class backgrounds tend not to
attend.

Another theory they cite is that society presents women more
often as sinners, which proposes that women are often overwhelmed
with guilt. That conforms to my earlier findings about how women
seem to take an unwarranted degree of responsibility for events that
go wrong (Day 2008), although this did not seem to incite them to
attend church. In my earlier study, the women who expressed such

sentiments included those who self-identified as religious and those who did not. Walter and Davie introduce a theory that women in their role as carers are disproportionately more likely to come into contact with both life and death or, as they describe it, 'the sacred'. And yet, as they describe, other studies of women reported that while they did feel a 'miracle' related to the birth experience, the miracle described was the experience to know and care for a baby, not a religious experience. They suggest there is a consciousness of women to bear suffering more than men, and to sacrifice their own needs and pleasures for their husbands and children. They discuss Gilligan's (1982) work, which proposed that girls have an ethic of care and boys have ethics of justice; just as God limits human authority, women can accept their authority is limited. Gilligan's work may appear essentialist, with insufficient exploration of socialization effects, which leads Walter and Davie to propose two main questions about whether religion reflects culture, and therefore gender roles, or reverses it. They also point out that women as carers see more death than men, and also outlive their husbands. They suggest this is at the heart of beliefs in the afterlife, but add a cautionary note that these beliefs may not be necessarily religious. In the final section of the paper they consider the effects of modernity, defined as (Walter and Davie 1998, 653) 'the conquest of nature by the techniques of science, capital accumulation and investment, the users of these techniques being imbued with the values of rationality, work and thrift'. Modernity erodes some people's vulnerability through, for example, the welfare state, and therefore it could be argued that the more people are involved in rationally oriented organizations, and can look more to the state than religion for welfare, the less religious they may become. Within a postmodern period, they argue, there is a shift from an external authority such as the church to the self. As churches are dominated by male systems of authority, it is perhaps unsurprising, they suggest, that women have left the churches. Walter and Davie do not offer any significant conclusions, drawing attention to the contradictory nature of the research findings. Trzebiatowska and Bruce (2012) ended on a similar point, concluding that the tendency for women to be more religious than men is probably a combination of many factors, not simply one. Devine's (2013, 485) study concluded that 'The data indicate strong support for the effect of socialisation in predicting levels of religiosity. In other words, having a strongly religious family background is associated with being religious in later life.' Similar findings were reported by Voas and Crockett (2005), who argued that decline in religiosity is strongly related to generational transmission. As each successive generation becomes less religious, the decline will continue, they said.

Another theory that has gained ground is risk aversion and its counterpart, power-control theory (Miller and Hoffmann 1995; Miller and Stark 2002; Stark 2002, 2009; Collett and Lizardo 2009; Hoffmann 2009). Briefly, the theory suggests that it is risky to be an atheist, more men than women are atheists, men take higher risks than women (as evidenced by crime studies), and that, they conclude, is why there are more male atheists than women. I never found that theory convincing, and after holding it in mind throughout my fieldwork, I came to conclude that it could be refuted on a number of grounds. I summarize and reflect on those in Chapter 9.

One aspect of the above discussion remains to be explored as it is, apparently, the most significant variable: prayer. Recent research by Pew delved into the gender differential and reported in detail how participation in the labour force seemed to narrow the gender gap.[1] As with other research, it also focused on prayer being a significant variable:[2]

> For example, women working in the labor force are more likely than men to pray daily by an average of 7 percentage points, whereas women not in the labor force are more likely than men to pray daily by an average of 13 percentage points. These patterns persist even after accounting for characteristics other than women's work status, such as educational attainment, age, marital status and religious affiliation.

If women report 'praying' more often than men, it raises a question about what they mean by prayer and why they engage in it more frequently than men. Other studies demonstrate, for example, that women participate frequently in prayer that focuses on the needs of family or immediate domestic problems (Wuthnow 1994; Day 2005). These practices may not indicate a gendered difference in religiosity

---

[1] <http://www.pewforum.org/2016/03/22/the-gender-gap-in-religion-around-the-world/>, last accessed 21.4.2016.
[2] <http://www.pewforum.org/2016/03/22/theories-explaining-gender-differences-in-religion/>, last accessed 21.4.2016.

so much, as it does in the kinds of labour women engage in. This is such a significant point that I devote a large section of Chapter 5 to discussing it in more detail.

While the particular theme here is the idea of 'generation', consideration is given throughout to the difficulties in generalizing, given the vast diversity of the women studied. While not as homogeneous a group as might have been expected, the majority have always attended since a child, with their families, but others joined later in life. Nevertheless, evidence about the particularities of wartime, nation rebuilding, post-war austerity, domestication, and the consumerist boom help draw broad strokes to characterize qualities of Generation A and their influence on subsequent generations. Generation A women were teenagers and young women during the Second World War, had careers and some raised families during the consumerist boom of the 1950s, and were often portrayed as the counterpoint to the counter-cultural and feminist revolutions of the 1960s. They did not have more 'time' than the current, unchurched generation, but chose to structure it differently (Gershuny 1983).

Before turning to the detail of Generation A, I will review some of the most pertinent concepts of generation that affected this work and set out the formative concept of 'active generation'.[3]

GENERALIZING GENERATION

Ideas about 'generation' vary, depending principally on whether it is conceived in terms of an ageing process or as a manifestation of shared values and interests unique to a specific age-related section of the population. Related terms such as 'cohort' and 'life cycle' are often conflated (for further discussion about the distinctions see, for example, Ryder 1965; Riley 1971; Buss 1974; Laufer and Bengston 1974; Glenn 1976; White 1992; Eyerman and Turner 1998; Edmunds and Turner 2002; Öberg et al. 2004; Biggs 2007).

Anthropologists accustomed to finely tuned ethnographies that do not claim wider, generalized significance are likely to be concerned about 'generation' being used to mask differences amongst individuals,

---

[3] An earlier version of the discussion about generations was published in Day 2013d.

and therefore raise questions for the ethics of representation. Different members of a social unit, be that a family or a nation, have different perspectives related to their own histories and locations in other socially constructed categories, such as age, class, gender, and status. As Wassmann notes (1995, 176): 'It becomes necessary to study individuals or categories of people in their own right rather than merely as some kind of cultural "subunits"'. The problem with large surveys purporting to represent 'generations' is the practice of logistical regression, which removes certain variables that complicate the story being presented. And yet the story is complicated. Generation is a complicated concept, understood differently by academics in a variety of disciplines.

My goal in this work was to try to grasp the importance of a shared period of time and situate the women I studied within it, while also appreciating individual and subcultural varieties. Burnett (2003) discussed how concepts of generation are inevitably tied to socially constructed ideas of personhood and time (see also Corsten 1999). Van Gennep (1960) proposed that movement in various stages of personhood could be analysed through distinct ritual moments. Halbwachs (1992) showed how shared rituals of commemoration embed events and ideas into social memory and identity.

Mannheim (1952 [1923, 164]) argued that although the job of analysing generation is difficult, sociologists should not be deterred from accepting the challenge: 'It seems to be the task of *Formal Sociology* to work out the simplest, but at the same time the most fundamental facts relating to the phenomenon of generations.' Mannheim's reference to formal sociology encourages the use of large-scale, survey-based, statistically analysed data, producing aggregated pictures of generation. Statistics alone cannot, however, provide insights into processes or meanings (Becker 1992; Becker and Hermkens 1993), nor illuminate internal heterogeneity. In his review in the *American Anthropologist* of Shmuel Eisenstadt's (1956) influential book, Bennett (1957, 722) observed that for all its useful data, the book 'may not make sense if one is not inclined toward sympathy with such broad analytical classifications'.

Nevertheless, Mannheim's key idea is attractive and will, for my work, serve as an ideal type. In his terms, a generation is not simply a cohort of people sharing similar birth years, but a collection of people born at a time of historical note and even trauma that has shaped their identity. He distinguishes between a generation and a concrete social group, such as a family or a tribe, with intimate knowledge of each other: 'union of a number of individuals through naturally developed or consciously willed ties' (Mannheim 1952 [1923], 165). Belonging to a generation, he argues, is different because it requires a self-awareness of that cohort's location in a certain time and place. He introduced the concept of a 'generation unit' for analysis by saying that it was not the fact of people being born at the same time, but that they experience the same kind of historical events in the same location that creates a unique, stratified consciousness. He qualifies this further by saying that the generation location is defined by historical and 'cultural region' (Mannheim 1952 [1923], 182), whereby some participate actively in sharing and creating a common destiny of that historical and social unit, exposed to the social and intellectual symptoms of a process of dynamic destabilization (Mannheim 1952 [1923], 183). According to his definition, generations are not defined by biology or time spans, but 'depends entirely on the trigger action of the social and cultural process' (Mannheim 1952 [1923], 191).

The term 'generation' is therefore tied intrinsically to an idea of active participation, and, at least in Mannheim's terms, acknowledges that not everyone born at the same time can participate equally in the same cultural and intellectual life of that time. Following Mannheim, Edmunds, and Turner (2002, 7) summarize the idea of generation as dependent on self-identity and construction.

The idea of generation thus far involves an apparently shared event affecting a cohort in a manner at least similar enough to produce a collective conscience, to which they will respond in an active rather than passive manner. That is a better way of expressing generation than by time frame alone, such as 'the sixties' generation'. Klatch's (1999) book about the 1960s focused specifically on the idea of internal variation, telling stories about young conservatives growing up in the 1960s at the same time as the hippies and radicals. While some members of that age cohort were smoking dope and listening to Bob Dylan, others were drinking ginger ale and reading the politically right Conservative Ayn Rand.[4]

---

[4] See also Cornman and Kingston 1996 and Riggs and Turner 2000 for discussion of variations within the so-called 'baby-boomer generation' and Elder 1974 for insights into children born in the 'great depression'.

A popular proponent of this idea of generation was Douglas Coupland's (1991) novel *Generation X*. He introduced readers to young people defined by their attitudes and practices and spawned numerous eponymous or at least similar works (see, for example, Lipsky 1984, Mahedy and Bernardi 1994, Nelson and Cowan 1994; Beaudoin 1998; Flory and Miller 2000; Pardun and McKee 1995; Rushkoff 1994; Roof 1993, 1999). He captured this approach to generations by exploring what he argued were shared attitudes, beliefs, and behaviours emerging at a particular time in American society and influencing a specific cohort of post-war babies born in the 1940s. From Generation X has followed Generation Y, and even, perhaps, generation Z or the 'Millennials'. My introduction of 'Generation A' is a specific reference to those alphabetically denoted generalities, where I am implying that Generation A, born in the 1920s and early 1930s, is, whether literally or metaphorically, mother, grandmother, and great-grandmother of them all.

The issue becomes more complicated when we add variations such as ethnicity, social class, or gender. The elderly women I study were actively involved in the workplace before and during the Second World War, but largely returned to the domestic sphere once the war ended. They were therefore less visible in the public, political sphere and may be considered less active, but only if we discount their unpaid labour that kept their husbands and children active and healthy, their homes clean, and, for many, their churches busy. More relevant for my field work was the Second World War and the terminology sometimes used to describe those who participated and were most affected. In the UK, the term 'air-raid generation' (and in the United States the GI Generation) is sometimes used to describe people who were young in that war and endured the hardship of constant deprivation and fear. Even so, variations render such concepts of commonality unworkable. One of my informants, for example, told me about her younger sister and brother dying in a bomb blast; another of my informants said she never heard a bomb nor saw an air raid shelter, but she did enjoy going to dances with the Canadian soldiers stationed nearby.

There is no single narrative that explains to everyone's satisfaction post-war social change and how, in particular, women were involved as either active or passive agents. Being closely involved with a segment of Generation A allowed me to observe and feel some of the values that seem to matter to them. Brown and Lynch (2012,

329–51) offer a perspective that seemed to fit best what I was finding with Generation A; the sense of a profound cultural shift between their generation and mine. My sense of that was moulded not so much by what they said, as by what they did. Brown and Lynch define a 'cultural account' (2012, 229–30). This involves 'not just thinking about culture (as any object of study), but thinking through culture (as a theoretical approach) to make sense of social life'. Their approach draws primarily on Raymond Williams's definitions (see Williams and Orrom 1954; Williams 1961) and other work on the subject of cultural change (see Cook 2004; McLeod 2007). They discuss the loss of a normative Christian culture in Britain with women rejecting traditional gender roles. The cultural changes of, primarily, the 1960s were vast, affecting music, social and economic structures, and expansion of higher education. These combined with significant global changes, such as increased migrations, modernizations, globalized economies, a neo-liberal turn, and changes in public and social media. As one woman I interviewed said, the period of change for her generation began in the 1960s with 'the hippy era, what was this, the sixties? [. . .] Yeah. I think that's probably when it started. It was the sixties I think, yeah.'

Brown's (2000) earlier work influenced me and other scholars at the time, and, while perhaps overly reliant on oral history, continues to have such an effect. Brown's main premise was that Britain underwent a massive and profound cultural shift after the 1960s which changed the way British people believed and behaved. His theoretical claims are based on his adherence to the theories of pre-modernity, modernity, and post-modernity, a position which he says divides the academy. Broadly, he asserts that social scientists have mistakenly observed secularization as a feature of post-Enlightenment rationality and relied on structural rather than discursive theories and methods (Brown 2001, 195–6). Brown's claim for the death of Christian Britain or, as he puts it, 'the demise of the nation's core religious and moral identity' (Brown 2001, 1), rests on what he perceives as a sudden shift in 1963 amongst the two generations who matured in the last thirty years of the twentieth century. These would be the baby-boomers and their progeny, the children and grandchildren of Generation A. The 1960s period was, Brown says, the time when the British population stopped going to church, marrying, getting confirmed, being baptized. What we saw then was not 'merely the continuing decline of organised Christianity, but the death of the culture which formerly conferred Christian identity upon the British people as a whole' (Brown 2001, 193). He discussed many reasons for this, but focused on a main gendered effect, whereby a gendered discourse had located piety in femininity from about 1800 to 1960 (Brown 2001, 195):

> the age of discursive Christianity then quite quickly collapsed. It did so, fundamentally, when women cancelled their mass subscription to the discursive domain of Christianity. Simultaneously, the nature of femininity changed fundamentally.

As a consequence, he said, the majority of churchgoers are older women. Importantly, Brown also focuses on the period pre-1960 when women of the generation I studied were returning to post-war domesticity. A brief religious revival between 1945 and 1958 may be attributed, he argued, to a need for redomestication to justify removing women from the workplace in favour of returning soldiers, and a wave of Evangelicalism spurred by the American evangelical minister Billy Graham's mission to the UK. Although Brown notes that of the millions who attended the rallies in the mid-1950s only a tiny percentage converted to that form of Christianity; their appeal reflected a general cultural discursive support of Christianity. The shift in the following decade was, he argued (Brown 2001, 176), sudden and violent, with a quick series of major changes as the 'institutional structures of cultural traditionalism started to crumble in Britain'. Those changes included weakening of book and theatre censorship, legalization of abortion and homosexuality in 1967, the liberalization of divorce in 1969, the women's liberation movement since 1968, and waves of new styles of pop music, youth culture, the popularity of drugs, new fashions, and student rebellions.

The arguments are persuasive, but what is generally absent from the record is any exploration of the role the mothers of the 1960s revolutionaries played. It was a question I often put to the Generation A women I talked with: 'You raised us: what kind of values did you instil that helped your children rebel?' Conversations would turn to the many demands on the modern family, together with increased leisure activities available to the modern child. There was a pervading sense that they, as mothers, had done their jobs in taking their young children to church, but if children who grew into teenagers and young adults chose not to continue to attend church, that choice was respected. As Guibernau (2013, 16) argues in her book, recent generations now reflect ideals of modern, capitalist society where 'the individual is now free from the bonds typical of pre-individualist society—nature, church and the absolutist state—and could enjoy the advantages of independence and rationality'.

It began to dawn on me that the choices the baby-boomers made were partly possible because they had been raised to be autonomous. Could the seeds of the cultural revolution have been sown by the women who raised their children in the 1950s and early 1960s? It is my contention that the post-war mothers were creatively engaged with the project of nation-building, and raising their children to be independently minded. In his study of British families in the 1950s, Kynaston concludes that (2009, 596, 597): '1950s parents were, taken as a whole, significantly less old school than the previous generation of parents [...] The overall sense is of parenthood on the cusp of fundamental change by the early to mid-1950s.'

If the children of Generation A became the generation most likely to select a category of 'none' or 'no religion' on the 2001 or 2011 UK censuses,[5] perhaps this is because they felt they had permission to decide such things for themselves. As Brown suggests (2012, 62), choosing 'no religion' is an act of commitment, not an absence of it.

Butler (1990, viii) described 'certain habitual and violent presumptions' about gender that shape the way it is studied. She points out that much understanding about gender presupposes a so-called natural state, locked in a fixed biology. In contrast, she argues that gender is socially produced through language, practice, culture, and the kinds of activities that encourage people to perform repeatedly gender identities in certain, culturally prescribed ways, thus further reifying them. Further, she provides an interpretation of power to show how it operates as a structure, defining and limiting the extent to which people can oppose or transgress that which appears to be natural. While I, and my contemporaries, may take for granted the need to upset apparently natural gender norms, it was not ever thus and neither is it the practice of Generation A. Reflecting on how contemporary

---

[5] The distinction refers to the 2001 census religious question option of 'none', which was subsequently changed in 2011 to 'no religion', reflecting, I have argued, the positive nature of that choice. See Day and Lee 2014a.

scholars are more attuned than their predecessors in noting androcentrism, Gross (2004, 17) wrote:

> Before that time, the term had been rarely used because it was not understood that there was any other way to conceptualize humanity or that we all operated with a model of humanity that put men in the centre of attention as normal and normative human beings and women on the periphery as a 'special case', and a bit abnormal.

The cultural, political, and sexual revolution of the 1960s began to shake those androcentric structures for many women. By the time the full force of the cultural revolution of the 1960s rocked the baby-boomers, the damage to church-attending habits and dispositions had been done. A turn from institutions, patriarchy, and authority was a turn away from everything Generation A had loved and held as sacred: God, the Queen, the nuclear family, and nation, represented by and revered in the solid, unchanging institutions of the Church of England and the wider Anglican Communion. My findings thereby challenge the stereotype of elderly Christian women as worthy, dutiful carers who just happened to have, somewhat inexplicably, raised a generation stereotyped as highly individualized, unchurched, selfish, shopaholic baby-boomers. My study reveals far more complex personalities, values, and behaviours. Generation A is, I argue, characterized by certain habits and dispositions, particularly a desire for a relationship with a church-based spiritual authority that supports the sacred institutions of their day: church, nation, family, law. As Kynaston (2009, 558) said about the post-war period, there were 'Normative assumptions identifying the moral and social health of the nation with the moral and social health of the family'. While those are characteristics I observed in Generation A and will return to throughout this book, I am not arguing that current generations no longer value, nor at times hold sacred, such normative assumptions. Particularly the strongly held emotions attached to nationalism, these are attachments that can lie comparatively quietly in banal, background forms (Billig 1995) to be activated when people feel they have been transgressed (Lynch 2012).

The kind of authority valued by Generation A is both masculine and 'traditional', embodied in the depiction of their god, their saviour, their priest, and the socially acceptable hierarchies of their day. They are also, above all else, religious women; holy women, defined and defending what they think is sacred. Religious change is therefore best explained through understanding how Generation A's sacred objects, beliefs, and practices are no longer held as sacred by their children and grandchildren.

The question I have been asking is: what did these women do, almost single-handedly, at least in the space of one generation, to bring down the Church of England? Other theories, such as they are, about women and religion like to emphasize their apparent qualities for predisposing them to being religious—they are caring, they are not risk-takers, they are stuck in a social time warp. Let me produce different questions: what do they do and why? What was their power and intent? What was, perhaps most importantly, their agency? To answer those questions, we have to understand first who these women were and are in a particular historical and social context, rooted here in my research in the global North and West. They belonged to, and believed in, a Church of England that represented certain ideals, beliefs, and structures. The values they represented were those strongly linked to England, or the West, at a certain time in those women's lives. They had fought in a war, not on the battlefields but in offices, hospitals, and factories, for certain values and ideas of nation. They did not want to forget those values and they did not much like it when the Church appeared to be rejecting or at least softening them. They were fighters and warriors. They had lost loved ones—brothers, fathers, uncles, fiancés, cousins. These women were teenagers and young women in the war, many of them working in factories or as part of the armed forces. When the war ended and peace returned, followed by a short period of austerity leading to prosperity, these women, as young mothers, were not particularly impressed by the counter-revolution of the 1960s which turned everything they believed in, belonged to, and had fought for on its head: that is why they resisted some of those changes. Why introduce new hymns when the old ones were so good?

I paused outside a church one morning where an elderly woman was sweeping the steps. I had chatted to her before and knew that her church had celebrated a Harvest Festival that week. When I asked her how it had been, she replied: 'Lovely. The hymns were lovely, the old ones that we know.'

When I attended 'hymn-sings', occasions where members of the congregation chose hymns, I noticed that Generation A chose the old ones they valued with phrases such as 'for those in peril on the sea', 'Abide with me', 'How great thou art'. Those hymns spoke to the values those women cherished: of nation, of family, of hard work and sacrifice. Those were the values embedded in their still-favourite guide to the liturgy, the Book of Common Prayer, which set out clearly the hierarchy of God, monarch, and country. They did not warmly welcome new musical styles, such as a long-haired hippy standing at the front of the church, strumming a guitar and singing in a monotone about giving peace a chance. As one Generation A woman described 'modern' church services:

> And, but they're much more modern too now than St. [...] is, my goodness yes. They do a lot of extra with guitars and all that. And what makes people think a guitar is better to listen than a beautiful organ, I don't know, I can't. I'm into music my entire life and I can't understand that one at all. And they're no good for leading a group of people singing, with someone's strumming one chord on the guitar. That's not my idea of music.

She is not just noting that the musical style is not to her taste, but she positions the group as more important than the music. The congregation, the church, is what matters more than the performances of one individual. This was the Church they had fought for, that their family members had died for, for which the British Empire had once stood. Changing the hymn book, another Generation A woman said, was just one of the small changes that increased over time to change the character of the church they so loved:

> So all of this had gone on for many, many years and gradually: it was very insidious, doing away with the prayer book, doing away with the hymns. No, we didn't want any of that.

Bergler (2012) argues that American Methodist, evangelical, Catholic, and African American churches tried to attract young people through diluting a serious Christian message through youth programmes and changes in worship style, a process he calls 'juvenilization'. The Evangelical churches followed that strategy, leading, he argued, to their success in retaining and attracting young people (who also, I would add, tended to attend with their families, possibly the most important quality to their retention). During my research, I sometimes heard from clergy that Generation A tried to prevent the Church moving towards more youth-oriented liturgies. As I will discuss throughout this book, I conclude reasons for the generational shift is more rooted in wider cultural changes than musical taste.

For British Generation A laywomen, the history of their Church is tightly tied to a history of politics, monarchy, and Empire, currently reflected in the vestiges of the worldwide Anglican Communion.

GENERATION A AND MISSION

I must position myself and this work as not just a work of a woman about women, but more specifically a work by a white woman about, predominantly, white women of the global North. Having chosen to elaborate on an age and gender perspective, I know that it is only one angle, and is implicitly racialized through its assumption of the normalization of whiteness and its failure to engage in depth with the history of exploitative white privilege and violence. More needs to be done by me and others in our fields of Religious Studies, the Sociology of Religion, and the Anthropology of Religion. While arguing at times against the dominance of men over women in the Anglican Communion, I hope I remain mindful that, as Mary Keller wrote (2004, 80]: 'in terms of a spectrum of social power, white women have always enjoyed the social power of being almost white men, a difficult and perhaps tenuous subjectivity [...]'.

A long period of missionary work has left a mark on the way that women see themselves and others across the Anglican Communion, partly because women performed distinctive roles as missionaries, often acting alone (not simply as the wives of male missionaries) and thus giving them roles of leadership and independence they could not have experienced at home in England. These generally conservative and well-educated women wanted to teach women in the colonies not just about God, but about the Christian ideal of womanhood, which was similar to their own Victorian values of domesticity and subordination, but also where their mission ideology 'emphasized the essential difference between white women and women of color: the former as liberated because of their Christian religion; the latter as ignorant and degraded in their heathenism' (Pui-Lan 1996, 254–5).

The traditional form of Anglican words and liturgy set in the 1549 version of the Book of Common Prayer is still favoured by women of Generation A, which explains why many church notice boards stipulate which services follow it. Pui-Lan (1996, 65) argues that the text is racialized:

> Today, the majority of Anglicans are people from the Two-Thirds World, who are not of English or European descent. Ethnocentrism and Christian imperialism undergirded the oppressive system of colonialism, and some of the language of the prayers for mission in Morning Prayer easily convey a feeling of superiority: 'Grant that people everywhere may seek after you and find you; bring the nations into your fold.'

Further, she notes (Pui-Lan 1998, 65) that the colonization process
followed the assumption that 'the white race was superior to all other
races. The Book of Common Prayer is full of imageries of light and
darkness, some of which can be traced back to the biblical tradition',
with darkness being a symbol of danger.

Both male and female missionaries worked in the global South to
impose northern styles of worship, dress, and vestments (Peiris 1998,
358), which explained, as I observed during my visits to three Anglican churches in Sri Lanka, the architectural similarities of churches
there to churches in the UK, United States, and Canada, right down to
the similar bronze eagle on the lecterns. The experience of missioni-
zation leaves a strange, strained, and sometimes stained legacy on
countries notably marked by histories of colonialism. It is 'Strange to
consider our common mother as a black woman of Africa', reflected
Bam (1998, 347), and stranger still when, as she says, black women
have been 'doubly cursed' by being oppressed both as Blacks and as
women. Yet, to further nuance an already complex story, she adds
(Bam 1998, 349):

> We are grateful to the people of the Church [...] I am a member of the
> Anglican Communion. I am glad to be able to say that. My great-
> grandfather was baptized and confirmed in this Church and with
> experiences of joy and pain in that membership over the years my
> family has been pleased to call itself Anglican since that time. I am
> Anglican. But I am not English and I am not male.

Women's involvement as missionaries and the impact of that on
future feminisms has been largely ignored. In her work on missionary
imperialism through the Church Missionary Society, (CMS), Francis-
Dehqani (2004, 126) states that: 'While traditional accounts of
Victorian church history have included little by the way of gender
analysis, contemporary feminist historiography has largely ignored or
treated with suspicion the religious element in women's history'. She
further criticizes the 1960s second wave feminist movement for the,
according to her, narrow view of equal rights for women. She argues
that nineteenth-century women were more concerned with basic
welfare rights for women, leading to them being generally excluded
from the historical women's movement. Francis-Dehqani (2004, 127)
continues by saying that although people involved in the CMS did not
use the term 'feminism', she employs it because 'no other term
adequately conveys the extent or intensity of concern regarding the

position of women or the sense of injustice at the oppression many experienced'. She further reviews discussions about the role of missionaries and imperialism and suggests there are two strands that run through those works: one links the missionaries inextricably to the project of British colonialism, while another embeds them into the history of evangelicalism and its influence on Victorian Britain and the lives of women. Following the latter version of events, Francis-Dehqani (2004, 128–32) argued that the then dominant evangelical culture promoted the idea that spreading Christianity was a moral duty, while simultaneously stressing that the future of Christendom was dependent on women maintaining their roles as wives and mothers. Such dominant narratives created a space for single Christian women to become missionaries. Taking as her example the missionary effort into Iran, Francis-Dehqani (2004, 132) says that: 'While the CMS women themselves rejected traditional roles as wives and mothers, they endeavoured to teach Iranian women about the inherent virtues of this mode, hoping they would adhere to it in the new Christian society imagined for Iran.' She develops the idea of the western creation of the Orient as 'other', while explaining that the women missionaries had themselves been 'other' in relation to men and therefore were reorienting themselves as the dominant self in relation to the Iranian 'other'.

The complexity of their roles was summarized by Bam (1998), who also reflected on the institutional racism of the Church itself. And yet, while she notes that the Church in South Africa supported the state and its apartheid policies for too long, the Anglican women on the ground performed, as always, important labour (Bam 1998, 350–1): 'while other people gave speeches and engaged in disputes, Church women's groups held the townships together by comforting and consoling the needy in many practical ways'.

Similar stories of Anglican women's practical labour through Church groups and the Mothers' Union are told throughout the Anglican Communion, with similar ambivalence. Women of Generation A were often members of the Mothers' Union, an Anglican institution created in 1926 to promote marriage (between heterosexual couples only) and help sustain families, both religiously and materially. It served both as a social club and a fund-raiser for mission overseas. In the UK, the Mothers' Union is presented as a safe, woman-centred organization led by Generation A designed to promote values of an idealized Christian woman as wife and mother.

The Mothers' Union, with four million members worldwide, continues to be active in the global South. In the global North it acts mainly to raise money for international projects and take on key campaigns: most of its revenue (nearly £4 million) is generated in Britain and Ireland. Like other Generation A linked organizations, its income from members, donations, and legacies is declining.

Some people have mixed memories of the Mothers' Union. Rose, now in her early nineties, told me that she had not been allowed to join the Mothers' Union when she was younger because it was only available to married women and she was single. The often troubling nature of the Mothers' Union was reported by Mombo (1998, 219–24) who, in discussing violence against women in Kenya, argued that abuse is rooted in 'a tradition reinforced by Judeo-Christian religion' (Mombo 1998, 220). She described the unfairness of women who, although numerically in the majority, are kept outside decision-making processes that affect women. Further, she argued, the largest women's group in Kenya is the Mothers' Union which, with its emphasis on the family, marginalizes single mothers and even ignores domestic abuse.

Swartz (1998, 188) comments that the Mothers' Union 'with its high (Western) ideals of family and marriage' marginalized many women, and yet women are the 'backbone' of the Church, family and community. Owing to employment practices forcing migratory labour, women need to keep things going while men work away, and yet 'Despite the vital role women play in the Church they are often disempowered—as in the community, the workplace and the home in this patriarchal society'.

The classed and ethnicized character of Anglican women of the global North may be a stereotype, but probably with good reason. The popular description of the Church of England today as 'the Conservative Party at prayer' is only partly tongue in cheek. In the United States, Episcopal women in the eighteenth and nineteenth centuries were significant fund-raisers for schools and hospitals, operating what was described as a 'parallel church' (Gunderson 1992).[6] Although smaller numerically than the Nonconformist and evangelical churches, the members of the Anglican/Episcopal Churches have historically been disproportionately represented in society's establishment and

---

[6] For a detailed insight into the history of American women and religion, see Ruether and Keller's (1986) comprehensive three-volume work.

perceived as the 'national' Churches. Reflecting on this phenomenon, Buchanan (1992, 310–11) wrote: 'the Episcopal tradition has always been small, exercising social and cultural influence vastly disproportionate to its size. More than any other Protestant denomination, it has been identified with the national power structure and destiny.'

THE QUEEN: A WOMAN OF GENERATION A

Heading the Church of England, Queen Elizabeth II has had a profound effect on Generation A, representing an Englishness and an Establishment which resonated with women I met in several churches and countries. That sense of a common history with the Queen, and her being part of their lives, was strong even amongst people not living in England. As an example, when my interview in Boston, USA, was drawing to an end with Generation A woman Doris, she wanted to talk to me about the Royal Family. She asked me when I was returning to England, and the brief extract from our interview indicates her enthusiasm for the Queen and family. She described herself as 'growing up' with the Queen and her sister, with her use of the collective pronoun of 'we' in reference to the recently born Prince George implying a strong sense that this was her family she was discussing:

ABBY: Well tomorrow I'm going to New York—I've got some churches to visit there, and, then I'm going back to England on Friday.

DORIS: Ohh, and we have a new baby, I've seen some pictures.

ABBY: Yeah—

DORIS: *[she interrupts me]* I can remember growing up, I grew up with the little Princesses, Princess Elizabeth, Princess Margaret-Rose *[laughs]*.

ABBY: Have you been to England?

DORIS: No, I always said you know someday, long ago though not now, I wanted to go see old England but we learned so much of it growing up [. . .] and my god-daughter, Virginia, went to England a couple of times and she brought me back a big picture of the Queen and she's still my favourite *[laughs]*.

Muriel, a Canadian Generation A woman, felt much the same way. We had been discussing what she liked about the 'traditions', as she described them, of the Anglican Church when she remarked that they were very 'English', adding: 'because the Anglican is the Eng... Church of England. The monarchy, way back, they took it away from Catholic entirely.' There seemed to be a nostalgia for an earlier period when she described how the Church was more 'traditional' than it is now: 'The early years, it was a very Anglican service, very English. We had a beautiful choir and we had altar boys.'

Another Canadian woman, Agnes, spoke specifically about the Book of Common Prayer being beautiful because of the English language:

> What else is traditional, now let me think for a minute. Well, it's the liturgy. See, they changed it, in the Book of Alternative Services, you know the BAS [*laughs*]. They don't have anything—one of the nice things about it is the, er, the kind of the poetry I guess. If you're brought up with the Book of Common Prayer, it's a sort of worship in itself. The English. I know that sounds silly but it's the truth. And, um, I just feel comfortable with it, and we have people who've come there because of the Book of Common Prayer and because of the service, who were with, one in particular was with a holy roller type place, you know, people falling on the floor and all the rest of it, and then they discovered the Book of Common Prayer and realised, you know, that this is so much taken from the scriptures itself and I think that this is probably the answer: it's full of scripture.

On 21 April 2016 Queen Elizabeth turned ninety, the same age as many of her most loyal subjects, the women of Generation A. As head of the Church of England, the United Kingdom, and, even nominally, Sovereign of fifteen Commonwealth realms, the Queen represents more than the face of England. Coming to the throne as she did at the young age of twenty-seven, in June 1953, Elizabeth was a young woman, mother, and wife at the same time as Generation A. Unlike her mother and previous generations, Queen Elizabeth has made an effort to present herself to the public not as one of them, but at least as someone who invited them occasionally into her life and home. The affection and respect with which she is held by the majority of the British public is well known, with 69 per cent believing Britain is better off with the Royal Family.[7]

---

[7] <https://www.theguardian.com/uk/2012/may/24/queen-diamond-jubilee-record-support>, last accessed 29.8.16.

It is the women of Generation A who are most likely to be unequivocal and undaunted monarchists, similar to their parents and grandparents, as evidence shows older members of the public have greater loyalty to the Royal Family. Republicanism, while only a very small rumble in British society, is much more a feature of youth: the number of over sixty-five year olds who believe Britain should become a republic, when the Queen abdicates or dies, is nearly half the number of eighteen to twenty-four year olds.[8] Indeed, when 'faith in God wears thin and trust in politicians sinks lower, the monarchy can at least market itself as a model of stolid continuum'.[9]

And yet, when the Queen dies she will not be replaced by someone who represents her own core values about marriage. Like the women of Generation A, her children have not all followed her example in matters of private marital fidelity and public face.

Now, having introduced broadly the themes and styles of the book, and its key conceptual apparatus, it's time to look more closely at the women and their religious lives. During the following six chapters, the ethnographic record will be foregrounded. In the final chapter, I will try to connect that record more tightly to the future of Anglican churches.

---

[8] <http://www.icmunlimited.com/data/media/pdf/OmBPC-May121.pdf>, last accessed 2.7.15.
[9] <http://www.theguardian.com/uk/2002/jun/02/monarchy.jubilee>, last accessed 1.7.15.

Section II

Holy Women

Although the women of Generation A are respected as the so-called 'back bone' of the Church, it is argued here that what is sometimes overlooked is how their belonging, identity, and labour all form them as religious, holy women. This section explores in detail their acts of, for example, keeping churches open and clean, and maintaining congregations bound together as a body of Christ.

3

Maintaining Open Churches

The title of 'maintenance' person conjures up an image of a man in overalls with a tool-box, but the more important role of church maintenance is actually carried out by women who ensure that the church is open and inhabited. The church is not just God's house, but their house: God may rule the universe, but it takes a woman to make the tea. Without their frequent presence and surveillance, the church could easily become neglected, fall into disrepair, and cease to be an attractive or viable site for either worship or community events. It would also mean a loss of public presence and evidence that the church is maintaining a useful purpose for anyone but its congregation. This kind of church maintenance happens on every day but on a Sunday, the day that usually commands the attention of statisticians and church auditors. During the rest of the week the members of the congregation most likely to be regularly seen in the church will be Generation A women and, sometimes, their priest. The women maintain an open church in three ways:

1. Through being in the church when there are no other activities, just to keep it open. This is known variously as 'church sitting', 'church watch', or 'church opening'.
2. Through hosting coffee mornings.
3. Attending weekday church services with their priest.

The most important work duty I maintained within my 'host church', St John's, for fifteen months was my active role as a member of the 'church watch/opening' team, maintaining a presence, in pairs, in the church on weekdays and Saturdays for an afternoon or morning three-hour session. Other churches have similar events known variously as 'drop ins' or 'coffee mornings': the intent and effect is the same and they attract similar types of 'regulars'. This is when Generation

A women keep the churches open and humming. It is also often dangerous, frequently uncomfortable, and a generally unacknowledged form of informal social care.

Along with my regular 'church watch' duties at my host church, I also visited regularly other churches nearby for their coffee mornings and mid-week services. As my fieldwork progressed outside my home town, I visited Anglican/Episcopal churches mid-week wherever I happened to be: other parts of England, Scotland, New York, Boston, Sri Lanka. The look and feel of those places were oddly familiar: outside service times there was usually a quiet, often empty church with one or two elderly women sitting at a table, sometimes offering a cup of tea and biscuit. The mid-week services generally consisted of Morning Prayer and Holy Communion on different days of the week, almost exclusively attended by Generation A women (apart from large city cathedrals that perform an entirely different function from a parish church), who help prepare the church and sacraments for the service, attend, assist, and clear up. Each service would therefore be populated by only a handful of people, forming a close, intimate grouping of older women and a (mostly male) priest.

In conversations with clergy attached to these churches, and with senior personnel at Church House, the pattern they identified was the same. They told me that, historically, their churches depended on Generation A to attend the mid-week services and to keep the churches open mid-week. More recently, those numbers have been dwindling. Fewer churches are staying open mid-week for services because of the loss of that generation, and even fewer have the mid-week coffee mornings/church watches.

The following ethnographic sketches may convey some of the feel of these events and provide documentary evidence of the activity. I conclude that these gendered, generation-specific forms of church maintenance provoke theoretical discussion concerning the nature of work, Christian service, social care, and gender roles.

YES, I AM MY BROTHER'S KEEPER

There is a verse in the Bible that contains a phrase probably familiar to religious and non-religious people alike: 'And the LORD said unto Cain, Where is Abel thy brother? And he said, I know not: Am

I my brother's keeper?' (Genesis 4:9). The line resonated with me as I wrote a short sketch of my first experience as a member of the church watch team.

It's a Saturday morning and I have been asked to help out at an event. As I approached the main door of the church I could see it was closed. Leaning against the wall nearby were two 'street people', a man and a woman. They watched me approach the door, try the handle, and knock hard. No one answered. I looked at them and saw that they were watching me closely. I asked if they had seen anyone come in recently. They shook their heads. 'Have you got anything to eat?' they asked me. I apologized and said I hadn't. They shrugged and looked away. I had seen people like them before on these streets, but until that moment I had never had any conversation with any of them, apart from when I might drop a coin in their cups and mutter 'you're welcome' to their 'thank you'. They were, I was to learn from my Generation A informants, not quite homeless, as most lived in nearby hostels or other temporary accommodation. They were often 'scruffy' but invariably polite and respectful when inside the church having tea and biscuits. As I had not had any experience as yet with them, it felt natural for me to walk away from the couple without further conversation as I went to investigate the possibility that another door of the church might be open. When I returned to the church the couple had left, but lying prone near the main door was a middle-aged, unshaven, unwashed male. I examined him more closely to determine that he was sleeping and, from the smell of alcohol, obviously drunk. I stepped around him to stand beside the church door and knocked again. Again there was no answer. I began to feel uncomfortably anxious, worried that I had got the day wrong or the time wrong, and therefore would not only miss an opportunity for an important fieldwork experience, but be viewed as an irresponsible member of the group. The downside of duty was becoming more obvious. Being regarded as dutiful in the sense of being trustworthy and reliable was, I recognized for what felt like the first time, an important part of my identity. It was also one of the most significant criteria of membership in this particular group and a means by which a sense of belonging was being fostered. I decided to wait by the door for another fifteen minutes before giving up. As I stood beside Drunk Sleeping Man, several people walking by paused to look at him, before asking me if he was OK. I assured them that he was; that he was obviously just sleeping off a heavy night. Somehow, my presence by

the church door conveyed on me a look of respectability and accountability, neither of which I felt I had earned. I was, like most of the
passers-by, merely a bystander. A few months later, after I had come
to know Drunk Sleeping Man and several of his friends by name, it
would become inconceivable to me that I had not taken a special
effort to nudge him gently to see if he was all right, and even urge him
to sit up or roll over on his side in case he vomited. Indeed, only a few
weeks later as I walked to church at 9.30 a.m. I saw him sitting by the
side of the road, looking sad and sick. I threw him a cheery 'Morning!'
and kept walking for another few minutes until I suddenly stopped.
How could I leave him looking so unwell? What if he needed help?
I turned around, walked back, and spent five minutes or so chatting
with him. He assured me that he did not need further help and urged
me to hurry off and not be late for church. Through the experience of
working in churches, often serving tea to men like him, the women
had trained me to lose my role as bystander: I had become my
brother's keeper. That transformation did not happen immediately,
but unfolded through several important stages I can now identify:

1. Opening a building that Generation A clearly viewed as God's
   house to offer a warm, safe, sacred space.
2. Creating commensality through offering refreshments and con-
   suming them together.
3. Becoming familiar with the lives and needs of others, lending to
   them a sense that they were cared about, and belonged.

OPENING GOD'S HOUSE: CREATING
SACRED SPACE

The first time I participated in a church event I felt privileged and
happy that I was meeting with the women's approval. The power of
an older woman's judgement, the maternal authority figure perhaps,
was evidently still strong within me, despite my having left home
some thirty years earlier. The first time I accompanied a woman to
the church door and she unlocked it I felt equally privileged. We were
alone in the big church, silent apart from the sound of our shoes
slapping on the stone floor. I realized I had never been in a church
by myself, or in this case nearly by myself. There was something

daunting about it, nearly spooky, but also, I felt suddenly, enormously privileged. This was, to many people, a sacred space occupied by their Lord and Master. My presence needed to be, I decided, deeply respectful, if not to God, who did not (apparently) feature in my own life, but to others, like the woman I was accompanying. She moved quickly down the nave, a woman with a purpose: she wanted to turn on the correct lights (altar and baptistery) and open the main door, to show that the church was open. It was a busy weekend and there would be hundreds of people walking by and potentially coming in. I poked my head outside the door and saw that the passing crowd had swelled in just the short time I had been indoors. I looked back into 'my' church and saw only an elderly woman laying out cups and saucers on a table near the entrance. During that Saturday I saw, in spite of the hundreds walking by the door, precisely five people come in and look around the church: a man and woman in their fifties who looked in and quickly left, a man in his fifties who said he was coming to a concert being held later in the day and was just checking the time, and a couple in their fifties who arrived, looked around the church, and left. The only others were the locals, mainly the 'scruffy' men who came in regularly for a chat, tea, and biscuits. That pattern was repeated without variation during all the twenty-five church opening duties I carried out over the following months: few 'tourists' looked around; most visitors were regulars. It was the same pattern at the nearby St Paul's 'coffee mornings' that I visited regularly but less frequently for comparison during the same period, and at several other churches in the region.

The women who kept the church open with me said that they believed it was important to be open to whomever chose to come in. In so doing, they were creating an unusual, perhaps unique, social space whereby anyone may walk into a warm, free, friendly environment and be welcomed simply and unconditionally. People sit together without any pressure to buy anything or join a group. There is a saucer on the table, and most people do add a coin or two, but there is no overt invitation to do so. Most of the people I talked to at church watches and coffee mornings recognize and value that space. The space can be conceived as sacred within the larger building known more commonly as God's house, not because anyone sprinkled holy water around it, but because it was marked off from everyday life for a specific purpose by those who considered it God's wish.

Sometimes, the sacred space is open for people who need the church for their own, not obviously religious, reasons. During one coffee morning at another church I was visiting a man walked briskly in, nodded to the elderly women sitting at a table, and continued down the nave to the piano. He sat, paused a few seconds to catch his breath, and then, without any sheet music, began playing Rachmaninoff. The women explained that he had been coming in lately because he knew someone who attended the church and had said it would be all right if he played the piano. They didn't mind his presence and, as I listened more, it was obvious that he was accomplished. Before I left I wandered over and had a chat with him, hearing that he had taken early retirement and was drawn to play music. He could not read music so learned everything by ear, and felt compelled to play for at least three hours each day. The coffee morning was exactly the right time period. He did not attend the church, and had no intention of doing so, but was grateful for the space and the piano.

One morning in June I bumped into a man I had seen in a church congregation. He was a tough-looking man, heavy-set, with a shaved head. On that particular morning, we were walking towards each other on a narrow pavement and as we drew closer exchanged smiles of recognition. We paused and said hello, and he told me he was heading to the church because, he explained, it was a Wednesday, the day he helped to clean. I suggested he must enjoy it, particularly because the women were so kind and friendly. He nodded, and then said forcefully: 'Gives me something to do. This is really good for me. I don't know what I'd do otherwise.'

The church space might be most important to a certain sort of people who use it informally, people resembling a social class that Savage et al. (2013, 243) describe as 'the precariat'.[1] Representing about 15 per cent of the population, these have the lowest social and cultural capital of all classes, are either unemployed or in semi- and unskilled occupations, and have the highest levels of insecurity across all forms of capital. Although their reasons for coming to the churches seemed, superficially, to be quite different, they had one thing in common: they had nowhere else to go. Given the class-ridden nature of UK society, this blending of class relationships is all the

---

[1] The area of social class will be dealt with more generally in Chapter 7.

more striking. In what other space would Drunk Sleeping Man take tea with women of an upper-middle-class background, or Shaved Head Man be accepted to push around a broom with a few elderly women, or Piano Man get unfettered access to a well-tuned piano?

WOMEN ON THE FRONT LINE

One church watch morning I noticed a poster on the wall near where my partner for the day, Laura, was sitting. It was a verse from scripture: 'Jesus says don't be afraid, only believe' (Mark 5: 36). I asked her if she, or any of the other women who joined her on church open days, were ever afraid. It struck me that the women were in a vulnerable position, alone, in a big empty church. Had they ever been given any training for this work? She laughed and shook her head.

A few weeks later Pat and I had occasion to be confronted by that vulnerable and, potentially, dangerous situation we feared when a confused, enraged man entered the church shouting that he wanted to see a priest. He was probably in his late twenties, dressed only in what looked like pyjama bottoms, barefoot, wild-eyed, and with his incisor teeth filed sharply into points like a vampire. My hand felt in my jacket pocket for my mobile phone. The three 'regular' men sitting at the table said nothing, and did not even look at him. Pat, meanwhile, rose to her feet graciously and said that the priest was not there but would be on Sunday, so why didn't he come back then? An exchange quickly followed:

SCARY MAN: 'I want to see a priest!'
   Pat replied that the priest was not in.
SCARY MAN SHOUTED: 'This is a fucking church! Where's the priest?'
PAT SMILED AND SAID, EVENLY: 'The priest does not usually come in on a Saturday. Is there something we can help with?'
SCARY MAN: 'I want to see a priest! I need some shoes! Can someone give me some shoes?'

By this time, I was feeling nervous and wanted him to leave. I suggested that he walk a little further to the centre of town, where he might find a hostel or maybe the Salvation Army where he could get some shoes.

Scary Man was having none of that. He said he wanted to see a Bible, and stood in front of us, shouting and swearing again that he needed to see a priest, and wanted shoes and a Bible. Pat picked up a few books that had been left in a corner, but they were all hymn books. She explained that there were no Bibles in that area of the church. Scary Man shouted: 'This is a fucking church and you don't have a Bible? What kind of stupid women are you?' I glanced over at the regulars, hoping they would intervene, but they were quietly staring into their tea mugs. The man was becoming more than just a nuisance, I felt. With him shouting abusively about women, I was feeling more anxious and worried that his aggression might turn into something physical. I then found myself turning to him with a smile and saying something which sounded both absurd and also completely appropriate: 'Would you like a cup of tea?'

'Oh, yes, thanks very much,' he said politely, and sat down. The tea seemed to calm him for a few moments, but then he started glaring at me and Pat again. Just when I thought I would slip out and ring the police another two regulars walked in. I asked them if they knew where any hostels were open that could help with a pair of shoes. They said they did, and they would give him directions. With that, Scary Man fell silent, and a few minutes later he left with the regulars.

The experience was unsettling, not just because it made me feel vulnerable but because it seemed that the women were on the front line, willing, kind, but with no training or resources. There could have been telephone numbers for them to ring for advice about hostels or other resources for the homeless and semi-homeless people who would come into that space. They could have had training in how to respond to people who were clearly mentally unstable and perhaps dangerous. On reflection, a call to the police might have been an appropriate reaction but Pat had ruled it out. That would not have been a 'Christian' thing to do, she said. Further, she explained, it is often the case that they just want to blow off steam. It is unlikely, she said, that they would hurt an elderly woman, which was why it had been a good idea, she added, that the male regulars sitting at the table did not confront and further agitate him.

There were other occasions when women sitting in churches became unsettled by those who dropped in. A church in the north of England I visited had a similar schedule to keep the church open. Annabelle told me about a young woman with a child who came frequently and asked for money. On one occasion Annabelle had to stop the young woman from stealing the tea lights laid out in the prayer candle area. She had told her: 'Think how upset the church warden would be to see the candles missing.' Overhearing us, Gladys added that she was very disturbed about the woman, always asking for money, even when she passed her on the street. As I began to frequent other churches in the area during their coffee mornings, I was to see the same woman and child, asking for money. It was obvious she knew which doors would be open, and when.

Sarah had been organizing coffee mornings at another urban church for many years, and agreed that occasionally people caused trouble, but she knew how to deal with them:

> It's very rare. I mean, we have had one or two that have been a bit stroppy but usually you can kind of calm them down, and walk them gently to the door and say, go and sit out there until you've calmed down, you know. You must never be confrontational because that would definitely spark it off, you know. It is a difficult one that, but we've never had a real incident in here. [*she knocks on the table*] Touch wood. [*laughs*] It could happen. But fortunately it hasn't. I mean, you do get quite a lot of alcoholics and homeless people around. But if they come in here they seem to be... You know, you offer them a cup of coffee, even if they're absolutely staggering. They think, oooh, not so bad in here. One or two have had little shouting matches and you say, be a good boy, you know, kind of thing—and it does calm them down, but you never have to be, none of this, get out of here! You're drunk! That would definitely spark it off [*laughs*], you know, so you have to be calm, you have to be, talk quietly, that kind of thing. And it usually works.

In the course of my research over two years, I consistently talked to laypeople and clergy about church opening practice and was consistently told there was no training or related support given to the people who performed those duties, mostly the Generation A woman. One man in Scotland I spoke with described how he and his daughter had done a church opening for many years, but quit when they were told they could not open a side door as well as the front door. He wanted it open because, he said, otherwise it was not safe:

> You never know who is coming in the main door because you can't see them and they can hide anywhere. Women shouldn't do it on their own. No one really takes control of security at the church. There's no alarm system. People can just wander in and hide, and later they could steal things.

One priest who has run training courses for his parishioners and others in the community told me that as far as he was aware, there were no similar programmes in the area. He agreed with me that the women were in vulnerable and potentially dangerous situations, and also that they were unable to give any practical help to people who came in. He said that in his city there had been a general training programme to create awareness of the resources available for vulnerable people. This awareness prepared people for giving useful, practical information to those who might drop into the church. A section on his church's website is unusual in that it draws attention to the role people play in providing practical information. The church is open every day from 8.30 a.m., it explains, staffed by volunteers who will answer questions about the church, and signpost people who may need particular services or advice. The act of opening God's house becomes, it seems, an act of informal social service.

INFORMAL SOCIAL WORK

We may not always notice 'them', I realized, but they notice us. More than a year later, we had a visitor who asked if he could look around the church and say a prayer. We told him that of course he could, and so in he went, re-emerging a short while later to say how beautiful the church was. He only lived around the corner, he told us, and he knew 'the vicar', as he saw him 'parking his car, lovely red car. Lovely fellow'. He shook our hands, introduced himself, and said he would come back. I never saw him again, but the incident, combined with the sorts of encounters described above, led me back to Davie's (2007) idea of 'vicarious religion'. Some members of the public expect the church to be open for their spontaneous use. Davie (2007) suggested that an 'unchurched' public believes 'vicariously' through others, such as church leaders, who believe on their behalf. Davie's ideas about vicarious religion follow from her theories about individualized beliefs, suggesting that vicarious religion conveys a specific kind of religious sentiment: 'the notion of religion performed by an active minority but on behalf of a much larger number, who (implicitly at least) not only understand, but, quite clearly, approve of what the minority is doing' (Davie 2007, 22). Davie argues that these performances relate to ritual, beliefs, moral codes, and creating discursive, unique spaces for debating unresolved issues. Notwithstanding considerable regional and denominational variation, as she pointed out in her earlier work (Davie 1994), the 'active minority' of whom she speaks is likely to be elderly and female.

Davie argues that the church is more than just a dependable service provider of life-cycle rituals for an unchurched public, but it is also a believer on their behalf. She describes how bishops, in particular, are expected to proclaim the key tenets of their faith, and when they publicly express doubts, they are criticized by people who rarely attend church. Davie's third point, similar to her example of believing bishops, relates to the issue of behaving bishops, and other clergy. The public expects them to uphold strict forms of moral codes, particularly with regard to 'traditional' family life. Of most interest here is Davie's fourth kind of vicarious religion relating to the symbolic value of a national church. She discusses how, for much of its history, the Nordic churches and citizenry have had a material, symbiotic relationship. All citizens were automatically members of the Church and approved that a proportion of their taxes supported it, unless they actively disassociated themselves, giving rise to an inversion of her 'believing without belonging' thesis: belonging without believing. This means that citizens participate in the ritual aspects of church performances 'and regard membership as part of national just as much as religious identity' (Davie 2007, 25). Further, she points out, a consequence of the citizens' contribution through taxation means that the churches are well maintained and act as a cultural resource. To add to the idea of 'belonging without believing', she adds that the Nordic populations do not attend church regularly and 'appear on every comparative scale to be among the least believing and least practising populations in the world' (Davie 2007, 25). I suggest that the act of keeping churches open performs a task, a duty perhaps, to allow the 'unchurched' public access for the occasional prayer or cup of tea. This suggests that forms of nominal religiosity represent a still-present historical association with the Church as an institution, representing not just religion, but safety, a sense of security, and a shared identity.

There was a strange sense I gained from the experience that the social service we were providing was accidental. Most of the women I talked with said that they had not originally seen their interactions with the vulnerable 'regulars' as the main purpose of their activity. As Fran told me, 'Originally the idea was to leave the church open in case someone wanted to come in and pray, then talk, and then maybe make them a cup of tea,' she said. 'In practice, no one comes in, looks around the church, and then pops in for a cup of tea. It's just the regulars.' At that moment a woman walked in whom I had seen before. I said we had been talking about the people who came in for a cup of tea, and that I wondered who they were. 'Only us,' she said. 'It's only the regulars that come in.'

Sarah reflected on their church opening sessions as central to her identity as a Christian. Keeping the church open and being kind to the people who come in was:

> part of our mission. I mean, we've got one particular fellow here that, when he first started coming, you know, he kind of crept in the door, we offered him a cup of coffee and he had about six thousand biscuits, you know, because he was hungry, and had no money, and he was renting a place fairly locally, which we found out after quite a long time, when he started to open up. Um, and now he's, he's got light in his eyes, he smiles, he chats, he tells us things about himself that he would have never have told us before. He's got little jobs that he does, he's got a bit of money in his pocket. He's got something to live for. And we feel very grateful for that. Because we feel that he was sent to us. We had to do that for him.

The variance in approach to what could be regarded as informal social work seems to be typical of churches. In her case study of the English northern town of Darlington, Middlemiss Lé Mon (2009) concluded that churches have conflicting views about their roles as social work providers. Her research used qualitative methods to explore the situation of religion and welfare in England, particularly at the local level, to assess the Church's role in welfare and people's perception about that role. Comparisons were made with Sweden to draw conclusions about the place of the established Church. One of her findings of relevance here is the ambiguous nature of social welfare, with her interviewees differing in their views about the church's role. She found that many people thought that the extent to which the Church provided welfare assistance was a matter for individuals to decide. I, too, found mixed responses to the church's social work role. At an event in one church where the connections with the surrounding area were being discussed, in terms of how much more the church could be involved, one elderly woman whispered to me that she was getting tired of discussions like this about social work: 'when I was young we had little, but we worked hard'.

Middlemiss Lé Mon also found that some people she studied realized that the age profile of the church made decline inevitable, and that attracting people through social work provision might be a way to increase numbers. The following passage illustrates the conflicting views (Middlemiss Lé Mon 2009, 220–1), beginning with one man's observation:

> The Church of England, which is what I am, you don't get a lot of people [...] you get the feeling that when these elderly people die off there is going to be nobody coming along. I just don't know what you do about that and I don't know whether that all stems from if the Church had a wider role in what we are talking about, whether that would bring more people in, give them a wider interest.

> Or as another put it: 'It may be that the only way that the church can go in Europe is to get involved more socially, otherwise it might decline severely' (G2 bm). The same man argued earlier in the same discussion that welfare work can be a way in which the church attracts members 'going out there practically to help people and then drawing people into the more formal aspects,' and, he continued: 'I think this is perfectly justified, even if it is slightly cynical' (G2 bm). Even if he is the only respondent to express his opinions in such strong terms there seems to be a general pattern of opinion amongst the respondents that if the Church were to be more active both in the community and in promoting what it already does it could attract more members and win allies in the public sphere, so that when it does speak out it would be taken more seriously.

COMMENSALITY

At first it was difficult for me to relax amongst the 'street people'. They tended to come in and sit for hours in many churches I visited, talking loudly and spoiling, I thought, the deep, comforting silence of the empty church. The women always sat with them. When they entered, usually only seconds after we opened the door, one of us would ask them if they would like a cup of coffee or tea, and in a mug or a cup. There was always a bowl of sugar and a milk jug on the table, a saucer for money (with a few coins we would put in to drop the hint), and a plate of biscuits. The biscuits at all such venues were generally low cost: Rich Tea, Oaties, Pink Wafers, or plain Digestive. For reasons I never worked out, occasionally there was with them a smattering of others that were more special, such as chocolate Hobnobs or Bourbon Creams. Most of the regulars were scrupulously polite, saying please and thank you, and only having one or two biscuits. At one church in England, I watched with fascination as one man continued to reach over to the biscuit plate and scoop up yet another handful. The Generation A woman sitting beside me caught my glance and whispered, 'One tries to be a Christian.' I nodded, but at the same time was aware of a feeling of resentment. The main reason I was taking the trouble to sit in the churches was because I wanted to get to know the women, to talk informally with them about their lives, about what they believed in, and how they acquired those beliefs. It seemed, however, I was not the only person who wanted to talk to them. Carol, a regular in her eighties, said she liked the company because her husband of some sixty years had recently died and she was lonely: 'you need to have people to talk to. You need to. You need to talk', she told me. Anna, a Canadian Generation A woman, made a similar point:

> If you were a woman who had no other activities and your husband all of a sudden died and you were lonely, you should come to the church. Whether you are religious or not [*laughs*]. Because there is something to do every day, in that church. It's a busy church. However, there are very few young people.

And then there was a slightly younger woman I listened to at an American church's coffee morning, who talked in long, disjointed monologues that eventually came around to the loss of her mother. The Generation A women I visited at those events told me that their 'regulars' rarely came to a church service. It did not seem to matter.

As the weeks progressed I realized one of my research tactics was failing. I was not, after all, going to be able to conduct and record the semi-structured interviews (or even what Yin 2003 would describe as a guided conversation) I had hoped for,[2] during these experiences. There were always other people around and, in any case, during any few moments alone it was generally at the end of a session and I had my arms up to the elbows in dishwater. On a few occasions early on in my fieldwork I excused myself from the group in order to sit apart and make notes. That seemed to be a better use of my time, until it occurred to me one day that I was missing a chance to observe an

---

[2] See Chapter 2 for feminist reflections on interviewing women.

important part of the women's religiosity: the performance of their core beliefs. The word 'commensal' is chosen here as it conveys the notion of eating together with a particular symbolic value. What happens when people eat together, and why do they choose specific people with whom to eat? Anthropologists have long noted the importance of commensality, loaded with ritual and other symbolic practices and meanings.[3] One particular feature of commensality that I will analyse here is the way in which it structured and replicated social relationships, and the important role played by its main non-human or, following Hallowell 1960, other-than-human actor: the cup.[4]

The role we 'church-women' played seemed clearly as 'provider' of both physical and emotional sustenance. This replicated and was reinforced by our unequal relationships with the 'regulars'. We were the keepers of the social space, the administers of tea and biscuits, the listening ear. While we also partook with the regulars in refreshments and conversation, we alone had access to the scarce material resources of biscuits, coffee, and tea, and the immaterial resource of time and social space. The church was opened and closed according to the schedule we created. We were also unequal in terms of knowledge and experience. The regulars lived precarious lives marked, according to their conversation, by (in almost equal measure) tedium and trauma. They talked about the deaths of people close to them, of their medical appointments, of what they had seen on the street that day, of a friend's absence because of an operation or a bout at the detox centre, their lack of control over their housing, and the constant sense of being neglected by the local County Council. Their worlds were foreign to me and to the women with whom I sat. One day, we ran out of milk halfway through the opening time. I said I would go to the local shop to buy some, but one of the regulars said I need not bother as she had a pint in her shopping bag and I could buy it from her. I thought that was a good solution and reached into my bag for my purse, hoping I had the right change, before realizing, with embarrassment, that I did not know the price of a pint of milk. She did, of course, because her world was regulated by short time periods in which she had just enough money to get through the next few days. My income (and access to easy lines of credit should I choose) meant

---

[3] For an excellent overview, see Mintz and Du Bois (2002).
[4] I return to the discussion of 'the cup' in Chapter 8.

that I could add a pint of milk to my Waitrose shopping basket without even looking at the price.

Our conversations generally avoided remarking on such details of disparity. This was the space where the women perform, not discuss, their Christianity. When I asked them if they ever talked to the regulars about God or Jesus, they drew back in mock horror. Certainly not! This was not a place to evangelize or put pressure on people, but just to do what Jesus would want them to do: listen, be kind, be calm. Katherine said:

> No, you don't preach. That frightens people away. You kind of, um, come alongside them if you like; put it that way. You show them friendship. Even if they're the dirtiest looking individual you could possibly find—you have to accept them, otherwise you'll never change their lives. They'll think, 'I'm not going in there again, so unfriendly, I suppose I suppose I'm not good enough for them'. And we never, ever want anybody to feel like that when they come through that door.

OPEN FOR SERVICE

The core demographic for mid-week church attendance was the same in most of the churches I visited regularly: largely Generation A, apart from the cathedrals that attracted a different group of people altogether: two students and a fellow conference attendee at Durham Cathedral for Morning Prayer; mainly male gay professionals in downtown Manhattan. The cathedrals also attract a tourist component for popular services such as Sung Evensong, particularly if the choir is well known.

At the parish churches, however, it is a different story. Women of Generation A attend church three times a week, more than the average married couple has sex.[5] The congregation at the mid-week services was almost exclusively Generation A, a pattern confirmed in discussions with priests from other parts of the Anglican Communion (the exception being churches linked to Church of England schools where children are taken by the school to attend special services). The women I saw attending the Sunday service would also attend Morning Prayer at 9.30 on Monday morning and Holy

---

[5] <http://www.kinseyinstitute.org/resources/FAQ.html>, last accessed 5.8.2014.

Communion at noon on a Wednesday. The weekday services in some churches took place in smaller side chapels, or even a smaller room near the vestry that had a small heater. Anyone who was not a regular but just wanted to attend the mid-week service would be unaware that we were there. The side chapel was just large enough to seat a small gathering, making our group of eight or so seem very cosy. At another local church the chairs were pulled into a semicircle in front of the altar. The combination of the spatial configuration and the handful of attendees created an impression of a private event, something a stranger might find intimidating, in the unlikely event that she were so inclined to pop into an unknown church for a mid-week service. To add to the feeling of familiarity and intimacy, the women did not even pick up their prayer books to read the words; they recited the prayers and responses by heart. Even at a large, prominent cathedral I visited for the mid-week morning prayer service it was apparent we were expected to know the liturgy. While reading the psalm, for example, we followed a definite rhythm, leaving a pause at the end of the first line of each couplet, but not between each. Anyone unfamiliar with the practice would be audibly outed from the start.

The liturgy, however, is only one part of the activity. On one visit to Morning Prayer I was aware of low voices, speaking almost in whispers around me:

> Where's Betty?
> And Jean's not coming any more?
> I don't know, haven't seen her.
> It's happened before, she usually comes again.
> I'll ring her when I get home.

By attending the mid-week services and the coffee mornings\church openings it is possible to know the daily movements of each member of the small congregation. If someone should, for example, have a fall at home and be unable to call for help, it would only be a matter of hours before one of the women would ring or pop round. The everyday religious lives of Generation A provide a pattern of surveillance and support for people living alone. The frequent, often daily contact also provides an opportunity for a sense of belonging. As Elaine, a Canadian Generation A woman told me:

> Church gives you instant community. Now whether that's being selfish or not, I don't know, but it does. [*Laughs*] Gives you instant community and you feel safe with the people you meet there.

As I left the services I would inevitably be joined by women asking questions: 'how are your children... will you be able to come to the church on Friday... are you coming to Bible study next week, it's *Ruth*, if you want to read up...' Although the women said that the services are open for everyone, their practice is one of a small, closed, tightly knit group, displaying embodied tacit knowledge of, for example, prayers, responses, seating arrangements, and movements (when to sit, kneel, or stand), and of each other. I was not able to observe regularly how the women incorporated new people into their group because strangers rarely appeared at either of the two churches I visited most regularly over two years.

The women's work was a gendered form of labour centred on stereotypical practices of food preparation, serving, and cleaning. Within the services they also reified the gender role of women in the pews and a man in the pulpit. This was overlaid with a generational character: only women of a certain age would be available for mid-week services or coffee mornings, either the older, retired women or young mothers taking a career break. No young mothers attended the services during my fieldwork. Also generational was the type of refreshment served—standard English tea, instant coffee, and mass-produced biscuits. There was not an espresso machine or organic flapjack in sight. The women's behaviour also followed gender and generational stereotypes of the passive, accepting woman. My observations here are not surprising, but what did surprise me was the quiet, unexpressed assumption that the women were in their own place. It may be God's house, but they opened it, closed it, and moved within it as if it were an extension of their own homes. Percy (2015, 234) observed:

> [the] making of homes is a profoundly analogical and literal reference to the function of faith. Making safe spaces of nourishment, well-being, maturity, diversity and individuation; our 'faith homes' (or households— *oikos*) are places both of open hospitality and security.

Looked at women's church space through a lens of 'home' it became more understandable why they were not in a hurry to professionalize their church activities through becoming priests. It is unlikely that as a priest they would feel more powerful or more involved than they already were. They already had unlimited access to the church building and they knew that they were the 'one body' that gathered in the quiet weekday mornings. Their priest arrived to pray with them or to serve them communion, after which they would linger for social time with each other and sometimes with him. It was a fairly exclusive group to which they belonged, and they were aware that without them the church was unlikely to be open apart from on Sundays. The Church of England's slogan stressing the importance of 'a Christian presence in every community' glosses over the demographic reality that the church's ability to be open on any day apart from a Sunday depends on a declining Generation A, and that the bulk of its informal social work is almost entirely dependent on that same generation.

The everyday manner in which women inhabit and behave in the space of the church achieves something more than just a sense of belonging and a warm confirmation of their Christian teachings: they owned that space, and they knew it. Their frequent, repetitive moves and constant conversations create and reinforce their individual and collective understanding of who they are in relation to the church and to others inside and outside the church space. Space, as the geographer Massey discussed (2005), is relational, a project in progress, a process (De Certeu 1984; Lefebvre 1991), composed of the relations amongst those who inhabit it and, I will add (to coin a new term), 'exhabit' it; the latter being those who create an external, peripheral area usually referred to as 'the community'.

The creation and maintenance of church space is performative, following Butler's interpretation of the power produced by repetitive discourses and practices (Butler 1990; 1993) and speech acts Austin (1962). It brings into being a social reality with what Butler referred to as the 'binding power' (Butler 1993, 225) of the acts. When Fortier (2000) studied Italian migrants in London through an ethnography of St Peter's Italian Church, she described 'performative belongings' with performative and belonging explored as constitutive of cultural identities that are both and at once deterritorialized and reterritorialized. She showed that cultural identities are created, performed, and embedded through socially binding linguistic acts and events such as processions, weddings, newsletters, and first communions.

Through research into how people discursively produce their sense of belonging to neighbourhoods, Benson and Jackson (2013, 806) usefully distinguish place-making from place maintenance, where place maintenance, 'while appearing relatively passive, is in fact a way of discursively producing place through action [...] focused on warding off unwelcome change...'

One of the most unwelcome changes feared by the women I studied is the possibility that falling numbers might force their church to close. At the time of writing, there were about 16,000 churches, with some twenty closing each year. The Church of England tries to manage the process sensitively. The congregation will be invited to join a nearby congregation and the public will be consulted on whether the church should be demolished or another use found for it. Statistics kept between 1969 and 2014 show that 1,902 churches were closed for worship.[6] Of those, 1,066 changed use, the most popular being for residential purposes (300), followed by use by other Christian groups (169), civic, cultural or community uses (149), and monument (150).

Church closure occurs for a number of reasons, but the key is finance, a function of attendance, fund-raising, gifts, and legacies. I will reflect more in Chapter 9 on Generation A's contribution to that mix, and the implications for the Church when they are gone, as most of the Church's money comes from their sort of labour: regular attendance, fund-raising, and legacies. Meanwhile, they know that keeping their church open and available to the wider public is part of the criteria for decision-making concerning potential church closures, as well as an important factor in gaining obtaining external funding. Viewed in this way, Generation A may have come to their informal social care role inadvertently, and in some cases reluctantly. In a time when churches are being closed almost daily, there arises a delicate balance in a parish between competition and collaboration amongst churches. A fight for resources will be, literally a fight to the death.

The inner city churches I visited in England and the United States were often located in areas that were, themselves, contested in the perceptions of those who worshipped and lived there. What is inter-esting and 'edgy' to some people may be squalid and dangerous to others. What was striking about the Generation A laywomen I talked to was their calm and defiant expressions when such subjects were raised: they were neither deterred nor discouraged by sights, sounds, and smells of dirty, drunken, or drugged local inhabitants. They seemed to exude a wartime spirit of strength and solidarity, a little like a siege mentality; they did not entertain possibilities of retreat. Theirs was a form of 'pew power'. As I will reflect in the following chapters, it was a form of power that rested on presence and an embodied knowledge of belonging.

---

[6] <https://www.churchofengland.org/clergy-office-holders/pastoralandclosedchurches/closedchurches.aspx>, last accessed 1.9.2016.

4

Powers of Purification

If ritual events in most religions have been historically performed by men, it is certain that behind them, invisibly, laboured a team of women. How else did his robes become so clean and smooth, his ritual artefacts so pristine, and the place of worship itself so clean? In the church, as in the home, the hard work of maintaining cleanliness, restoring order, and preparing for rituals is carried out by laywomen; in the church, this has been largely carried out by Generation A. Such labours are typified by their generation, often stereotyped as passive 1950s housewives, dutifully cleaning their houses, their family's clothes, and preparing the family food. It earned them distaste and derision by their daughters, the feminists of the cultural revolution of the 1960s. In this chapter I reflect on my fieldwork experience during which I became familiar with the jobs of cleaning and preparation, and how it contributed to my impression of these women as active agents in creating and maintaining the 'purity' of their church and its family. Further, I was to realize that we feminists only ever knew half the story of what we saw as labour-theft and subjugation, unaware of the deep pleasure and power such work can give to a holy woman committed to her priest and her god. As this chapter will detail, the intimate acts of cleaning and preparation are not best interpreted as selfless, sacrificial labour performed by a worthy generation tied to each other and the church mainly through bonds of obligation. Generation A treats the church building as their extended home. Through their physical and spiritual labour, they renew and reimpose a sense of order, ownership, and care, extending to the building, the priests, and the congregation. The work includes the regular church cleaning, often physically demanding routines of dusting, polishing, and sweeping, shifting furniture, and carrying heavy objects. At once spiritual and embodied, the labour is typical of women's work: tough, mundane, routine, and exhausting. As this generation ages, more churches are employing professional cleaners. And yet, as Beckford reminds us, religion depends on the labour of human beings (Beckford 2003, 1–2, 214). What is hidden from the public view is the communal, meditative, pleasurable, absorbing nature of the tasks that embed the women, literally, in the fabric of the church, and, many believe, through their good works, contribute to their salvation.

The experience of cleaning with women brought me into a deeper relationship with them and their church, understood now both as a building and a family. It was a feeling of intimacy, framed in a specific social space, but strangely resonant of other social spaces such as a home or a club. I introduced the idea of 'home' in the previous chapter, and will develop it further here, in the context of safety and refuge. It reminds me of a question I had discussed several years earlier in the course of another project, when I asked a woman how she would define 'home'. She said that home was a place where she felt safe, where nothing bad would happen to her. This sense of their church as their home also prompted me to think of the notion of 'sanctuary' as not just a physical place at the top of the church where the altar stood, but as something experienced more deeply, as a safe place, or place of refuge. Still lingering in the popular imagination is the idea that a church is a place to which people can flee when they are running from the police, as if the police cannot enter it or arrest them there. My question typed into Google 'Can you get arrested in a church?' brought 87,600,000 responses. An exchange on a popular website revealed the extent to which this notion persists.[1] Several people wanted to know if churches were still safe havens. Within the apparent safe haven of their church, the women do more than polish and dust. They are engaged in what Douglas (1966) understood as a political act. This spoke, for me, not only of cleaning but of 'place', and reminded me of how 'matter out of place' was how Douglas defined 'dirt' as objects (or people) that do not belong. She argued throughout her work that harnessing power depended on recognizing and managing divisions, primarily related to purity and impurity. She focused on disorder which, she says, is usually construed as dangerous and powerful. Cultures try to tame it or use it as a creative ground from which order can re-emerge through ritual. The discomfort people

---

[1] <https://uk.answers.yahoo.com/question/index?qid=20090427073130AA5JFwL>, last accessed 17.10.2015.

feel about disorder relates to ideas about pollution and purity, where that which is out of place, does not belong, is seen as anomalous and dangerous. Keeping a church clean and ritual artefacts pure and in their right place is the necessary step to maintaining order and positions of power and privilege.

CLEANING 'DEEPLY'

I am waiting at the appointed time on the lane beside the church for Florence, who is responsible for church cleaning. We have not met before, but she was introduced to me by a friend at St John's when I explained I wanted to study other churches in the same city. She arrives on schedule, unlocks the heavy door, and motions me inside. She makes her way very carefully, leaning on her cane. She is an old woman. I ask her later if she finds the cleaning tiring. Yes, she tells me, it is very tiring, which is why, she adds, she is sure to make her own house clean and her lunch and dinner prepared for the day before she comes to the church. Once she has finished the church in the morning, 'I'm done for the day, exhausted', she says. It is much worse in the winter when the church is not heated during the week, she said. I wonder why not . . . if it can be heated for a service on a Sunday, why not for three hours per week day so that the old women can clean without becoming even more exhausted through fighting the cold?

Not being a regular cleaner, and a newcomer to that congregation, I depended on Florence to tell me what and how to clean. She explained that they had a system that rotated different cleaning tasks: on Mondays they give the whole church 'a good old sweep'; on Tuesdays they polish the wood (mostly the pews); on Thursdays they do the floors with a broom; and they polish the brass 'as and when'. She said that today I should dust the side pews and she would follow me and sweep; that the best dusting method in her opinion was to spray the cloth first and use it to wipe the pews, rather than spray the pews and wipe after. The four pews were long, 9 metres each, and it took me half an hour to clean them. Along the top, down the backs, along the seats, over the sides, down to the floor, with Florence following behind with the broom. She was right about spraying into the cloth. When I tried once to aim it directly onto the wood my nose was instantly filled with the moist, acrid, spray. Cleaning pews is a

long and physically demanding job. Many churches have removed
their pews and therefore no longer have the need. A member of a
congregation, Emily, mentioned this during a conversation we were
having about how the church had changed over the years. She said
she is glad that even though they are difficult to clean, the pews have
not been removed and replaced by chairs. She realized, she said, that
cleaning the pews is time-consuming and arduous, and the cleaning
rota spent several hours each week cleaning the church. Even chairs
would need to be cleaned, she noted, and one good thing about pews,
she added, motioning to her arthritic knees, is that you can lean on
them for support when you stand up.

One morning when I was cleaning we were joined by one of the
male members of the congregation. He sometimes comes, Florence
explained. I watched him dusting the pews just in front of me: *my*
pews, in fact. As I worked my way along in silence I wondered why no
one had told him not to bother, as it seemed like an unnecessary
duplication of labour. I was also slightly irritated when Florence
announced we would stop for a tea break: I had only two hours
available and had so much more to clean. Florence whispered that
they only stopped for a tea break when others dropped in. He was,
I knew, one of the more vulnerable members of the congregation who
was deeply in need of kind conversation and small treats, such as tea
and biscuits. I was beginning to realize something important about
the labours of Generation A: efficiency, outputs, and measurements
were not their organizing principles. As spiritual practices, team
cleaning was an act of communion, meditation, and belonging.

Our embodied social practices thus reflected knowledge shared by
the women who had come before us and in turn reflected the ideas of
the Church, which in turn reflected wider social norms: we were one
body, a family, joined in our shared beliefs and practices of cleanliness
and purity, performed through our physical bodies. Social ideas and
practices are manifested, expressed, and produced through our physical bodies. As this generation ages, churches are turning to other
sources of labour for cleaning acts. A few can find volunteers from the
sons and daughters of Generation A, but many need to turn to
commercial services. The result may, indeed, be a clean church, but
the consequence is a church less organically alive and the ties less
tight amongst the congregation that remains. It also removes, for a
particular kind of woman, a particular kind of service, or a way of
'doing theology', as I discuss in the next chapter.

At one service I was struck by the reading from scripture concerning church cleaning. This contained a slightly troubling picture of Jesus rebuking a woman called Martha. The text relates (Luke 10:38–42):

[38]   As Jesus and his disciples were on their way, he came to a village where a woman named Martha opened her home to him. [39] She had a sister called Mary, who sat at the Lord's feet listening to what he said. [40] But Martha was distracted by all the preparations that had to be made. She came to him and asked, 'Lord, don't you care that my sister has left me to do the work by myself? Tell her to help me!'

[41] 'Martha, Martha,' the Lord answered, 'you are worried and upset about many things, [42] but only one thing is needed. Mary has chosen what is better, and it will not be taken away from her.'

That seemed a bit harsh, I thought, and I decided to ask Sue, who ran the Bible Study group at one of the churches, what she thought this told us about women cleaning. She explained that:

> SUE: I think in that particular instance Martha was busy and therefore her busyness came between her and listening to Jesus, and the interesting, the important thing in that instance was that she should be listening to *him*.
> ABBY: So that context, at that particular time—?
> SUE: Yes, in that particular context. Of course it doesn't mean that cleaning is not important; it's very important.

Jesus may have preferred that the women should listen to him, rather than clean, but in today's context there may be an added, unexpected dimension of spirituality to our labour. It was while I was dusting the pews one morning while Florence and Mary worked nearby on their cleaning acts, surrounded by a deep silence broken only by the *shhhhhhh* of a broom as it swept across the floor and the *clunk* as it met the wall, the occasional *pssssst* of the furniture spray, and the *ting* as the container was put down on the floor, that it struck me the first time I had participated in silent, focused group activity had been eighteen years earlier during a Zen Buddhist retreat led by the Vietnamese monk Thich Nhat Hanh. He taught us to 'look deeply' by walking slowly around a garden, pausing briefly every now and then to stare into the greenness of a tree, drinking in deeply its colour, shape, and texture. Immersing oneself deeply in observation and participation is a key Zen spiritual practice, popularized more recently as 'mindfulness'. Since then, I have taken several groups of students on 'Zen walks' to show them the benefit of focusing on what is present, in the here and now. In the church that morning, I recalled those Zen walks and sensed deeply that, although separated by time and religious tradition, our cleaning acts that morning felt qualitatively the same as a walking meditation at a Zen retreat.

Of course, this was not a Zen retreat and I was in the church to practise ethnography, not meditation. Indeed, the impression I had gained from the literature in my field of Religious Studies and Sociology of Religion was that meditation and other so-called spiritual activities were practised by baby-boomers, but not the oldest generation.[2] I looked over to where Mary was sweeping and I wondered what she was thinking, or perhaps praying about. I wandered over to her and asked her if the women always worked in silence. She paused in her sweeping and said yes, she supposed they did; they enjoyed the peace and quiet. I asked her what she thought about when she was cleaning and she said she was 'just sort of meditating'. On anything in particular? I asked. She thought for a moment and then said 'it depended'; it was never the same thing every time. On that particular day, she said, it was the presence of several homeless people she had seen on her way to the church that had make her think about the scale of vulnerability that humans share. We are all vulnerable to some extent, she explained, as we are all emotionally and physically damaged in some way: it is just our place on the scale that differs. Our place on the scale... of course! That is all that separates us. It was a good thought, an important insight—a flash of satori, perhaps, when our oneness with others seems so fleetingly obvious.

The meditative, rhythmic, dreamy quality of cleaning struck deeply on another occasion when I found myself cleaning the pews under a war memorial on the south wall. I put down my cloth and read the names silently, looking at them 'deeply' as Nhat Hanh might say. Several shared the same family name; brothers, cousins, fathers. I sensed over my shoulder Florence polishing in silence and wondered what her story of the war might be. Who had she lost, how many, and at what cost? The word 'sacrifice' came to mind, and for the next few pews I meditated on that word, and the significance of it for Generation A, sometimes described as the 'air raid' generation.

---

[2] See Chapter 5 for further discussion of that literature.

How significant, sacred even, for them must be the 'England' in Church of England, as the institution that embodies and honours sacrifice, commemorating it in national events such as Armistice Day, in the names carved in the church of father, son, husband, brother, boyfriend, cousin.

The understanding of 'sacrifice' is essential to religion. Jay (1992) reviews early religious theories beginning with totemism and observed that these theories, created by white British and European men, assume society's structures and morals are created by men, with women as either passive observers or victims of men's desires. She refers (Jay 1992, 132) to work on violence and sacrifice that only emphasized the violent and sacrificial acts, and not the feasting—a practice presumably made possible through women's labour of cooking and serving. Most rituals involve some notion of sacrifice, which itself encompasses gender dichotomy, as only adult males (real or metaphorical), have traditionally performed sacrifice. One function of sacrifice may be that it secures the lineage of the dominant male: 'Without sacrifice there can be neither a hierarchical priesthood nor its institutionalized genealogy linking males in unilineal descent' (Jay 1992, 123). Jay's study made me realize that the sort of work carried out by Generation A women, such as cleaning, making teas, and raising money, is perhaps ignored, or at least not valorized, because it is not linked to sacrifice.

A Canadian Generation A woman (Bays 2012, 45) writes of declining membership amongst women. This is a difficult time for members, most of whom, she says, have been part of a close-knit group all their lives:

> sharing the joys and sorrows of everyday life, had the fun of working and studying together, and now are in their senior years with less energy to work in the kitchen but with a deep appreciation for the Christian companionship and support of the group. To some, it seems as though something precious is being cast aside, not valued.

Although we were deep in our own meditative, spiritual practice, our moves were pre-recorded. Florence told me what the morning routine would be, how I would dust, and how she would follow me and sweep; that the best dusting method in her opinion was to spray the cloth first and use it to wipe the pews, rather than spray the pews and wipe after. Our embodied social practices thus reflected those shared by the women who had come before us and in turn reflected the ideas of the Church, which in turn reflected wider social norms: we were one body, a family, joined in our shared beliefs and practices of cleanliness and purity, performed through our physical bodies. Shhhhhh, psssst, clunk, ting, shhhhhhh, psssst, clunk, ting. Social ideas and practices are manifested, expressed, and produced through our physical bodies, mirroring a relationship between the 'individual' and 'society'.

TECHNOLOGIES OF BELONGING

Those embodied practices are learned through the repeated acts of doing, and such things take time, as Mauss (1935) noted in his reference to the skill of digging the trenches in France during the First World War. English soldiers did not know how to use a French spade, which meant 8,000 spades had to be exchanged each time French and English troops relieved each other: 'This plainly shows that a manual knack can only be learnt slowly. Every technique properly so-called has its own form' (Mauss 1935, 71). It is here that Mauss (1935, 73) introduced the concept of *habitus* that was to influence generations of scholars (notably Pierre Bourdieu) meaning culturally created, collectively learned habits. For my purpose here I want to draw attention to a specific aspect of his formulation: prestige. Successful transmission of *habitus* occurs through people imitating the techniques of those who have successfully performed them 'by people in whom he has confidence and who have authority over him' (Mauss 1935, 73). The cultural upheaval of the 1960s meant that feminist children of Generation A neither had confidence in nor accepted the authority of that older generation. As Matthews (1987, 222) suggests, 'By the 1960s, the woman who was supposed to provide emotional support for her family and in essence underwrite the psychological well-being of her society was all too likely to be herself in a state of demoralization.'

The way the women incorporated their physical moves into a religious experience recall what Mellor and Shilling (2010, 30) called 'body pedagogics', an approach that moves attention about contemporary religion from easily measurable data such as church attendance to:

> an investigation of the central institutional *means* through which a religious culture seeks to transmit its main embodied techniques, dispositions

and beliefs, the *experiences* typically associated with acquiring these attributes, and the embodied *outcomes* resulting from these processes.

They suggest (Mellor and Shilling 2010, 29) that an emphasis on measurable data, such as church attendance or affiliation, has led many scholars incorrectly to advance arguments in favour of secularization theses. Indeed, the analysis and argument about religious transmission is limited to the obvious religious rituals of, for example, Christian communion or Muslim salat; the kinds of embodied practice evidenced by Generation A, in contrast, demonstrated religious transmission through everyday practices of church attendance, church monitoring, cleaning, and socializing. They trained me, for example, to know how to listen to people I described earlier as members of the precariat; how to adapt to a cleaning rhythm in a sacred space that opened up time and directions for reflections and how to alter my schedules to account for new forms of time-making.

The more I observed Generation A women and talked about their lives, the more I realised that their church attendance and related activities did not occur because they had more 'time' than, for example, their sons and daughters do now. Some had worked when their children were older, some had no children at all and worked full time when they were younger, many were caring for old or sick relatives. Most relevant to my work is the anthropological discussion about time, reminding me to appreciate both specificity and universality. Munn (2012, 116), writing on the complexities of time from an anthropological perspective, observed that it is 'difficult to find a meta language to conceptualize something so ordinary and apparently transparent in everyday life'. Gell said (1992, 9):

> There is no fairyland where people experience time in a way that is markedly unlike the way in which we do ourselves, where there is no past, present and future, where time stands still or chases its own tail, or swings back and forth like a pendulum.

As my research continued, the idea of time became increasingly important as I found myself becoming embedded in St John's, to the point that it became difficult to leave the group even when my fieldwork had finished. That realization led to me explore the awkward sense that I had been hooked, trapped even, and analyse what exactly the women had done to me. Over time, I developed a model

Holy Women

upon which I will reflect wholly in Chapter 9, consisting of seven
stages I identified: Recognition; Social Intimacy; Integration; Routinization; Obligation; Ritualization; Internalization. Its relevance here is
to highlight the sense of routine that had quickly developed as a result
of my commitment to the tasks in which I was now involved. Very
early on in my research I had realized that it was easy to tell who
belonged and who did not belong, simply because there were not that
many people in the congregation, as is typical of a Church of England
mainstream church. The Evangelical churches within the Church of
England may number their average Sunday congregations in the
hundreds or even thousands (Holy Trinity Brompton reports an
average Sunday service of 4,500), but these are exceptions. On a
'usual Sunday' the average congregation size in a Church of England
church is sixty-nine, and given the large numbers in the Evangelical
urban churches, it becomes easy to see how many church congregations would number in their tens. As reported in the latest available
(2014) Statistics for Mission:[3]

> It is possible to talk about an "average church" (which had 69 people
> attending each week during October 2014, 92 at Easter, 171 at Christ-
> mas, and which carried out 10 funerals, 9 baptisms, and 3 marriages),
> but it is important to recognise that many churches are far from
> average; the largest 5% of churches have a usual Sunday attendance of
> 160 or more people, whereas 8 or fewer people attend the smallest 5% of
> churches.

Typically, the churches I visited regularly had between thirty-five and
fifty congregants on a Sunday, with another five to twenty making up
the officiants and choir. I therefore knew that I could recognize easily
the people who were there regularly; there simply were not that many,
and strangers were a rare sight. I also saw that they learned to
recognize me, and that they were getting to know me, first as a
researcher, and then more as a near-neighbour, mother, and daughter. Over post-service coffee and tea, they would ask me more personal questions—'ah do you live here, oh that's nice, do you have a
family, do you have children'? They may have also recognized me as
an Anglican, as our holy moves are learned and rehearsed. As I had

---

[3] <https://www.churchofengland.org/media/2432327/2014statisticsformission.pdf>,
last accessed 14.5.2015.

been, as a child and teenager, a regular attender with my family at Church of England services, I knew how to behave: when to stand, when to sit down, when to pray, how to take communion. I could also see how difficult it was for people who did not know the moves. One priest I interviewed at a different church said to me:

> It's so embarrassing when we have some particular service and it's an important service, so let's say the mayor comes and some people from the town council might come. They always sit in the front row because they're important people but this means they can't see what's happening and so I have to tell them to sit down or stand up, because they don't know the moves, they weren't regular church attenders.

All these moves and moments of recognition form part of the knowledge, the body pedagogics, held and practised by Generation A, and, to a decreasing degree, passed on to future generations.

PURIFYING PLEASURES

Church cleaning was also, I learned, a pleasurable experience in some ways. This must have been felt particularly keenly when the women were younger, busy with children, and, in some cases, in paid work. The hour or two of church cleaning gave them a break. Sue also told me, reflecting on those days, that:

> When my children were small, I valued a few moments in church enormously and, I have to say that, when they're very tiny and climbing all over you etcetera, I really felt the loss of that quiet space and time. So, in fact, that made me—that was a spur really for me to consider contemplative prayer. I realized I had a need within myself for times of quiet and silence.

I was looking forward to finding quiet and silence when I arrived at the church for my second experience of cleaning. Obtaining enjoyment from cleaning was an unfamiliar sensation for me. The idea that it was possible had only arisen the day before in conversation with my mother, a Generation A Christian laywoman. My week had been busy, I recounted to her, but, I added with a tone tinged with regret, I was going nevertheless the next day to clean the church. 'Oh, good,' she replied. 'You can relax then.' The thought that cleaning would be relaxing had never occurred to me before. When Florence asked me how I had been lately I answered that I had been too busy:

> ABBY: It's nice in a way to come here and clean. It's so peaceful, isn't it?
>
> FLORENCE: Course it is.

These are surprisingly selfish pleasures, even more surprising given the church's emphasis on selflessness and duty. Listening one Sunday to a layperson's prayers from the lectern I was struck by her plea to 'remind us gently, kind father, that our labours are for you alone'. She obviously had not spent weeks on the cleaning rota and learned that the labours are also for the people who perform them. While I was reflecting on this theme, I discovered that some contemporary women feel the same. A blog-writer from the Church of Latter Day Saints discussed 'The joy found in cleaning the church' and specifically mentioned the sorts of pleasures I had discovered:[4]

> In a way it is like the celestial room, where peacefulness reigns and one can consider life at different level. Often I find it almost soothing and on days where my concerns are overcoming my life it is a welcome break.

Another writer, from a Catholic church, wrote along similar lines:[5]

> Scrubbing floors. Mopping and sweeping. It may not be glamorous work, but it's a wonderful way to serve the Lord and give back for all of His blessings. Indeed, we are often told that 'cleanliness is next to Godliness'. [. . .]

One woman who regularly cleaned said she and others of the 'Women's Guild' included women who had been doing the job for decades, scrubbing floors, wiping down pews, and cleaning 'the most sacred parts of the church'. As they aged, professional cleaners were hired to clean the largest part of the church, while 'the more sacred spaces—the sacristy, altar, and chapel' were cleaned by the women. The experience of cleaning allowed women to develop 'a closer relationship with Him by being within the church and being a part of the church physically, as well as emotionally'.

---

[4] <https://bannerswordshield.wordpress.com/2008/06/02/the-joy-found-in-cleaning-the-church>, last accessed 12.4.15.
[5] <http://www.stjohnmililani.org/news/parish-newsletter/206-february-2015/file>, last accessed 12.4.15.

Pleasurable as it is, the cleaning can also be frustrating and ultimately fruitless. On the Sunday following a cleaning week I noticed
something disturbing as I walked down the side aisle after communion. 'My' side pews were, only a few days after I had dusted them,
dirty from crumbled bits of stone that had fallen from the ceiling.
'Needs a good clean,' I muttered to myself, and instantly felt a wave of
hopelessness. As de Beauvoir (1949, 470) put it, 'Few tasks are more
like the torture of Sisyphus than housework, with its endless repetition.' An English expression of comparing an endless task to 'painting
the Forth Bridge' came to mind, as Australians would say about the
Sydney Harbour Bridge: as soon as you get to one end, it's time to go
back and start again. As Germaine Greer, whose work introduced
me to feminism in my childhood, said, housework is 'a typical
vicious circle; work makes more work and it goes on' (1970, 327).
I wondered how Generation A women bore the boredom of housework at home and cleaning at church without, as Friedan (1963)
predicted, losing both their minds and spirits. Or maybe they did.
Maybe the second-wave feminists with their calls for 'consciousness-
raising' were right; perhaps Generation A women merely stupidly
stumbled through the 1960s without seeing their true potential, their
noses and brains polluted by so much cleaning spray that they
couldn't think straight or, as De Beauvoir predicted, find any 'escape
from immanence and little affirmation of individuality' (1949, 470).
Perhaps. At that stage in my fieldwork, I couldn't decide. Feminists
have criticized a 'second-wave' focus on collective identities in favour
of embracing diversity and subversion in a 'third wave', itself problematic as it links to other unstable categories such as individualism
and choice.[6]

The pleasure of cleaning resulted not just in an outcome, a clean
church, but included a process, one which was tactile, sensual. Here,
in the half-dark of the church, we ran our hands along pews and felt
their nicks and smoothness; were aware of the fine gradient of the
stone floor; and traced the intricate wings of the brass eagle with our
finger tips. Morgan observed (2010, 8) that for most religious believers the transcendent 'does not come to them as pure light or sublime
sensations in most cases, but in the odour of musty shrines or
moldering robes or the pantry where they pray'. We were close to

---

[6] See Budgeon (2011) for an excellent overview.

our material objects in our material places: brooms, chalices, and vestments, some of which are physical, self-evident sacred objects, but others are more pragmatic and acquire their specialness through use. The objects we gather and display speak to our social relationships and connections. Miller (2008) argues that attachment to and 'comfort' in 'things' shows how people maintain their relationships in an increasingly fragmented world. He suggests that (Miller 2008, 295) 'Households have become more like societies which create a cosmology, to a greater or lesser degree linked to wider religious and cultural norms'. For households here, I can read, on behalf of the women I studied, 'churches'.

Indeed, church cleaning is a job with no end, and that sense of a predictable eternity brought its own comfort through the rhythm of its production, at once practical, material, emotional, and spiritual. It will, however, soon be ended for the generation that has carried it out for most of their lives. As they die and are not replaced, the church will be cleaned less often and, in the wealthier parishes, cleaned by professional companies. This will have several, possibly unintended, consequences.

First, it removes from the congregation one strong tie that binds. The women who do this work not only renew and strengthen their own connection with the church but the recognition of their labour reinforces the character of the church 'family'. The only people who clean for nothing are typically women looking after their homes and families. The cleaning team's job, mirroring the actions and apparent values of a family, will be lost. That may be a good thing, for feminists of my generation who view housework as tedium and the family not as an unequivocally desirable institution, but also as a site of patriarchy and control. But, for women of Generation A, it is a sacred institution inextricably linked to another sacred institution, their church, and their work is valued and respected by their fellow congregants.

Second, depending on their location, many churches leave their doors unlocked when the women clean. On some occasions, regular members of the congregation drop in to say hello, and the opportunity is there for strangers to have a look or even a short visit and a chat if they like. The cleaning rota is one means of keeping a church open on the days when there are no services or other events. I asked Sue if she thought there was a danger of the church being closed more often if the regular rota of women disappears:

> That will be a danger that church won't be open as often and that will be a great mistake because people will miss out. The sad thing really is that I don't think people realise what they're missing, if they haven't got some kind of contact with spiritual values, they seem to me to live life at a sort of secondary value, rather than being in contact with something that can give them real appreciation of life.

This effect may only be felt by a few, largely invisible people; a loss that is impossible to quantify or generalize. As I mentioned earlier, sometimes vulnerable members dropped in occasionally to help out. What they, and others like them, might do otherwise when the handful of women who give them some comfort and self-respect die is something that will likely not be picked up by large-scale surveys measuring impact and social cohesion. Theirs are the small, quiet voices of the, typically, generally ignored poor and troubled.

Third, the employment of commercial contractors continues a trend towards professionalization and commercialization that is already being felt in other areas.[7] A Generation A woman I talked with on the topic of a local arts festival told me that in previous years she and many other people had freely given their labour to perform a number of tasks connected with the festival's organization and successful running. More recently, those jobs were being done by a specialist commercial company. She and others cannot volunteer any more because, she said, 'now it's a business'. Her experience provides an alternative interpretation of the frequently discussed phenomenon of what Putnam (2000) described as 'bowling alone': Americans enjoy bowling, but do it less in organized leagues than was common a few decades ago. He was concerned that social groups would fragment, with individuals left to create their own, more atomized, senses of meaning and morality. Putnam argued that there appeared to be a trend in American society away from civic engagement, resulting in a loss of 'social capital'. Others have criticized that work and shown that it is neither applicable to the UK nor explains declining church attendance (see, for example, Hall 1999 and Bruce 2002), but my point here is that far from wilfully withdrawing their labour, what may better explain the diminished numbers of

---

[7] An interesting example is the professionalization of Women's Aid, a once voluntary group set up to provide refuges for women and now transformed into a professional organization, with attendant successes and tensions (see Dean 2010).

volunteers is increased marketization in an increasingly neo-liberal, capitalist society. I will return to this analysis more fully in Chapter 9.

The Generation A women I cleaned with think, pray, speak occasionally to each other, but mostly soak up the silence and smells of old buildings holding familiar old stories reaching back in time and space to a quiet, uncomplicated relationship with their god. To be allowed to join them in those quiet times felt like a privilege, and had the effect of drawing me more intricately into their church lives. This, I reflected later, was another stage in the process of moving from just 'friendly stranger' to becoming much more significantly involved with what they were doing and how they felt about each other, and about me; moving from recognition to intimitization and obligation.

SACRED SACRISTANS

During the same fieldwork period I observed and talked with two sacristans of two different churches. Theirs is the task of cleaning the 'vessels and vestments' and preparing the correct items for the rite of Eucharist or Holy Communion. Their practice overlaps the spaces of home and church. They take the cloths home, laying them out to dry or rolling them up, returning them to the church, and arranging them in a prescribed order. They clean the silver and place the chalice and related objects in a specific arrangement. This labour-intensive practice involves the invisible, private female labour that supports the mainly male public ritual. While the public performance of religious ritual has usually been the preserve of men, behind the scenes it is often the work of a woman. Describing in 1927 the work of the sacristan, a priest writes that such a person's tasks are performed while 'moving about sacristy and sanctuary with loving devotion laying out vestments, replacing candles, filling cruets, and changing linen, that the Divine Mysteries may be celebrated with cleanliness and godly fear on the morrow'.[8] He notes that the sacristan is often a woman who can, he says, perform some tasks that a man cannot do as well, such as sewing and washing.

---

[8] Rev. S.E.B. Serle, Project Canterbury, The Sacristan and Server <http://anglicanhistory. org/misc/sacristan1927.html>, last accessed 6.4.2015.

As I found in my fieldwork, the 'sacristan' is often a woman of Generation A. The usually long-serving woman is not only highly skilled and experienced, but increasingly anxious that her role is being accomplished often single-handedly, and with no replacement in sight as volunteers for the job fail to materialize.

A sacristan I came to know agreed to have a chat while she busied herself preparing for Holy Communion. The ritual of Holy Communion, or Eucharist, is a symbolic re-enactment of the final evening (or 'Last Supper') Jesus Christ spent with his twelve disciples, and a reminder of what happened next: death on the cross, and resurrection. Although the precise style of some aspects of the Eucharist may vary amongst Anglican churches, what does not vary is its importance as a 'sacrament', a rite believed to have originated with Jesus Christ as means of receiving spiritual grace. Two sacraments recognized by all Christian churches are baptism and Eucharist.

The ritual act of eating bread (represented by a flat, tasteless wafer) and drinking wine follows the instruction Jesus gave to his disciples to 'do this in remembrance of me' (Luke 22:19). In practical terms, the Eucharist is 'celebrated' by the priest and helpers preparing the altar and the people. The altar is prepared by the priest placing a large silver goblet, called a chalice, and a tray of wafers, called the host, in the centre of the altar and mixing a little water with wine (not grape juice: Anglicans are required to use the fermented juice of the grape) from a glass bottle, or vessel, into the chalice. A large wafer is sometimes broken to represent the occasion when Jesus shared a loaf of bread amongst the disciples, and to symbolize one community, or family, eating from the same loaf. While some churches break the wafer into small pieces for the congregation, or communicants, to eat, most use small, round wafers that are given individually. While the priest prepares the bread and wine, prayers are said to prepare the congregation. After the altar has been prepared the congregation is invited to come forward. They stand and move, beginning with the front row to the rear, into the nave (the central corridor of the church) and then to the altar. Some churches have a rail, where people kneel to receive the bread and wine, while in others the congregation gathers in a semicircle near the altar. The priest, with helpers, comes to each person in turn, giving them first a wafer and then, on a second round, a sip of wine. Depending on the church and individual preferences, a person may literally sip from the cup or, instead, may dip the wafer into the wine and eat it.

None of the detailed ritual of the Eucharist could be carried out if all the objects were not expertly cleaned and prepared in advance. The sacristan's job is to look after, as she describes it, the 'vessels and vestments': clean the cloths and clothes, prepare the objects for Holy Communion for the Sunday and Wednesday services, and, on Wednesdays, arrange the chairs in the small chapel where Communion will be celebrated. Only a dozen are put there and these, in my fieldwork experience, are not all required. There were never more than ten when I attended, and mostly were Generation A women.

To prepare for Holy Communion, all the silver is washed in hot water and carefully dried. She shows me how the large silver cup called the chalice is set out with its pall on top (a stiff white card), paten (small silver dish to hold the wafers), and purificator (linen cloth) carefully folded in three and draped over. It is important, she tells me, to pull down each side of the purificator carefully so it is even.

At another church I visited, I overheard someone asking a member of the Altar Guild what happens if some of the wine spills on the cloth after it has been blessed, and therefore made sacred. I had read somewhere that such cloths were considered desecrated and had to be burnt. The woman laughed and said, 'We don't have to do that any more! It's supposed to be separate and use separate cloths and then burn them', but she says, 'I don't have a big enough kitchen, I just use one pot!'.

Women in the Church of England frequently take the role of sacristan, but it is more common in the wider Anglican communion for the same role to be performed by several women in an 'Altar Guild'.[9] The Altar Guilds are, traditionally, women-run and take care of the kind of work Madge does as sacristan, plus organizing the altar flowers and performing church cleaning chores. As Gunderson (1992, 116) wrote, the Altar Guild is unique in the church because women are given a high privilege through performing acts of service in the

---

[9] In pursuing this point, I asked a Canadian clergyman about use of the term there, and he explained that the term 'sacristan' has been used but mainly in association with cathedrals. This is a person who is charged with the care of the contents of a church, especially those dealing with the sacred vestments and vessels. The sacristan may be a priest, a layperson, or sexton, whose principal duties were to see to the cleaning of the fabric, ringing the bell, and digging graves. He combined the duties of both door-keeper (an ancient office) and sacristan. When the duties were split between the two, the name sacristan became obsolete.

'sacred' areas allowed to them around the altar. An elderly American woman, Doris, recalled the work:

> Let me see I, you know, we had meetings like evening groups and things like that and then I also was on the altar guild so I would come in and, you know, during my work come in on Saturdays and Sundays and do that, and anything else that needed to be done I was always happy to help [...] You know just set up like pouring, getting the wafers and the silver, the wine and the urns and go out and set up outside by the altar, and all the things they'll need out there and stuff like that ...
>
> ABBY: So while you were working as well, full time I guess, you were coming in here on Saturdays and Sundays. How often would that be, once a month or—?
>
> DORIS: No every week, every week, oh, yes, faithfully.

They take their work seriously, and strive for a high level of perfection. A guide written in 1952, by Generation A woman Constance Murray Ribble,[10] was sprinkled with sections in full capital letters for emphasis:

> 13. Have a plain linen cover on the credence table itself. It may hang down slightly over either end, but not in front. DO NOT COVER THE ELEMENTS ON THE CREDENCE TABLE. (Ribble 1952, 5)
>
> Duties After Service
>
> I. (When Morning or Evening Prayer):
>
> 1. Remove flowers, wash the vases and put them away. If heavy brass vases are used with liners, remove the liners and leave the vases on the re-table if you like. NEVER LEAVE FLOWERS ON THE ALTAR AFTER A SERVICE AND NEVER LEAVE WATER IN THE VASES. The flowers may be sent to the sick or shut-ins. but they should not be used just as a pretty bouquet in anyone's home [...] Carefully remove the vessels to the workroom or sacristy. They should be rinsed and polished before putting away. If in the country where there is no water in the church, DO NOT LEAVE THEM UNWASHED UNTIL LATER. TAKE THEM HOME AND WASH THEM THOROUGHLY AND POLISH. (Ribble 1952, 6).
>
> The linens should be washed by members of the Altar Guild and NEVER given out to a laundry or laundress. This phase of the work of the Altar Guild should be done to the glory of God just as surely as any other of the duties. (Ribble 1952, 19)

[10] <http://www.acanedio.org/library/altarguildmanual.pdf>, last accessed 8.4.14.

GIFTS, DUTY, AND THE PERSISTENCE
OF 'PROPOSITIONAL' BELIEF

As I emphasized above, the process and outcome of cleaning, restoring order, and purifying involved two emotional drivers, personal pleasures and a feeling that one's duty was being done. It may be possible to connect and theorize the two through the idea of 'the gift'. Mauss (1954) is widely credited in anthropology for his conceptions of 'the gift', itself a notion argued first by Malinowski (1922; 1926): in terms of self-interest: one gives in order to receive. That reciprocity is not necessarily material; it is sometimes returned through feelings of obligation. Parry (1986) offered a critique of how scholars have adopted ideas from Mauss uncritically and ahistorically, imposing a contemporary idea that sometimes gifts *should* be pure and disinterested. He points out that the small-scale tribal societies that Malinowski and Mauss studied differed from world religions mainly through not being based on a notion of salvation that needs to be earned through good deeds: 'An ethicised salvation religion, in which rewards are contingent on conduct, is clearly likely to have the effect of orienting the ideal goals of social action towards a future existence' (Parry 1986, 467).[11] That insight stretches the idea of duty from being a feeling towards the larger group, or as Gilligan (1982) argued, a gendered ethic of care, to being an obligation laid down by a religion. As will be discussed throughout this book, these holy women took seriously the edicts of their religion.

And so, while undoubtedly the acts gave women personal, pleasurable moments of contemplation, they also counted in some divine score-card measuring good deeds.

That kind of belief determined the nature of their belonging and the kind of church-based actions they performed. It is unlikely that they would share those beliefs and not belong, as Davie (1994) might argue. Those tenet-beliefs, sometimes described as 'propositional' or 'creedal', matter to them. Anthropologists from Needham (1972), Ruel (1982), Asad (1993, 2003), Lindquist and |Coleman (2008),[12] and contributors to a special issue of *Culture and Religion* I edited with Simon Coleman (2010), and to an issue of the *Journal of*

---

[11] That broad generalization ignores differences within the 'world religions', as Parry (1986, 468) notes, but applies, I would say, to Anglicanism.
[12] See Day 2011 [2013], 3–7 for a review of how the disciplines of anthropology and sociology have analysed 'belief'.

Contemporary Religion I edited with Gordon Lynch (2013), are nearly united in their cautionary notes to avoid prioritizing 'belief' over other constituents of religiosity. They have argued persuasively that belief, which they tend to understand as 'propositional', is a limited concept not applicable to many religions outside Christianity. Work towards broadening that category and showing how it interlinks with, say, felt or emotional belief (Day 2013f) is limited. The Anglican Generation A women I studied did, of course, feel, embody, and perform belief, but they prioritized, I argue, the creedal form which they regarded as non-negotiable instructions from their Lord. They sometimes referred to the more Evangelical wing of the Anglican church as 'happy clappy': that emotive, relationship-with-Jesus form of religiosity neither suited their dispositions nor their rule-based set of beliefs. It is also the kind of expression favoured by the 1960s cultural revolutionaries who not only turned from the church, but also its style of belief-centred religious orientations and practice.

In conclusion, I suggest Generation A women were not only cleaning the church and its sacred objects, but purifying and protecting a certain kind of religion. If that was a form of duty, then it was a form designed to both honour the promises they had made to God and the church, and to save their souls. Future generations may not have been attracted to that kind of god, church or the business of saving souls, but that is not to say that they were without obligations or a sense of duty. They had, after all, been raised by their Generation A mothers, even if the objects of duty and manner of exercising it had changed. Following Foucault (1987, 49) who said that 'historic-critical investigations are quite specific in the sense that they always bear upon a material, an epoch, a body of determined practices and discourses', my analysis of Generation A has been to situate them in a specific time and culturally defined space. It is ahistoric to suggest that their understanding of 'duty' and belief would be seamlessly transmitted to their children.

My experience and further analysis of cleaning and ritual preparation practices reinforced for me the material aspect of a lived religion and how in these cases it strengthened the ties of belonging. Conventional descriptions of the embodied practices involved in religion is limited to public practices such as partaking in Communion or attending services, whereas this chapter has focused on the more private, invisible, mundane practices of Generation A through church cleaning and preparations for ritual.

5

Doing Theology

Generation A's role as 'lay' was one many Generation A laywomen specifically embraced. They were often historically opposed to the ordination of women and also, later, to their admission as bishops. The reasons for this opposition given in public, usually voiced by male bishops rather than women, speak of biblical inerrancy based on Christ not having female disciples or teachers. The verses usually quoted to explain this are:

> Let your women keep silence in the churches: for it is not permitted unto them to speak; but they are commanded to be under obedience as also saith the law.
>
> And if they will learn anything, let them ask their husbands at home: for it is a shame for women to speak in the church.   (Corinthians 14:34–5)
>
> Let the woman learn in silence with all subjection. But I suffer not a woman to teach, nor to usurp authority over the man, but to be in silence. For Adam was first formed, then Eve. And Adam was not deceived, but the woman being deceived was in the transgression. Notwithstanding she shall be saved in childbearing, if they continue in faith and charity and holiness with sobriety.
>
> (1 Timothy 2:11–15, King James Version)

The lived experience on the ground is variable, differing not only geographically but by what is meant by speaking and teaching. It was my observation that many Generation A laywomen would have been uncomfortable with women priests not only because of the theology, but because they were not men: the male priest, uniquely, was part spiritual leader, part son, and part husband. If the church is the family, Generation A is its matriarch. This chapter considers several fieldwork case examples and further historical evidence to construct a profile of Generation A as teachers, lay preachers, readers, biblical scholars, and activists. The term 'theology' is being used widely, to refer to how the women understood, explained, and practised their Christian beliefs and their images of God. As Percy (2015, 232) observed:

> All doctrine is pastoral, biblical and applied. All theology is contextual. All of it is historical, ideological, philosophical and to some extent sociological. Theology refuses to be neatly organized. It cannot be coaxed into neat silos.

The main activities I observed as 'doing theology' include practices of regular church attendance, Bible study and discussion, praying for people, and participation in specific rituals. Together, they helped form a picture for me of complex women who are both what I would have expected in terms of conventional, church-based conformity, and also surprisingly unconventional.

SPIRITUAL BUT ALSO RELIGIOUS (SBAR)

The word 'spirituality', like 'sacred', was markedly absent from my conversations with the women. At first, that did not strike me as strange, informed as I was by hundreds of conference papers, journal articles, book chapters, and books all confident of their shared, largely uncontested paradigm: baby-boomer 'seekers' and their Generation Y and X children and grandchildren are spiritual, not religious. Their turn away from institutionalized religion to less formal kinds of spirituality will spark what Heelas and Woodhead forecast as a 'spiritual revolution' (Heelas et al. 2005). The largely unspoken corollary was that their mothers and grandmothers, the Generation A, were different: religious, certainly, but not spiritual. I prefer now to think of them as spiritual but also religious (SBAR).[1]

Ammerman (2014) studied the idea that, although the 'spiritual but not religious' banner is popular amongst academics trying to explain contemporary religious landscapes, such a separation did not occur with many of her research participants. Through lengthy

---

[1] This is a deliberate inversion of what is sometimes called Spiritual But Not Religious (SBNR), where people want to explicitly index spirituality in their lives, but distance themselves from what they see as unattractive, institutionalized religion. For a general overview and also a specific discussion of the Canadian case, see Beaman and Beyer (2015).

discussion and storytelling, the boundary blurred, apart from amongst Conservative Protestants who actively emptied 'religion' in favour of a deep spiritual relationship with Jesus. She concluded (Ammerman 2014, 50) that: 'in the vast majority of our participants, religious participation and spiritual engagement occur alongside talk that intermingle the two' and, correspondingly, spiritual and religious disengagement talk is also similarly entangled.

She found a 'Theistic cluster' that represented people who talked about spirituality linked to God, both in belief and practice. This cluster was found to be most relevant to the oldest group she measured: 93 per cent of those aged over sixty-five settled there, as compared to 67 per cent under the age of sixty-five. The 'Extratheistic' cluster was populated by those who do not reference a god in relation to their spirituality, but nonetheless feel a sense of reaching beyond the ordinary, whether through art, music, or beauty. Only 36 per cent of people aged more than sixty-five years old were found here. A third category was those who represented the 'Ethical Cluster', corresponding to Ammerman's (1997) earlier work on Golden Rule Christians, with a discourse that stretched across all clusters.

Her findings fit with mine. Generation A's practice of attending church services regularly, participating quietly in structured, predictable services, reciting their service-book prayers, singing hymns both ancient and modern in difficult-to-reach registers, performing their duties as a form of obedience to scripture, and listening respectfully to a sermon preached by a man in robes seemed the antithesis of what people imagined as 'spiritual', and yet, by spending time with women of Generation A, in services, bible study, social events, and voluntary labour, it slowly became obvious to me that their 'spirituality', were I to label it as such, was embodied, practised, implicit, and deeply pleasurable. They are not the sort of people who would generally speak of such things, just as they would not speak of sex, or family scandals, or illness, or other private matters. Of course, like all those matters, that they may be unspoken does not diminish their presence or importance. The spoken, written nature of their sons' and daughters' spiritualities tend to outnumber that of their elders' and has proliferated to generate thousands of books lined up under various bookshop headings of 'spiritual', 'new age', 'mind-body-spirit', while the Bible, prayer books, exegesis, and other commentary fall under 'religious' or 'Christianity' labels if they are labelled at all. Bruce (1999, 161), for example, found that books related to 'mind-body-spirit' in

Oslo's leading bookshop took up 60 metres of shelf space, while 'Christianity' occupied less than a metre. With all those distinctions in mind, I was therefore surprised to find two Generation A women who wanted to tell me about their personal, intensely emotional experiences of communicating with God. What I found was more complex, reflecting what Woodhead (2012, 3–22) described as 'entanglements', where Christianity and spirituality are mutually constitutive and, as she charts, have been so through the centuries. Bender (2010) in her study of contemporary mystics, found that their spiritual identities drew, even unintentionally, on history and memories, and therefore had their own 'traditions', just like religion.

Felicity, for example, told me that she had attended the same Anglican church for fifty years. She had not been religious all her life, she said, and had never attended church when she was younger. But one day, she explained, something happened to change all she felt and later practised. When her son was born he was very ill and not expected to live beyond a few days, she told me. She was desperate with worry and fear and, although she had never been to church regularly before, and had not been in any way a religious person, she prayed that night and promised God that if her son lived, she would have him and her other children baptised and take them to church regularly. Her son lived, and she, she said in a typically Generation A-formed phrase, 'upheld my part of the bargain'. She began attending her local church and has never stopped. From the first time she walked into it, she felt at home, and even discovered that she knew several of the people. She had her children baptised, as she had promised, and became, and has since remained, active in many parts of church life. The bargain she struck with God was not simply a technical arrangement. She quickly grew to know and love Him, she told me. Her children did not remain active churchgoers, but Felicity was not particularly disturbed about that, so confident is she in her relationship with God: 'He wasn't calling them,' she said. 'He was calling me.'

Another woman, Clare, approached me one day at an event, saying she had heard about my research and wondered if I would like to talk to her, as she fitted the age range I was studying. We arranged to meet a few days later, and from the moment I sat down in her living room she never stopped talking about her experience. It seemed that she urgently wanted to share it, as it was one of the defining moments of her life. She described how earlier in her life she had felt for years that she wanted to feel something directly from God. She was not in the habit of attending churches regularly, but she and her husband often visited them when travelling, as they were interested in churches 'from a historical viewpoint', she said. During those occasions she would often sit quietly in the church, she told me, hoping that a religious-like emotion would touch her. Nothing ever happened. As time went on, she attended church services occasionally just to see if something would happen. One day it did, in a spectacular fashion. She was sitting in a pew when, during the service, a light shone in front of her and completely covered her view of everything. She could no longer even hear the voices around her or see anything but the white light. She described the feeling to me as being 'bathed in love'. That was not only how she felt at the time, but has done ever since, she said. She joined her local church and has been a regular churchgoer, and active member.

BIBLE MATTERS

The Bible appeared to me to be important to Generation A women: they all owned one, they referred to it through quotes, and they seemed to rely on it as a source of guidance and truth. Field (2014, 513) described its role succinctly:

> The Bible is the cornerstone of the Christian faith, at once its inspiration, authority, and evidential basis. As well as offering a spiritual route-map for the believer, it has provided the moral framework for Judeo-Christian civil societies.

Its use and relevance to people is, as Field found (2014), generationally and gender marked. He examined what he described as 'Bible-centrism' against five criteria—ownership of the Bible, readership of the Bible, knowledge of the Bible's content, belief in the Bible's veracity, in general and specifics and influence of the Bible in everyday life. Survey data collected by 123 surveys between 1948 and 2013 show a clear pattern. Older women over the age of sixty-five are much more 'Bible-centric' than other members of the population.

During fieldwork, I participated in regular Wednesday afternoon Bible study groups, hosted at the home of one Generation A woman. The afternoons were structured around readings, discussion, and prayer.

The sessions began with a cup of tea and a biscuit while the group gathered and settled. The usual 'chatting' was briefer than that I experienced on other events such as church socials. There was a feeling that this was a more business-like occasion. On the occasions I attended the sessions there were never more than six people, and most were Generation A women. During some of my visits the group was attending to 'Lent', a forty-day period in which Jesus was said to have fasted and prayed alone in the desert before his crucifixion. The beginning of that period has been secularized to a large extent, with the day known as Shrove Tuesday being popularly marked as Pancake Day. Adherent Christians may partially fast during Lent, or at least refrain from eating or drinking a particular favourite, such as meat, chocolate, or alcohol. The Lent Bible Study sessions were structured around the Archbishop of Canterbury's Lent Book, an annually commissioned book that combines reflections on a specific theme with scriptural references. I discovered that this form of study was common in such groups. A Canadian woman I interviewed, Audrey, told me that her Bible Study group had handbooks it followed and that she has purchased them for her own use at home:

> Well, I haven't actually done any college courses or anything, but I do read a lot. Just a sec, I want to show you something I have here. I got connected recently in the last year or two with the [...] ministries. They put out this magazine once a month; there's a lot of theology and that in there, and I find it good. It's a daily reading plus extra ones, and when I read them, I find myself—that there's a reference there and I end up reading the whole, I've even read a whole book, one of those small books—a handbook for Bible study.

During the group I visited, we were asked to each read a section of the handbook and offer a comment on it. I was aware that I felt nervous and apprehensive about what they might ask me about my own religious beliefs. As it turned out, I need not have been concerned: I was with Anglicans, after all. And so, when someone asked me how I felt about the theme of 'abiding with God', my answer that I was somewhat ambivalent about it was met with quiet smiles and nods. I was also nervous because I knew that I was out of my depth. The women were highly religiously literate and more aware than I of the provenance and different interpretations of the passages. We were also encouraged to discuss how certain passages may have relevance to us in our daily lives. As they discussed verses and related them to both global and more personal current issues and problems, they struck me as scholars doing serious practical theology.

Another moment of 'doing' Lent theology occurred at a special Maundy Thursday service I attended. Maundy Thursday is part of what Christians call Holy Week and commemorates what they refer to as the Last Supper (John 13:1–17). This was a traditional Passover meal, an important event in the Jewish calendar, and the last evening that Jesus spent with his disciples before being crucified on Good Friday. It is an important occasion for two main reasons. First, the meal they shared came to symbolize the relationship Jesus demanded of his followers. The word Maundy is related to a term for 'commandment', deriving from the Latin *mandatum*, referring to the commandment Jesus gave then to his disciples to love each other (John 13:34) and remember him through a ritual known as Holy Communion, or the Eucharist:

> And he took bread, and gave thanks, and broke it, and gave unto them, saying, This is my body which is given for you: this do in remembrance of me. Likewise also the cup after supper, saying, This cup is the new testament in my blood, which is shed for you. (Luke 22:19–20)

Maundy Thursday also commemorates another event said to have occurred during the Last Supper, when Jesus washed his disciples' feet, telling them that this was to remind them to service others (John 13: 3–17):

> When he had washed their feet and put on his outer garments and resumed his place, he said to them, 'Do you understand what I have done to you? You call me Teacher and Lord, and you are right, for so I am. If I then, your Lord and Teacher, have washed your feet, you also ought to wash one another's feet. For I have given you an example, that you also should do just as I have done to you. Truly, truly, I say to you, no servant is not greater than his master, nor is a messenger greater than the one who sent him. If you know these things, blessed are you if you do them.'

There is an interesting series of debates within Christian scholarship as to the possible presence of women at the Last Supper and the significance of the act of Jesus washing a woman's feet. The foot-washing that took place at the service I attended was mainly participated in by the Generation A women and the priest. It began with the priest, Father David, announcing that the ritual was about to begin: 'Anyone who would like to have your feet washed by me, put your right foot out.' First one to be washed was a Generation A woman, Irene. As Father David bent down, a server handed him a bowl of water. Irene placed her hand on his shoulder as he gave her foot a gentle, thorough wash. They smiled at each other as he dried her foot carefully. I watched as he slowly got up and felt sorry for him; the hard, stone floor must have been a cold, uncomfortable place to kneel. He made his way along the pews looking at people, most of whom shook their heads. Three other people, all women, nodded to him. As he washed their feet I looked more closely at the towels, and realized they were an odd assortment of mismatched tea-towels. That gives the ritual a warm, domestic touch. In all, five women and one man had their feet washed. I found it very touching, moved by that small group's familiarity with each other and sense of belonging.

Foot-washing was a ritual performed traditionally by the monarch, being also the head of the Church of England. The tradition of the monarch washing the feet of poor people (the number determined by the monarch's age) and giving them gifts and money on Maundy Thursday began with Henry VIII and continued until the eighteenth century, when the foot-washing component was abandoned. 'Maundy Money' was introduced by Charles II and continues in the same form today: Queen Elizabeth presents it to elderly people (as many as her own years) who have been nominated by churches. A total of 6,710 people have received Maundy money, coins minted especially for the occasion, in recognition of their service. The Queen has attended fifty-six royal Maundy services in forty-three cathedrals during her reign, only missing some because of royal tours and royal babies. I observed the ceremony on television on 2 April 2015:[2]

The Queen, in matching teal coat and hat, stepped from her car unaided and walked into Sheffield Cathedral to the sound of church bells ringing and crowds of thousands of people cheering. Inside were the eighty-nine chosen men and eighty-nine women, who stood in the nave awaiting her. Some looked older than others, which is to be expected as to qualify as 'elderly' they only have to be aged more than seventy. As the Queen moved from one to another, smiling broadly and looking genuinely pleased, handing out the small purses of money, at least one woman cried. They received the purses with hands extended and cupped, in exactly the manner of receiving the

[2] <http://www.telegraph.co.uk/news/uknews/queen-elizabeth-II/11512515/Queen-hands-out-Royal-Maundy-alms-at-Sheffield-Cathedral.html>, last accessed 14.6.2015.

wafer at Holy Communion. Those specially minted coins are made to recognize older people who have been active in volunteering in their churches and communities. An example of the generational nature of that ritual comes from the *Telegraph*, read by older, Conservative readers. In welcoming the Maundy Thursday event, the *Telegraph* writer warmly welcomed such a practice. The journalist, Christopher Howse (whose blog note says that he writes about the world's faiths, particularly Christianity, and the uses and abuses of the English language),[3] opened with a headline to his story about the event, adding a subheading that 'The Queen's gifts today are a refreshing change from look-at-me rituals like Red Nose day.'[4] This is a reference to a popular biannual national charity event begun in 1988 by young celebrities and charity workers. The article continues with a short history of Red Nose Day, part of the wider charity Comic Relief, by remarking that 'but it seems to me a welcome change from personalised rituals like Red Nose day. The Queen and Yeomen and Almoner will go about their arcane tasks solemnly, not joshing to the camera', the reference being a coded criticism of the highly visible Red Nose events and television coverage. Howse concluded that Maundy Thursday's 'whole performance does no earthly good. It does not even pretend to be a work of social welfare. That is all the better.' I cited his work here to suggest that there may be a connection between the thoughts of the older, conservative, cohort of *Telegraph* readers and Generation A.

PRAYER AS WOMEN'S WORK

The Bible Study group I attended during Lent often created, as I discussed above, prayers to accompany the readings. In those moments I was reminded of my earlier work (Day 2005) with Baptist women and my intellectual struggle with one of the leaders in my field of the sociology of religion, Robert Wuthnow. I briefly alluded to gendered prayer in Chapter 2, when discussing how researchers

---

[3] <http://www.telegraph.co.uk/comment/columnists/christopherhowse>, last accessed 14.6.2015.
[4] <http://www.telegraph.co.uk/topics/easter/11508877/Royal-Maundy-Money-does-no-earthly-good.html>, last accessed 16.6.2015.

typically find that the largest gender gap in religiosity occurs through private acts, such as prayer, with Christian women consistently reporting that they pray more often than men.[5] Work exploring prayer from a sociological or psychological standpoint examines the impact of prayer primarily as related to frequency, rather than content and form (Mason 2013, 23). It is the content, I will argue, that explains the gender differential.

Most scholars with a sociological or anthropological background (see Giordan and Woodhead 2015) rely on the grounding offered by Mauss in his unpublished thesis of 1909 (Mauss 2003) where he defined prayer as a social phenomenon, just as is religion (2003, 33):

> Even when prayer is individual and free, even when the worshippers choose freely the time and mode of expression, what they say always uses hallowed language and deals with hallowed things, that is, ones endorsed by social tradition.

That definition departs from how James (1982 [1903], 31) described religion, as mostly an individual, psychological event:

> Religion, therefore, as I now ask you arbitrarily to take it, shall mean for us the feelings, acts, and experiences of individual men in their solitude, so far as they apprehend themselves to stand in relation to whatever they may consider the divine.

Theologians tend to be uncomfortable with the notion that prayer is grounded in social traditions, as discussed by Burley (2012, 137) in his discussion of Wittgenstein and D. Z. Phillips, particularly with how Phillips (1965) had positioned prayer as an act of talking to God.

> Phillips first notes that what theological realists fear is 'that belief in God is being reduced to ways of talking about forgiveness, thankfulness and love' and then emphasizes that this is not what he is doing [...]

Burley explained that Phillips had really meant that prayer was about talking to God about God-given matters, such as forgiveness, thankfulness, and love, thereby firmly coupling prayer to God. That is not what Mauss, or other sociologists, argued. Weber (1922, 26) saw prayer as stemming from magic, with petitioners having to please, influence, cajole, or collaborate with a magician-like God to show

---

[5] <http://www.pewforum.org/2016/03/22/the-gender-gap-in-religion-around-the-world>, last accessed 21.4.2016.

why they are deserving. In his review of the sociological history of prayer, Mason (2013, 9–26) showed that the Weberian materialistic view of prayer was inadequate as sociologists have found prayer to be often oriented away from material goods or even the self.

As Collins (2015) observed in his study about prayer requests in hospitals, most prayers were about friends and family. While that may not have been surprising given the context, it conforms to a Maussian understanding about prayer as a social phenomenon, he explains (Collins 2015, 200): 'The literature on prayer is dominated by theologians and clerics, who attempt in their writing to lead people to "true prayer".' One difficulty with Mauss, Collins argued, is that he tied prayer to ritual action. This leaves a gap in explaining other forms of prayer of which hospital prayer requests are one, and would also include, I suggest, Bible-study prayers, sweeping-the-church-floor prayers, driving-the-car prayers, and so on. Collins also observed behaviour in the hospital chapel, and surmised that there were probably more prayer requests submitted by women than men.

Baker's (2008) analysis of data from the Baylor Religion Survey (2005) in the United States found that women, African-Americans, and those with lower incomes pray more often. These findings may support Norris and Inglehart (2004), who have argued that those suffering most from deprivation or existential insecurity are most religious, assuming that women are those sufferers. Baker found that prayers that might be described as immediately self-oriented, such as requests for financial gain, were the least frequent type: most prayers were for family and friends, or for a deeper relationship with God. That is the sort of work that conforms to how labour is differentiated in late modernity. As I noticed in my earlier work with Baptist women (Day 2005), this was not the sort of labour some male theologians or sociologists of religion are likely to regard as 'theology'. In his work on small groups, Wuthnow (1994) focused on prayer groups such as the one I had visited and observed similar practices, commenting on them in a somewhat dismissive tone. His interpretation of what the women were doing was pointedly different from mine which, I suggest, revealed more about our interpretative frameworks than any truths within the 'data'. Wuthnow's research into small groups addressed what he argued was the vulnerability of a religion whose adherents prayed for practical items, such as whether they would find a good parking space. Wuthnow expresses concern about what he calls the domestication of the sacred, something he says has been worrying saints and sages for centuries who fear that (Wuthnow 1994, 255) 'Sacredness ceases to be the *mysterium tremendum* that commands awe and reverence and becomes a house pet that does our bidding'. I suggest that 'house pet' is an emotive, gender-coded term for what appears to be everyday activities linked to women's religious practice. Further, he criticizes the orientation towards application, which 'becomes more important than whether that application is grounded in truth', favouring intuitive insights rather than 'the wisdom accrued over the centuries in hermitages, seminaries, universities, congregations and church councils' (Wuthnow 1994, 358). That gendered statement implicitly refers to the status of men, who populated the hermitages, seminaries, and so on, and the less valuable contribution of women. That contribution is, as is often the case for women, given freely in support of other people.

Prayer is a form of emotional labour and, like most emotional work, it is usually assigned to women in a society structured through a gendered allocation of responsibility for care, moral integrity, housework, and religious transmission (Hochschild 2003 [1983]; West and Zimmerman 1987; Hochschild and Machung 1990; Day 2013e.) That allocation is a prime characteristic of contemporary Euro-American societies, an important point to be recalled when situating arguments about gender. Mukhopadhyay and Higgins (1988, 486; see also Skeggs 1997) argued that:

> First, gender must be studied with reference to historical, economic, social, and conceptual context; understanding gender requires more than exploring its relationship to biology and economics. In addition, gender theorists must be alert to how androcentric and Eurocentric folk views influence scholarship.

Saying a prayer for an unemployed husband to find a job, a daughter to find a friend (Day 2005), or for a parking space while out on shopping chores corresponds to the sort of everyday activities women perform in their domestic work. Perhaps, indeed, the ideas explored in Chapter 2 that women are more religious than men are themselves folk tales, or even tropes, by which I mean a sort of tale, a story, that symbolizes a distinct cultural belief or fantasy. Looked at it differently, it is not difficult to explain that when women get together to discuss religion, as did, in my studies, the Baptist women and the Anglican Generation A women, their conversations centre on the needs of others rather than themselves. This is not something some male theologians or sociologists of religion respect or even consider to be proper religion, preferring to characterize it as therapy or self-help. In the language they use, it is interesting to note how one of the most sacred places for women, the home, is seen as a threat to the men who traditionally have commanded religions from male-dominated spaces, such as monasteries. Once again, the preference is for a leadership to turn women away from focusing on themselves, and on their sacred domains of home and family. And yet this apparent obsession with the self is remarkably absent from other studies. It is rarely the case in my observations that women pray for themselves. Even young people, often seen as less religious than older generations, more frequently pray for others rather than themselves (Mason 2015; Collins-Mayo 2008). Those lightly coded criticisms of women have been remarkably absent from real, by which I mean qualitatively grounded, studies about women, both religious and non-religious. In my longitudinal study of belief and belonging in the UK, I found that women of all ages and religious orientations spoke in a similar way about their sense of connections and obligations to their families. One woman I interviewed, Nicola, aged thirty-seven, a care-worker and mother who lives with a partner, found it difficult to even think about what she wanted for herself (Day 2011 [2013], 149–50):

> She said her purpose in life was 'to bring my family up', to look after her children until they leave home, at which point she will spend more time on herself. Until then, she said, if she had a spare day and no one to look after, she would not know what to do. She explained why: And that's because I don't spend a lot of time on myself. I might have a bath, I might do my toe nails, I might take the dog out, but that's about it. I don't really—I can't remember what I like to do.

Throughout our interview she returned to her narratives about being caregiver, not attending to her own needs, but looking after her family. Laura, a twenty-three-year-old single receptionist described her sense of what was morally right as 'trying to abide by the law and trying to keep everybody happy, not just yourself'. Lindsay, a fourteen-year-old student, said she prays and she believes God answers her prayers unless it was a 'selfish' prayer. When I asked her what she meant by a selfish prayer she said that it would be about something just to do with oneself and not anyone else.

Anna, a Generation A Canadian woman, talked about going to church to feel close to God, but, she explained, she also often feels close to God at home when she prays. The way she emphasized the strength of her act of praying, and the implicit sense that she was praying for, or about, something or someone close to her, spoke of strenuous emotional work:

> And you can pray at home and I often do; there are times when I pray *very, very* hard at home, when something... [*pause*] and God has been good. But I just find that it's important for me to do [*go to church*].

Prayer is an act women participate in as an extension of their socially determined role as carers. In conclusion, I suggest that the gender differential in prayer reflects socially constructed gender roles rather than an apparent general inclination of women to be 'more religious'.

IDENTITY POLITICS AND THE CULTURAL TURN

Wuthnow is not alone in his depiction of people being more self-oriented now than in some generally vaguely constructed past era. Wilson once wrote, referring (2001, 44–5) to the modern family being 'split apart', with parents insufficiently present to take a role in the moral inculcation of their children. This, he says, is not only because family structures have changed but also because individuals are being encouraged today to 'discover their own identities', to 'be themselves', to 'do their own thing'. Bauman (1992, 35) describes an absence of:

> A reference to the supercommunal, 'extraterritorial' grounds of truth and meaning. Instead, the postmodern perspective reveals the world as composed of an indefinite number of meaning-generating agencies, all relatively self-sustained and autonomous, all subject to their own respective logics and armed with their own facilities of truth-validation.

A problem for the post-modern theorist has been to balance the unequal weighting given to the idea of the free-floating, autonomous self and the connected, relational self. Are people composed of some sort of essentially stable self-identity, or do they exist only in relation to others? To apply that question to women of Generation A is tricky because it is necessary to separate social theory from social practice. The kinds of social theories that influenced what has been described as new social movements appeared in the writings of academics, public intellectuals, and activists during the 1960s, a critical period in the lives of many Generation A women and their baby-boomer daughters. The forms of social activism began changing. Generation A women perform their Christianity in social contexts that were tightly connected to the institution of their church and existing networks. Their insular interests and preferences were striking, and markedly different from other organizations composed of women from the same generation. The Women's Institute group I regularly visited with one of my Generation A church friends, for example, included women who attended churches and many who did not. Most people knew each other and had done so prior to joining the group. They enjoyed hearing guests talk about a variety of topics, from growing vegetables to creating music on unusual instruments. They supported charities who helped women in Africa and signed petitions created by their head office on matters important to women. In contrast, the Generation A women I visited through churches were almost wholly focused on the needs of their immediate church. When I talked about the Mothers' Union I heard stories about church-based meetings, social events, and causes. Most of the money they raised through fund-raising events, one woman told me, went directly to church funds for maintenance and enhancement of the church building and fabric. These were tangible, material outcomes, embedded in the fabric of the church and their daily church activity. It was their immediate surroundings and their church institution that mattered to them most. This is not reflective of current trends in civil society, as the reach extends from the local to the global. Most Mothers' Union activity now takes place in the 'global south' with funds raised from the 'global north'.

During the last few decades much scholarly attention has turned to the similarities and differences between social movements and new religious movements, both of which began to proliferate around the same time. Social movements eschew institutional roots and associations, formality, clearly defined boundaries, and explicit criteria for membership (see, for example, Della Porta and Diani 2006; Koopmans 1993) in favour of looser, emotionally significant, network-based connections (Castells 2012). Nynäs and Lissander (2015, 457) summarize the key characteristics of such movements as: lacking stability, as compared to institutions; non-dogmatic; containing a central value usually based on experiences of oppression or misrepresentation; united in a longing for change. Those are precisely the opposite of the characteristics and preferences held by Generation A. In their discussion of the LGBT movement in Finland, Nynäs and Lissander described the difficulty of finding support in the established Church for LGBT 'Rainbow Masses'. The religious LGBT movement in Finland reflects what they describe as 'contemporary Western trends' (Nynäs and Lissander 2015, 467) for reflexivity and subjectivity; again, values that would not be shared by a generation less disposed to self-contemplation.

While many feminist theorists rightly critique the idea of an autonomous self as a fiction, it became a necessary fiction for the baby-boomer generation that sought to deliver itself from what appeared to be soulless institutions, such as church and family, empty of meaning and significance. It is, perhaps, this mistaken idea that the cultural revolution of the 1960s was solely centred on the female 'self' that prompted the sorts of seething condemnations expressed by some theorists such as Wilson and Wuthnow above. I suggest that what may have irritated male academics and male leaders of institutions such as the church was not the emphasis on 'self' (philosophers have valorized the self as embodied independence and liberty for centuries) but rather the threat it contained to male leadership, power, and position. And, for Generation A laywomen, the male positionality in the church provided a certain female positionality that permitted their particular form of pew power. Together, they could regard themselves as dedicated members of a society that had been shaken and badly damaged by war: they had a job to do, and rebuilding their sacred institutions of family, church, and country was their priority. Further, to focus most specifically on the 'self' and the cultural position it may have taken for Generation A would be to undermine the central proposition so important to their lives as religious women: their model is Jesus Christ, always positioned as selfless in his sacrifice.

The construction of gender within the sociology of religion has tended to follow one of the most dominant, yet problematic, themes within the sociology mainstream: the apparent binary between self and society, and, consequentially, the apparent rise of individualization as a means of explaining the decline in mainstream Christianity. As I have argued earlier in this book and elsewhere (see, for example, Day 2011 [2013]), this thinly veiled attack on women usually takes the loftier form of discourse concerning five main but interlinked causal explanations:

1. A focus on the individual rather than a wider social set of, for example, family, community, or society.

2. Consumerism—the so-called turn from obligation (or duty) to consumption.

3. The apparent tendency of women to shop around, 'pick and mix', and create their own forms of 'do-it-yourself' religion.

4. A preference for religion or spirituality to become a means of personal therapy.

5. The 'feminization' of churches, which has alienated men.

That a stark binary exists between individual and self is central to most political, philosophical, and economic theories, and their influences on such contemporary notions within debates about religion, such as the 'rational choice' theory (Stark and Finke 2000) that individuals are self-interested creatures intent on maximizing personal gains. And yet, in practice, the boundary between self and other blurs in women-centred work.

DOING THEOLOGY THROUGH MINISTRY

As I described above in relation to the Bible Study group, the work of exegesis and contemplation created a different tone from many of the other church-based activities of Generation A: there was little of the light-hearted banter found at coffee mornings or jumble sales. And yet it was at the coffee mornings and jumble sales that many of the women commented that this was their way of doing God's work. This emphasis on 'good works', or what academics may term 'practical theology', resonated with what I often heard at the Women's Institute (WI) meetings and social events I attended, where careful attention is paid to the work of fund-raising, campaigns, and social action. The serious, labour-intensive work of social action and change is usually ignored in wider, popular discourse about the WI, which favours the softer gloss of 'jam-makers' or 'flower ladies', perhaps revealing a popular preference for women to be safely contained in a domestic sphere.

There is a tension between the historic work of women missionaries and women priests, as I discussed in Chapter 2. In the nineteenth and early twentieth centuries, women often performed dangerous and challenging work as missionaries, both working to spread the gospel and also, embodied through organizations such as the Mothers' Union, to inculcate an image of the civilized white woman in British colonies.[6]

Campaigns to allow women to be ordained as priests in the Anglican Communion have been particularly problematic for many women of Generation A. Although many women I talked to supported the move, several others did not. Sarah, for example., said that she did think it was a good idea, and referenced her Bible Study group and the theology she had learned as evidence:

> I personally do. I don't see any reason why they shouldn't be. I know there are people in the Church of England that don't agree and they have their own theological reasons. But personally, you know, doing Bible study and that kind of thing, I haven't found any evidence in the Bible that excludes women from senior offices in a church, whether it's from the beginning of the church or over a period of time. It's almost— it's like a lot of things, it's a man-made rule that's developed over the years. And don't forget, in past centuries, um, most situations have been very much male dominant; that's the way it was. But we're in the twenty-first century now.

The possibilities for women to be ordained as priests in the Church of England began with a report in 1966 which opened the discussion; Generation A women would have been aged in their thirties and forties. The General Synod, the governing body of the Church of England, reported in 1975 (when Generation A women were in their forties and fifties) that there were no fundamental objections to women being ordained, but because there were objections at the diocesan level, potential changes were not taken forward. In 1987, women deacons were admitted; in 1994, the first women priests were ordained. Generation A women would have been in their sixties and seventies. In November 2012 the Synod narrowly rejected a move to allow women to become bishops because of opposing votes in the House of Laity. Nearly half of the opponents (thirty-three of the seventy-four) were women, drawn from the Conservative Evangelical movement and the Anglo-Catholics; it was the Anglo-Catholic constituency that reflected the Generation A women of my study. The opponents were not seen as representing the majority view in their dioceses, forty-two of which, out of forty-four, were in favour of

---

[6] See Pui-Lan (1996) and discussion in Chapter 2.

women bishops, although 2,000 women had signed a petition opposing women bishops.

Canon and Cambridge Divinity Professor Sarah Coakley drew
attention to this point, commenting that:[7]

> Recent elections to Synod allowed conservatives (both Catholic and
> Evangelical) to push forward more candidates into the House of Laity
> with precisely this vote in mind; and it has long been noted that the
> House of Laity contains more than its expected share of conservative,
> elderly or bureaucratically-inclined church people.

The Synod voted again on the issue several months later, and the
motion was passed. In the wider Anglican Communion there are
twenty female bishops in Australia, Canada, Cuba, India, Ireland,
New Zealand, Swaziland, South Africa, and the USA.

Most of the Generation A women I talked with were broadly
supportive of women priests, apart from a few who had chosen to
go to churches which refused to have women priests. Those who
opposed did so, they said, for theological reasons. Agnes, a Canadian
Generation A woman, was clear about her position on women and
gay priests as being scripturally based:

AGNES: The new people we have or *they* have female bishops and
    people like that. But that's not according to the scriptures, the
    way we interpret it, you know.
ABBY: So your church wouldn't have female ministers.
AGNES: No.
ABBY: And you wouldn't have female bishops, obviously.
AGNES: No, no.
ABBY: And also I understand that there is some dispute between
    some churches on particularly homosexuality.
AGNES: Umm hmm.
ABBY: And whether or not—whether or not what? That is per-
    missible or you can be a minister or you can be married or
    what?
AGNES: Now I read something this morning that kind of covers
    it. The fact is it's not, it's not right according to the scriptures,
    and we take that view that, er, I don't think people put you

---

[7] <http://www.abc.net.au/religion/articles/2012/11/23/3639111.htm>, last accessed
7.8.15.

out of the church for it, but I think it's a case of, it's not condoned. [Pause]

ABBY: So you wouldn't have ministers who you knew were homosexual?

AGNES: No, no.

ABBY: And you wouldn't have marriage, homosexual marriage, or, as we call it, gay marriage, you wouldn't have that?

AGNES: No. Well, the scripture speaks against it and I mean it's that simple, I think. And not only that, but—not that I know much about it—it's not a good thing anyway. Probably not for everybody, just that is, it's like everything, there are always people who are just on the edge and you say there's nothing wrong with those people, you know, but the very essence of it is not good.

Had women such as Agnes remained in an open congregation, with gay people and women priests, they might have found that their theology changed, as occurred with people in a study conducted in the 1980s. Between 1983 and 1984, Peberdy conducted doctoral research amongst six Church of England parishes to explore people's responses to women's ministry. She analysed and summarized the research in a short but richly detailed pamphlet (Peberdy 1985). As women were not yet admitted to the Church of England priesthood, the women ministering were deaconesses, the nearest equivalent to a priest. To compare her study with my study conducted between 2012 and 2014, I will infer that the women I was studying aged in their late seventies, eighties, and nineties would have been in their forties, fifties, and sixties at her time of writing. Covering a wide geographical range from the south to north of England, she interviewed ninety laypeople using open-style interviews with only a few questions to guide her. Her questions focused on how women were received in their ministerial roles, what actions they performed, and how they felt about their roles and levels of acceptance. A major finding was the lack of correlation between the 'churchmanship' or theology of a parish and the extent to which the congregation accepted the role of women in ministry. In the Introduction to her pamphlet (Peberdy 1985, foreword) John Tinsley, former Bishop of Bristol, chastized those who considered the issue of women's ordination to be a matter of theology:

This is to do theology badly because an incarnational religion like Christianity impels us to do our theological and other thinking inductively working from actual facts, real data and considered experience.

As Peberdy spoke with people about women's priests, she noticed that most people with good experiences of the deaconesses were in favour of women in priesthood, thought it was 'normal', and found it difficult to remember their earlier positions of opposition. 'Such forgetting of earlier views is a normal part of the adoption of new attitudes' Peberdy noted (1985, 23). She quoted (Peberdy 1985, 24) one man at length to illustrate the effect of being raised in a parish that had been strongly opposed to women's ordination. John, an accountant in his late thirties, was speaking about Penny, their deaconess, when he admitted that his views had changed significantly. He explained that earlier, before Penny arrived, he:

> always thought that there was something wrong with a woman leading a service simply because I was brought up to see a man doing it ... but I've changed my mind because of the way Penny conducts services and now my feelings against women preaching and so on have completely disappeared.

He not only found it acceptable that Penny carried out the role, but he changed his mind to accept wholeheartedly the wider principle of women's ordination. One woman expressed her fears that a woman priest might not engage sufficiently with the women of the congregation. Given that they did most of the church labour, such a concern is understandable. 'Pat' said that she liked the deaconess because (Peberdy 1985, 18): 'She's let us have our say and then drawn us on starting from our level [...]' It is that concern, that an incoming female in a structurally superior position might not respect, or might interfere with, the women's work, that, I suggest, drove much of the women's resistance.

Generation A women had long accepted that, although they were not in a position of priestly power, they had important roles to perform. In her study of an Australian Anglican church, Manville (1997) observed that the lay labour in the church, called 'team ministry', was performed on gendered lines. Tasks of cleaning the church, organizing flowers, and cleaning the altar linen and vestments were performed mainly by women, as was the work of food preparation and serving. When men were involved, it was because they were 'helping' their wives. One of the women I cleaned with, Mary, described the job as 'a form of ministry'. Said by a woman whose generation fought, and won, the right to become priests and bishops in the Anglican church, this opened up a different way of thinking about ministry and one that seems to conform with the desires and habits of women who in many cases resisted the movement for women's ordination. To consider dusting and polishing as a form of ministry fits with an idea of ministry as something more than work carried out by ordained people. Percy (2015, 229–30) writes:

> Ministry is easy to describe on a day-to-day basis in terms of tasks; and supporting paradigms—rooted in people and practices drawn from the richness of Christian tradition—are numerous. Yet curiously, ministry remains difficult to *define*, and the roles increasingly hard to articulate.

In the sense in which Mary was using it, the concept of ministry would be applied not just to serving God, but to the wider congregation. Another woman in a different church told me that the cleaning work is generally seen as specifically the task of certain women. She had overheard someone complain, saying 'there's been a sweet wrapper in front of my pew for the past three weeks'. She laughed as she repeated the remark and shook her head. Why didn't they just pick the wrapper up themselves, I asked. It wasn't their job, she remarked. Given that she was an active member of the congregation, it did not seem sensible to interpret her remarks as an abdication of her wide and varied duties, but rather to place them in the context of the congregation as a group whose strength comes partly from being bound tightly by strands, each of which has a particular character and role.

Many Generation A women do theology through simple acts of ministry and mission. As described in Chapter 3, the women involved in maintaining open churches often see that act as a way of carrying out their faith. Sarah, whom I quoted there, explicitly framed such work as a form of mission, saying that she 'had' to do that. Other women do their theology through helping with social or fund-raising events. This is what Percy (2015, 235) described as the ministry of 'deep hanging out' through many activities, from visiting to offering open house: 'Much as Jesus was, simply walking from place to place.'

6

Sacred Sundays

A significant insight gained from the intense fieldwork schedule was the embodied realization that Sunday services were felt as a welcome relief after the week's labour. On the seventh day we, briefly, rested and watched the men perform work for a change. Sundays are a sacred time, perceived by Generation A as a day of rest during the week, although they will be constantly busy once the service ends providing after-service refreshments and then washing up. The church service also structured the day itself. For Generation A, Sunday was a special time to dress up, greet friends, make a Sunday lunch, and be with family. Particularly as they have aged and friends and families drift further apart, a Sunday church service structures what might otherwise be a lost and lonely day. Generation A is unequivocal about the importance of church attendance. The Church of England hierarchy is reconstructing its idea of belonging to include a wider 'worshipping community', but Generation A discuss the matter differently: attending church is, and should be, a non-negotiable aspect of being a Christian. It is, they explain, what Christ commanded. More than for any other reason, Generation A attends church for worship. A Canadian Generation A woman, Anna, explained:

> I try definitely not to get into the politics of the church, into the small, what, disagreements in a church, into the humanity of the church [*laughing*]. I go there because I'm close to God, *closer* to God in the church than I find myself at home because I'm occupied with other things. So that's why I'm an Anglican.

The threat posed by other forms of church activities, such as small prayer groups, never materialized for Generation A, who remained loyal to Sunday attendance (Brown 1992, 252). A Tearfund research report conducted in 2006,[1] six years earlier than my research (Ashworth and Farthing 2007, 20) found that 'Worship, mass or communion is the most popular reason for attending across all age groups but peaks among over 65 year olds at 79%'. In contrast, the slightly younger generation (fifty-five to seventy-four year olds) is the group most likely to attend for church and community events not linked to worship: they seem to have inherited the party, but not the piety. The cohort most likely to attend for private reasons such as confession, prayer, or reflection is younger still, aged between thirty-five and forty-four. It is also, I observed, a means of marking and protecting the group of regulars who count as members of the 'church family', to be discussed in more detail in Chapter 7.

The sense of what was sacred and profane and how women are rendered invisible can be strikingly obvious in a church's design and its services. There remains to this day a black line in the floor of Durham Cathedral over which women were not permitted to cross. Even more modern church 'furniture' accomplished the same result to some extent, with women often made less visible when reading from oversized lecterns. If women have been accorded a less visible status than men, this is even more obvious when analysing what is made visible and explicit. The hierarchy of prayers recited, for Church in the world, bishops, the Queen, down to lay prayer requests, emphasize the importance of 'institution' and what is held sacred at the heart of the Church of England such as England, nation, the Establishment, tradition, patriarchy. One only has to stand on the banks of the Thames and see the grand buildings of the Houses of Parliament on one side facing the equally grand Lambeth Palace, London home to the Archbishops of Canterbury since the thirteenth century, or sit in the public gallery at the House of Lords and see the bishops in their robes, speaking and voting on matters of public concern,[2] or recall that the Head of State, the monarch, is also the head of the Church of England to feel the symbiotic, mutually constitutive relationship in the UK between Church and State.

---

[1] Tearfund is a Christian agency devoted to development. This research was carried out on a representative sample of 7000 UK adults over the age of sixteen, capturing the views and habits of churchgoers and non-churchgoers: <http://news.bbc.co.uk/1/shared/bsp/hi/pdfs/03_04_07_tearfundchurch.pdf>, last accessed 20.7.2016.

[2] There are twenty-six Church of England bishops in the House of Lords, the UK's second, unelected house of parliament.

WORK AND RITUAL

Women work. From the time we wake up, to the moment we fall asleep at night, we rarely stop. We cook, clean, organize cleaning, shop, write lists, go to jobs, remember birthdays, organize parties, ring friends, family, and neighbours to check they're OK, arrange deliveries, rearrange deliveries, look after children, find childcare, book dentists and doctors—and it's not even lunchtime yet. Single, partnered, widowed, a mother, or childless, it is no different. We rarely stop, rest, or have fun.

Fun is a feminist issue. Women do not have socially sanctioned rest periods for fun, such as football games, golf, cricket, or—Britain's most popular 'sport'—angling. This, almost exclusively male pastime, involves sitting on a river bank with friends, drinking beer, and observing a fishing rod in the water with line trailing. In the occasional moment when a fish may actually be caught, excitement is brief until the fish is dutifully thrown back. This wholly leisured activity does not result in a fish brought home for the family table. Meanwhile, women are out doing the weekly food shop, taking men's suits to the dry cleaners, and cleaning the family home. There may be a hair appointment squeezed into an already packed day, or, for 'treats', a manicure; but even finding times for those is stressful. No wonder women suffer heart attacks more than men, although the popular view is that men are more at risk. Women work and we rarely stop. And so, one Sunday morning at the end of a typically manic week, I found myself slipping into my regular pew and breathing a nearly audible sigh. First, there was the sense of having my place. Everyone sits in the same place, week after week, and I even witnessed on a number of occasions elderly women suddenly becoming quite spry as they clambered over someone who, just because they were visiting and did not know any better, had sat in her place. At another church I visited one week, I watched a woman take her place and then nod at a man sitting nearby in conversation with another man.

WOMAN: You're sitting somewhere different.
MAN: Oh, just for a minute.

He then finished his conversation and moved down a few rows to what I assumed was his usual place.

The tangibility of 'place' provided important fieldwork insights. Within only three weeks of fieldwork it was easy to identify who was a church-family member and who a stranger; by the sixth week I was finding myself both encouraged by and slightly suspicious of new people who attended. One obvious marker of belonging is the place people sit. Many people remark on the apparent habit of regular members to always sit in the same place every week in the church; I encountered an embodied realization of that importance by the third week into my observations when it was apparent that I had 'marked' my place. I headed to the same corner at the back on each occasion, and saw that no one else had claimed it. This sense of place, however, is both a sense of belonging and excluding. I noticed how strangers did not seem comfortable in the churches where my ethnographic experiences allowed me to know who was a stranger and who a regular. Their discomfort was partly evident by how the strangers would enter during a service, pause briefly, and then leave, as if they had been taken by surprise and had not expected there to be a service. Indeed, given the lack of general public participation in church services, the collective memory of when and how services occur has inevitably declined.

The other reason I felt relieved as I sat in my pew was because I knew I could rest. The setting was by now familiar. I recognized the thirty or so regular attenders, knew the order of service, was confident that my presence was accepted and felt the fieldwork was on track. It had been an otherwise busy week. For Generation A women, the hour of a Sunday service or a midweek service is the only socially acceptable time in the week when they do not have to work. Knowing the liturgy by heart makes it easier. No thought or planning is required. Stand up, sit down, kneel, turn the page, read the words, stand up, sing the hymn, sit down, offer the peace, accept the peace, take communion (be waited on by men!), listen to prayers, offer some in a moment of silence, put the envelope in the tray, stand up, sit down... Their daughter's generation rejected the idea of such repeated rituals. A characteristic of the 1960s was a turn to informality, away from structured religiosity. According to social historian Brian Harrison, what later became known as 'new age' 'owed much to the long-lasting influence of the sixties outlook: an open-minded eagerness for self-expression, novelty and freedom, and a youthful impatience with formal and hierarchical structures' (Harrison 2010, 379). During the 1960s, he noted (Harrison 2010, 370), 'In their share of the UK population, those claiming to be Christians fell from 80 per cent in 1950 to 64 per cent in 2000, and members of Christian congregations fell from 24 per cent to 13 per cent.' All other aspects of institutionalized Christianity also showed decline, he continued, including church attendance, Easter Communicants, the number of clergy, and proportion of religious marriages as a share of the total, falling in England and Wales from 70 per cent in 1960 to 53 per cent in 1980.

The children of Generation A turned from the very quality of religion that their mothers valued so much: familiarity, repetition, and structure. What the children saw as boring, inauthentic ritual, their mothers experienced as meaningful. Douglas (1973, 1) empathized with the valorization of ritual, arguing that 'Ritual has become a bad word signifying empty conformity'. She continued (1973, 3):

> It is fair enough that 'ritualized' ritual should fall into contempt. But it is illogical to despise all ritual, all symbolic action as such. To use the word ritual to mean empty symbols of conformity, leaving us with no word to stand for symbols of genuine conformity, is seriously disabling to the study of the sociology of religion.

She 'will take ritualism to signify heightened appreciation of symbolic action' manifested by belief in the 'efficacy of instituted signs, sensitivity to condensed symbols'(1973, 8). She suggested that sacraments are socially determined signs that are assumed to act as divine channels, which is why people at different points in history are more or less sensitive to different signs. Those perceptions and interpretations are what she calls condensed symbols. These would include, for Christians, the Eucharist or the Catholic (pre-Vatican II) Friday meat abstinence, and, for Jews and Muslims, pork abstinence. If the condensed symbol represents important signs for Generation A, we should not be surprised that they were not shared by their children, who turned away from religious institutions with the 1960s cultural revolution.

The familiar routines of the Sunday ritual gave Generation A a break, allowing a few moments for quiet reflection without worrying about the next task on the list, when they can sit back and watch the men in the front do the work for a change. This is an hour, a precious hour, when women can be swept along with the familiar pattern of Sunday worship. It is a rare hour, and one mandated by their God: 'Six days you shall labour, but on the seventh day you shall rest' (Ex. 20:9). A sacred hour, part of a day that is in itself, for that generation, a sacred day.

It is the sacred day amongst an otherwise, recalling Durkheim, profane week.

SENSING THE SACRED

The term 'sacred' has multiple, often implicit, definitions and associations. That point was well made by Evans (2003, 32) who reviewed a
single issue of the *Journal for the Scientific Study of Religion* and found
that the word 'sacred' was used differently in three different papers: as
a more interesting term for 'religion', as something that encompassed
a transcendent or supernatural view of reality, or as something that
was 'set apart', while not being necessarily supernatural. The first
meaning, as sacred being a more interesting term for 'religion', is
primarily of interest to academics who do battle in their conflicting
views about secularization. Nearly ten years later, I conducted a
similar review for comparative purposes, choosing the *Journal of
Contemporary Religion*. An analysis of three papers in the same
issue reflected Evans's findings, with an added quality of the sacred
being sometimes presented as 'authentic'.

My ethnographic experiences with Generation A illustrated for me
the importance of the second and third meaning above—as sacred
being something with a transcendent reality, being set apart. From
social science, the classic functionalist approach to 'the sacred' was
Durkheim's formulation wherein he defined religion as being composed of beliefs and by a separation between the sacred and profane.
Durkheim did not need to define 'sacred' because his point was that
'the sacred' did not exist as an *a priori* entity or quality, but it was
whatever the group decided it was. Durkheim rejected the idea that
religion presupposes a belief in the supernatural or divine beings, and
defined religion as follows (1915, 47):

> A religion is a unified system of beliefs and practices relative to sacred
> things, that is to say, things set apart and forbidden—beliefs and
> practice which unite into one single moral community called a Church,
> all those who adhere to them.

The sacred–profane distinction existed to maintain order and social
cohesion between what might be declared sacred and profane or, as
Douglas (1966) later argued, pure or polluted.

Demerath (2000) argued that is more useful to recognize 'sacred' as
the term of most consequence for people. Religion is just one expression of the sacred, with 'secular' sometimes being a partner with
sacred rather than its opposite. He suggested an analytical method
that first distinguishes between sacred experiences that are either

confirmatory, where a sacred experience is one that binds the individual to another or to a group, or a sacred experience that is compensatory, where it comforts or relieves. That analytical distinction is useful when considering the communal act of Communion from a non-functionalist perspective. Further, Demerath proposed distinctions between sacred experiences that are marginal, that is, self-consciously outside the mainstream, and those that are institutional. Those intersecting distinctions result in four separate kinds of sacred: the integrative, the quest, the collective, and the counter-cultural. Applying this to the generational dynamic at the heart of this book, I suggest that the church-based sacred experience enjoyed by Generation A is more typical of the integrative and collective, whereas their children's experiences, particularly those claiming a more non-institutional, spiritual path, would reflect the 'quest' and 'counter-cultural'. A useful, perhaps unintended, consequence of Demerath's model is to replace the discourse of generational conflict with one of generational preference.

Lynch theorizes the 'sacred' by describing it as a culturally embedded 'communicative structure' (2012, 245) that reflects social conceptions of morality. He allows for 'multiple sacreds' that exist simultaneously in any society, with people experiencing 'different kinds of gravitational pull over their lives' (2012, 246).

Sacred Rituals of Religious Belonging

Theologians and religious people such as the women of Generation A embrace the idea of the supernormal sacred. Otto (1958) viewed a sacred object as other-worldly, with a power to create awe, desire, and fear, as did Eliade (1959), who conceived of an other-world, pre-existing, *sui generis* sense of a sacred power. The idea of another world positioned away from the everyday is, feminist and eco-theologians have argued, implicitly sexist because it privileges 'spirit' rather than the 'material', 'natural' world and everyday (see, for example, Ruether 1993 [1983]; Rose 1993; Raphael 1996; Eaton 2005). The women I met of Generation A, who do not describe themselves as feminists, are aligned to both other-worldly and this-worldly sacred experience. While their daughters' generation of academics have urged scholars to turn from such binary definitions as 'sacred and secular' (see, for example, Day et al. 2013) it is that binary, that demarcation, that Generation A upholds. During our conversations they seem to be in no doubt that they believe in God, that He has the power to transform their lives, and that they go to church not only for the communal experience, but to worship God. As one Canadian woman told me:

> Well, I'll tell you what my faith means to me. I believe in the Lord Jesus Christ is my saviour, which is an evangelical thing. And I believe that He is in us and we are in Him, that's something that's in the Bible, and it's in our liturgy too, the Anglican liturgy [. . .] what else is traditional, now let me think for a minute. Well, it's the liturgy [. . .] it's a sort of worship in itself. The English. I know that sounds silly but it's the truth. And, um, I just feel comfortable with it, and we have people who've come because of the service, who were with, one in particular was with a holy roller type place, you know, people falling on the floor and all the rest of it, and then they discovered us and realised, you know, that . . . it's scripture.

An Englishwoman remarked, simply, that Christians ought to go to church because that is what Christ told them to do. It is a Christian obligation, in her view. Another Englishwoman explained why she went to Church:

> Well it's to do with one's *faith* . . . and you see the Church as being the way that God operates in the world. I suppose you could say the Church has perhaps a hotline to God or God has a hotline to the Church because the Church is seen as Christ's body and therefore you want to be a part of that and you want to work in the world through His body, if that makes sense.

Having a hotline to God is a privileged position to be in, but the position is not, according to that formulation, individualistic. It is through the Church that one has the hotline. The requirement to attend Church and be part of that body is, for the religious women of Generation A, non-negotiable. This recalls a definition of the sacred proposed by Anttonen (2000, 280–1):

> The sacred is a special quality in individual and collective systems of meaning. In religious thinking it has been used as an attribute of situations and circumstances which have some reference to the culture-specific conception of the category of God, or, in non-theological contexts, to some supreme principle of life such as love, freedom, equality or justice. Sacrality is employed as a category-boundary to set things with non-negotiable value apart from things whose value is based on continuous transactions . . . non-negotiable

value apart from things whose value is based on continuous transac-
tions . . . People participate in sacred-making activities and processes of
signification according to paradigms given by the belief systems to
which they are committed, whether they be religious, national or
ideological.

Once again, the lines are drawn between the 'sacred' and non-sacred.
Creating and maintaining those boundaries requires both belief and
practice, often performed in religious contexts through ritual, and in a
specific place. With their adherence to church attendance, Generation A
was, even tacitly, recognizing the connection between a place and
the memories attached to it and what those memories represent.
What Connerton (2009) theorizes as place-memory is salient here:
the process of emplacement both facilitates and enriches the coded
practices that are essential for value transmission. Connerton (2009,
31) describes the 'encoding power of place' whereby habitual practices are 'sedimented'. The church, and specifically the Sunday service, is the locus of such sedimentations. Generation A was right to
assume church attendance was important for transmission, a point
Connerton made in an earlier work (1989, 3–5): 'images of the past
and recollected knowledge of the past, I want to argue, are conveyed
and sustained by (more or less ritual) performances'. While others,
such as Halbwachs (1992), also argued that memory is carried
through social spaces, Connerton (1989, 38) stresses that it is not
sufficient, for memory transmission, that any one group retains social
memory but that 'it is necessary also that the older members of the
group should not neglect to transmit these representations to the
younger members of the group'. Sunday service ritual in the Church
was the most important means by which Generation A tried to pass
their tradition on.

One of Turner's definitions of ritual (1977, 183) was as 'a stereotyped sequence of activities involving gestures, words, and objects,
performed in a sequestered place, and designed to influence preter-
natural entities or forces on behalf of the actors' goals and interests'.
Taking that definition as a starting point, I suggest that the women
I studied were performing a ritual of religious belonging through
attending and participating in church services. As they come into
the church they chat to each other before taking their seats, although
in two churches I visited regularly I noticed that the (male) clergy was
trying to shorten that period. New service leaflets had been printed

with a suggestion that people take their seats more quickly so that they could experience a few more moments of prayer and reflection. By that stage in my fieldwork I was familiar enough with the women's social practices to know how unwelcome that suggestion would be. Theirs was not inconsequential 'chatting' but important social labour that reinforced the sense of belonging.[3] After taking their seats they tended to be quiet and focused on arranging their personal effects, checking the pages for the hymns, and getting their envelopes ready for the offering. They remained seated, looking forward, never backwards, and rarely obviously stretching to glance from side to side. If they caught someone's eye, they would smile warmly. Once the service began, they refrained from conversation or other forms of social contact, with the exception of the practice of 'sharing the peace'. This occurs about halfway through the service at the invitation of the priest to 'show one another a sign of the peace'. Everyone stands and turns to the people nearby, shakes their hands and says 'peace be with you'; some may even move about the nave and stop at each pew. The conviviality of that practice is in sharp contrast to their behaviour during Holy Communion.

Considering the rite of Holy Communion, I took the perspective on ritual initially proposed by van Gennep (1960) and then worked out more intensely by Turner. The tripartite, processual model presumes three stages: one, where a person leaves behind the old life; two, where there is a no-life, no-identity, in between; and three, where the person is admitted into another social group that confers identity. Turner was particularly interested in the first and second state, when actors are 'neither here nor there; they are betwixt and between the positions assigned and arrayed by law, custom, convention, and ceremonial' (Turner 1969, 95).

Contemplating the Holy Communion experience every Sunday drew my attention more and more to the second phase of the ritual. The beginning of the ritual appeared straightforward and was marked by the priest leading the pre-Communion prayers and blessing the cup, wine and bread (symbolically represented by the thin, dry wafer, or 'host'). The congregation remains in the pews, reading along and praying as directed. The priest, reading from the Book of Common Prayer, suggests that those who want to take Communion should first

---

[3] A point I made and discussed in my earlier study of a Baptist women's prayer group (Day 2005).

'make your humble confession to Almighty God, meekly kneeling upon your knees'. Looking around the congregations I visited during my research, I was struck by how many elderly people did as they were told, unlike the few younger members present who seemed to remain sitting as if, I felt, they were not inclined to bow to such an authority.

When the priest turns to the congregation and invites them to 'draw near with faith' they rise by row, usually when indicated by one of the sidesmen (or women these days). This, I suggest, begins the second, liminal phase when they are no longer in their places but moving towards the altar, where they pause and are given the bread and wine. At that moment, accepting what the priest says is the body and blood of Christ they are, according to their theology, experiencing the presence of Christ and becoming transformed by his spirit. They then, in the third phase, return to their seats and remain in silence, or in prayer. What caught my attention was the sombre nature of the second phase when they steadfastly avoided eye contact or acknowledgement of any kind. This was not a moment of convivial playfulness or joyful collective effervescence, as Durkheim described ritual performance. But it was, I sensed, a period of 'communitas', or comradeship, as Turner discussed (1969, 96–7). The communicants moved, as their theology suggested, as 'one body', together experiencing the destruction of their old, sinful self and the reformation in the new, forgiven, divinely graced self. The journey to the altar is taken by ghost-like creatures who have left their old bodies behind: this is a marginal, unformed state. The reason they did not want to have eye contact or greeting was undoubtedly partly because they were acting formally as their ritual practice demanded, but also because they were not, in their sense, themselves. Who was the Abby who would smile at Rita in recognition as we walked along, when we each had left our old selves behind us? It was not until the ritual was complete and the priest finished the Communion prayers that we were fully renewed, and fully in the knowledge, for the faithful, of being in one body with each other and Christ.

That 'sacred' experience was so because it clearly delineated in space and time the moment of transformation sensed as 'other' as completely different from every day, the human directed—the profane. Sacred rituals, such as communion, are effective because they are set apart and constituted with the premise of divine participation. The experience of Communion is one ritual that conforms to a wider anthropological understanding of 'sacred time'.

Sacred Time

Time is variously experienced and defined,[4] although I would agree with Gell (1992, 9) as described in Chapter 4: some limits can be set; time is not a pendulum. And yet it is often perceived as such, and accounted for differently in how activities are described, how people perceive having more or less of it, and how they try to slow or reverse it. Leach (1971), for example, argued that there are two types of time: profane time is directional and forward, whereas sacred time is backwards, through ritual, restoring us to an original state. The experience of Communion conforms to that second type of time. Lynch (2012, 20) suggests something similar in describing 'fleeting moments of ecstasy, transgression, creativity, and *communitas*, which give life by temporarily releasing people from cultural structures'.

Durkheim (1915) considered rituals as a way of creating a sacred time away from ordinary or profane time when, through communal ecstasy or 'collective effervescence', groups experience a sense of awe that they project onto the idea of a deity. Such group identity is then maintained through coming together again for periodic renewal, as Generation A recognized through their adherence to church attendance.

Profane time is the type discussed by Generation A, as I explored in Chapter 4, where a lack of time is often given as the reason their children have not followed their own church-attending habits, as if the only time that counts is a capitalist-based time of paid labour. They ignore the time they spend in buying presents and cards for grandchildren, nieces, and nephews, going to the post office to mail them, doing housework, shopping, cooking, looking after less able family, friends, neighbours, cleaning the church, and so on, and on.

When Leach (1971, 133) talks about the 'rate' of time, he is getting at how and why people impose measures to track it, a little like the cycle of church-based tasks and festivities I experienced during my fieldwork. Leach says the time between festivals is named, variously, a week or a year: for Generation A women attending mid-week Communion, the interval is only one to three days. Although sometimes people talk of measuring time, what they are actually doing, says Leach, is creating time by imposing intervals between festivals.

---

[4] For a fuller discussion see Day 2017 (forthcoming).

TEACUPS AS CONDENSED SYMBOLS

At many churches, the tea and coffee service after the main service is an important part of the church-attending event. It is, I suggest, part of the larger ritual of religious belonging, mirroring, through material objects and bodily movements, the Eucharist itself. Generation A women have traditionally taken the main responsibility for the after-service refreshments, offering a cup of tea or coffee, on a saucer, and a small, dry biscuit to a congregant, who has lined up with others, just as the priest did only ten minutes earlier at the altar. At one Church I observed there were two types of cups and saucers—the green ones used for events such as coffee mornings and fund-raisers, and the white ones used for the after-service refreshments on Sundays. The white cups, being a colour associated with purity, and the process of producing two different categories of the white and green are means of marking the sacred through 'setting things apart' (Durkheim 1915, 40–1, 47) and the pure from the polluted (Douglas 1966).

Part of the duties for the volunteers attending Saturday events was to set out the white cups and saucers in the Church, ready for the Sunday service and post-service refreshments. I made several mistakes on my first attempts to help. In the kitchen, Vera gave me a bag containing the cups and saucers. I took it into the Church, set it down beside the table and returned for another bag-full, at which point Vera told me to first lay out the cups and saucers I had taken in already before returning for another bag. I did as I was told, but was interrupted by a member of the congregation who was also volunteering that day. He began to rearrange the cups so that all their handles pointed in the same direction. Nodding towards the women in the kitchen, he whispered 'they are very particular'.

The work of Gell (1998) helped me resolve what initially seemed as a contradiction. How could the women be so 'particular' when the cups were transported in bags and stored haphazardly? If these were, as I was beginning to postulate, sacred objects, should they not be stored, like the chalice used for Communion, in a special, secure place? I had found that the cups and saucers were stored in a crate in a crowded cupboard along with a box of candles, two tins of artichokes, a bottle of olive oil, and a jar of pâté. It seemed to me that something so important, so potentially symbolic of significant values and beliefs should have an equally special storage space. Gell (1998), and later Latour (2005), drew anthropological attention to how objects participate in the networks of human relations in which they play a part. Although mainly discussing art objects, Gell's (1998, 6) idea that we need to pay attention to what objects do, and what their 'practical mediatory role . . . in the social process' may be, helped me think this through. As I observed the way the cups and saucers were used in practice, it became increasingly clear that, unused, they had no intrinsic value unlike, for example, the silver chalice which was brought out for Communion but could equally be, in the wrong hands, melted down for the base silver value.

During my fieldwork I was able to participate in all phases of the coffee service at my host church and sometimes at others—setting up, serving, washing up, and, of course, partaking as an ordinary member of the congregation on many occasions. The job of serving was not as easy as it looked, primarily because members of the congregation often made our task difficult. We made tea in a large, metal pot that needed to be frequently topped up to ensure the tea did not get too strong, and also so that it went a long way. Coffee was made to order through adding a teaspoon of instant coffee to a cup and then filling it with hot water from an electric urn plugged into a socket near the table. The urn had to be switched on halfway through the service to get ready, which it did with a soft 'whoosh' I could hear from my pew. I recall a day when I didn't hear the whoosh and, looking around, could see that the person usually responsible for that job was not at church. It did not seem anyone else had noticed, most likely because most were too old and deaf to hear the 'whoosh' signalling the urn's operation. I didn't know what to do. Turn it on myself? I didn't know how to do that, and would everyone notice and be distracted? I had no idea what to do and found that I could do nothing. I could not disturb the quiet conformity of the assembled congregation, now immersed in the service, and nor could I assume that the urn operator had not made some other arrangement with someone who might yet appear. That surprised and irritated me. Duty was something to be taken seriously. Duty is mutual. If I did not turn up for one of my 'duties', there could be havoc. One of the rules of doing church watch/ opening is that at least two people need to be present. My not turning up might mean in that case the church wouldn't open, which would have consequences for the whole church 'family', and for me. I would find that the trust they had in me would be diminished. It might be recoverable once, but not twice. That I was participating for my research would not provide me with any excuse. The idea that the researcher has more power and can just walk away is flawed. If I walked away from those people and neglected my duties I would lose credibility with the group and my project would be damaged, or might even be dropped. That would influence my project, my standing in the group, my standing in the academic community, my relationship with my funder, and my institution. My career may not be quite over, but it would certainly be diminished. As I recognized that there was a consequence for both of us, I better understood the point of 'duty': it has costs and benefits as it co-implicates everyone involved.

I was frozen by structure and role: no wonder, I reflected, anthropologists analyse those categories so carefully. I sensed, with some irritation, the agency of the urn, the other-than-human actant (following Latour, 2005) that, with its now-absent operator, was determining the success or otherwise of the after-service ritual. As the service drew to a close I realized I was dreading the moment when those on the rota would realize the problem. Would I tell them that I had known all along? Would I get in trouble? Their matriarchal power and dominance was, I felt, an almost palpable force. Maybe I should just leave—run away like the naughty child I had somehow, in the space of thirty minutes, become. It was, however, too late in the development of our relationship for that. I was implicated already. There were previous phases in our relationship of recognition, intimitization, integration, and routinization, but this was something different. I was fixed to the spot through another web of belonging: obligation. I began to think about how to help with the cold urn situation after the service. I was not part of that rota, but I imagined that the two elderly women who were would find it difficult to go back and forth to the kitchen with kettles of hot water. I, however, could do that more ably and would therefore offer that assistance. Somewhat calmer, I felt stronger about breaking the news to one of the women as the service ended. I quickly explained the situation and asked if we should turn the urn on now, or was it too late? 'I have no idea,' she replied, 'not my department.' Yet another demarcation, a boundary, a structure. And so it was that on one particular Sunday I found a new role, the kettle boiler, who kept the teapot hot and the coffee cups full.

On an occasional Sunday and, more frequently, at other events, I was asked to be part of the serving pair. This required some dexterity as cups needed to be filled and passed to a waiting hand while not bumping the arm of the other server doing exactly the same thing in a small space. Typically, we were serving thirty people, many of whom, I was to discover, were surprisingly picky about the sort of coffee and tea they wanted: a little more water or a little less; not so strong or a little stronger. Any decaf? Any herbal? I would sometime mutter to the woman next to me—what are we, Starbucks? This was not the place to order your double decaf skinny latte caramel top, and why, I wondered, would anyone imagine it to be? This was being served by the generation of proper tea and ginger biscuits, thank you very much, and count yourselves lucky that on a special day you might get a slice of Victoria sponge.

I was to overhear many conversations during my fieldwork that centred on cups and saucers. For example, one Sunday morning in a busy church I was visiting in London, I listened carefully to a conversation between two women I'll call Sandra (who had been doing the washing up) and Hazel (who was sitting at the large communal table set up for the refreshments):

SANDRA: Whose cup is that? (pointing to a nearly full cup of coffee in a saucer)

HAZEL: I don't know.

SANDRA: Is it Mark's?

HAZEL: Don't know.

SANDRA: I wonder if he's coming back for it.

HAZEL: I'm not sure. Maybe he finished it.

SANDRA: He didn't finish it. It's nearly full.

HAZEL: It must be cold.

SANDRA: And whose is that? (pointing to an empty saucer)

HAZEL: I don't know. There's no cup there.

SANDRA: No. I wonder where that is.

HAZEL: I don't know. Maybe it's Mark's.

SANDRA: No, I think that's Mark's.

HAZEL: I don't know. Maybe.

SANDRA: I think I'll take it to the kitchen.

HAZEL: You might as well.

SANDRA: I'm going to take it. It's probably cold anyway.

HAZEL: Yes, He's probably done.

SANDRA: He hasn't touched it!

HAZEL: No.

SANDRA: I'll take it now.

HAZEL: Yes, that's a good idea.

SANDRA: I'll take the saucer too. But I don't know where the cup is.
HAZEL: Maybe someone else took it to the kitchen.
SANDRA: Maybe. I'll take it anyway. [Sandra leaves with the cups.]

I puzzled over this for several hours. The exchange felt like a set piece from a play and reminded me of what Evans Pritchard had said about the Nuer and what he termed 'linguistic profusion'. Evans Pritchard had absorbed himself in the life of those he studied with his detailed observations moving anthropological thinking along in several ways, probably most notably in showing how social systems and people's cosmologies, or world views about meaning and causation, intersect and are mutually dependent. For example, through observation Evans Pritchard saw the importance to Nuer society of cattle—there were more expressions for cattle than for anything else. As he put it (1940, 41): 'Linguistic profusion in particular departments of life is one of the signs by which one quickly judges the direction and strength of a people's interests.'

The cup and saucer is probably the most important material object to symbolize the women's roles and sense of importance. The cup and the saucer are important things, but, as Morgan asks in his description of material culture (Morgan 2010, 70), what is a thing?

> So what is a thing? What goes into our experience and evaluation of a
> material object? Certainly its physical properties—its weight, texture,
> size, shape and colour. But also its relationship to other objects and its
> placement in the space we ourselves may inhabit next to it, above or
> below it, or from afar [. . .] Things are social.

Things are also sacred. Religious material culture, Morgan suggests, 'consists of the objects, spaces, practices, and ideas in which belief takes shape' (Morgan 2010, 73). Most objects considered to be part of the religious material in a church are overtly religious, such as the cross, or the chalice. But, central to the women's performances of being Christian through commensality is the cup and saucer: the everyday green set and the special Sunday white set. The cup and saucer are not just what the women use; they are the material embodiment of what they do in the church and the extra-church activities such as coffee mornings and church openings. It is also how they become visible. With the passing of the cup and saucer to a stranger comes an offer of hospitality and possibly friendship. Sitting down and drinking together from identical cups equalizes part of the relationship. Washing the cups and saucers and putting them away again is the act of preparation for the next event. The relationship to these objects is one of care, concern, and affection. The objects themselves have their own agency that affects the women signifi- cantly. Without the cups and saucers there would be no framework of the coffee morning or after-church teas and coffees. Those are the spaces where the objects and women perform an event that makes the women visible. Without these events there would not be a visible space for these women, who reject the possibility of becoming priests. In churches without an after-service event the women file out the door like everyone else and disappear. In churches that are open without the coffee and tea service, there may be a woman volunteer to answer questions about the Church, but there would not be space for lengthy conversations of a more mundane, personal nature. It is the cup and saucer that create the opportunities for conversation and command attention on the women.

The importance of sharing time over a cup of tea has an English, 'Anglican' quality that has long been noted and often pinpointed as peculiar to an English disposition. In her book section called (appro- priately for this book and my own disciplinary obsession) 'tea beliefs', the anthropologist of Englishness Kate Fox (2004) suggests that English people believe that 'a nice cup of tea' has magical properties (Fox 2004, 313), capable of healing bruised limbs, broken hearts, confused minds, and awkward social situations. Reflecting on how hospital chaplains try to create social intimacy, Simon Coleman (2015, 219) contrasts the cup of tea with the communion chalice:

> This time, the tea is not one that is carried through corridors, but rather one that provides a semiotic replacement of, and functional equivalent to, communion wine; in other words the kind of tea that a chaplain usually finds themselves making as they attempt to create an instant intimacy with patients (and sometimes medical staff) who may be facing physical and emotional extremes, and for whom the generic sociality represented by 'a cuppa' is often far more effective than the liturgical formality of a Eucharistic cup.

Women play a parallel role with the priest, who uses the cup, or chalice as it is usually known, to offer wine to people taking commu- nion. The sacristan, often a woman of Generation A, has prepared the chalice through laundering the altar cloths and setting up the chalice with its various coverings for the communion service. The priest blesses the wine in the cup to make it sacred; the women clean it afterwards and prepare it for its next service. The purpose of taking communion and drinking from the chalice is to show oneself as a member of what the priest describes as one body, being in communion with each other and Jesus, who will take the heavy burden the communicant is carrying: 'Come unto me, all ye that labour and are heavy laden, and I will give you rest' (Matthew 11:28–30).

The purpose of drinking tea at a coffee morning or church opening is to show oneself as a member of the group of fellow 'regulars' and, through conversation, to feel better about oneself as the women listen with a non-judgemental ear, conferring a sense of absolution. There is one more quality of the 'cup' in this case that reflects in particular Generation A: most homes today in Euro-American countries would more commonly have mugs than cups and saucers. A question on the website 'Yahoo Answers'[5] posed the question: 'When did we start to use mugs?'. Responses generally pointed to a generational shift over the past fifty years or so, as these extracts show:

> Growing up we always had cups and saucers for the adults and beakers for the children. During my teens (60's) I remember getting a mug for the first time.

> When I got married in 1976 I was given 3 tea sets as wedding presents (with proper cups and saucers). To be honest, I never used them as we always used mugs.

> I was born in 1959 and we used mugs all the time. Cups and saucers were only used if my parents had people over for dinner as they matched the best dinner set.

> Delicate tea cups are no longer popular and most are pretty decorations sitting on shelves. And most owners do not want them to be touched or used.

In conclusion, I suggest that the Sunday service celebrates and reinforces that which Generation A holds sacred: their day of rest, the sacrament of Holy Communion, the sense of belonging with their congregation, and the wider social influences of nation and Establishment. That final point may help explain one aspect of the generational change I have argued is a result of a clash of certain beliefs and values between Generation A and the generations that followed. The

---

[5] <https://uk.answers.yahoo.com/question/index?qid=20101026080227AadyOVt>, last accessed 2.10.2015.

1950s political commentator, Henry Fairlie, popularized the term 'Establishment', which he described in a *Spectator* column as a powerful matrix of official and social relations, including the Church.[6] Those Establishment figures included, he suggested, 'the Prime Minister, the Archbishop of Canterbury' and heads of media, military, and powerful families. As 'sacred' as the Establishment might have been to adults in the 1950s, it was its antithesis that sparked the anti-Establishment 1960s cultural revolution. Prayers to protect it must have, almost literally, stuck in the throat of the 1960s teenagers dragged by their mothers to the Sunday service.

[6] <http://archive.spectator.co.uk/article/23rd-september-1955/5/political-commentary>, last accessed 7.12.2015.

Section III

Ties that Bind: The Pew Power of Generation A

What may seem as innocuous social events are read here as carefully constructed means of involving congregation members through bonds of belonging and obligation. A seven-stage Model of Belonging is introduced to show how newcomers can be integrated into the 'church family', a unit distinctly different from the external 'community'. Finally, the book's data and arguments are drawn together to conclude how Generation A's passing will affect certain sectors of the church and external community.

7

Family and Community

A tension exists between the close church-based 'family' and other, external people often referred to as the outside 'community'. The reference to a regular congregation as a 'church family' is not merely metaphorical. A network analysis of my host church revealed strong kin relationships, a theme that was identified and discussed in interviews at other churches and found to be replicated, with many women speaking about it as a source of pride: 'My son was one of the first altar boys', one woman said. 'And we had a children's choir besides the piano choir, and since I was in music, I trained the children's choir for some years in the church.' One woman reminisced about her early church days, when it was her father that encouraged them to attend the local Anglican Church:

There were four or us, and I'm the youngest, and we all went to Sunday school, and the people up the street had four kids, we all went together in a *group*. Everybody went to Sunday school. And, er, the Anglican Church, ours was St [...]. Anyway, I guess we were, I was baptised 1936, when I was 6 years old. What happened, my father influenced my mother and all of us got baptised together, and then my mother took quite a role in the church . . .

The pattern of close family ties is supported by Schwadel (2008) in his discussion of religious teenagers, to which Smith and Denton (2005) and Regnerus et al. (2004) add friendship networks. Although it is sometimes argued that 'family' is a victim of modernity, other research challenges that notion by showing the persistent importance of family relationships, albeit sometimes constructed differently (see, for example, Bengtson 2001; Bengtson, Biblarz, and Roberts 2002; Cannell 2005; Day 2011 [2013], 79–85; Danely and Lynch 2013; McKinnon and Cannell 2013).

Most women I talked to had long histories of Anglicanism. One Canadian woman said she had been 'paddling in Anglicanism since I was a little girl':

> We all went to Sunday school, and the people up the street had four kids, we all went together in a *group*. Everybody went to Sunday school [...] And er, so as we grew up we went to Sunday school and then when we got older, we taught Sunday school and were in the choir and things like that [...] used to have Sunday schools on the beach and things like that. So, there were a lot of Anglicans in that, and a lot of people [...] were in the Anglican ministry [...] we had a lot of Bible study and outreach and when I got married my husband was an Anglican so we went to the Anglican church.

With a history of connection to both Anglicanism and, often, to a specific parish or church, it is not surprising that the observable religious life of the church is self-focused. The church as a congregation is a larger unit of the individual selves that constitute it and most of its activities are concerned with the betterment of those selves. For example, it was observable during the prayers that were requested by members of the congregation, and sometimes by visitors who had dropped in, that people were well known to each other. The prayers were sometimes written on pieces of paper, or pinned to a board at the back of the church. During my visits to churches I would always read the requests and each time note that the majority were for family members—mostly for people who were ill, but sometimes for those who were experiencing family break-ups or alienation. Apart from prayers for members of the nuclear family, there were others for members of the 'church family': 'for Frank to be restored to the church family', for example.

The 'family' mirrors the nuclear family institution, with priests as the male head/husband/father and the Generation A woman as the matriarch. They and other women are assumed to perform the kinds of domestic labour found in nuclear families. Even the 'social work' happens in the church home. As I discussed in Chapter 3, most of the money raised and caring activities performed occur for and in the church. For those unmarried, childless women I met in the churches, their extended family networks were just as important to them as the nuclear family was to others. In one Generation A woman's home I visited, her walls and tables were filled with photographs of nieces and nephews, and as we spoke regularly over the course of my fieldwork, she would update me on her latest news of graduations, engagements, and christenings. She mentioned one day that she must remember to go to the shop and pick up a birthday card for her niece. It occurred to me then that the days are numbered for the greeting card business—it is no longer the norm for people to send physical cards when a message or Facebook post will do.

The inclusion today of women priests complicates that family structure—in the eyes of Generation A, they can be seen variously as family members or as interlopers. Other markers of difference, such as 'race' and social class, are not always easily assimilated when the identification as church as a family is often seen through the lens of literal and metaphorical genealogy, with a special, institutionalized place given to motherhood.

OF MOTHERS

Reading a popular UK morning newspaper one March morning, an advertisement from Legal and General, an insurance company, caught my attention. The timing was important as this was 5 March 2013, five days before what is known in the UK as Mothering Sunday. The advertisement, with timely ease, led with a prominent line telling the reader that although mothers are priceless, research conducted by Legal and General had been able to show that they are actually worth precisely £31,627 per year, calculated in terms of household tasks. Following through that idea, I checked on Legal and General's website and found the relevant page:[1]

> Imagine Mother's Day without Mum: What would your loved ones do without Mum to rely on for comfort and support? Help financially protect them with life insurance. Buy before 31st March and receive a free £50 M&S voucher.

The page quantifies a mother's worth. A section headed: 'The Hardest Job In The World' explained that:

> At this time of year we appreciate how important mums really are. According to our 2013 'Value of a Parent' research, the unpaid household tasks Mums do are worth £31,627.

[1] <http://www.legalandgeneral.com/life-cover/campaigns/mothers-day/press/>, last accessed 22.6.15.

> The emotional support mums provide is priceless, but when you consider how much it would cost to replace the job they do, award-winning life cover from just £6 a month could make all the difference.

To cover oneself for the possibility that mother might not actually die, but might simply become too ill to conduct her household responsibilities, the next section detailed how to obtain 'extra peace of mind' with 'Critical Illness Cover':

> You can add Critical Illness Cover to your life insurance policy at an additional cost. We cover 40 conditions in total including heart-attack, stroke and some forms of cancer.

> Life insurance policies are not savings or investment plans and have no cash value unless a valid claim is made.

Given that sudden reminder that mothers were irreplaceable for anything less than £31,627 it might seem prudent to at least buy the old dear a card. Nowadays, that might not be as straightforward as one might like if Mother is a member of Generation A. The number of cards that state 'Mothering Sunday' are few compared with those that state 'Mother's Day'. Perhaps this reflects an increasingly global, or Americanized, economy, or is an example of the secularization of religious festivals, but to many women of Generation A it marks the difference between a secular and a sacred event.

Mothering Sunday in the UK, in contrast with Mother's Day in other parts of the world, is an explicitly Christian observance, falling on the fourth Sunday in Lent. The day is not fixed in the calendar but moves in relation to the Christian festival of Easter, itself a mobile event depending on the lunar calendar. Mothering Sunday therefore has sacred temporal roots in 325 CE, when Christian bishops were called by the Roman Emperor Constantine to set certain policies and doctrines for the Christian church. Before Nicaea, Christians had relied upon the Jewish calendar to determine Easter. Many had become dissatisfied with that arrangement, and at the Council of Nicaea it was established that Easter would be held on the first Sunday after the first full moon occurring on or after the spring equinox, approximated as 21 March.[2]

The history of Mothering Sunday is generally told with charming, mythical tones. For example, the Religion section of the BBC website

---

[2] While that is relevant for Anglicans, and most other Christian churches, it would not be so for Orthodox churches, which follow the Julian calendar.

reports that Mothering Sunday was formerly a day when domestic servants were given time off to visit their mothers.[3] Nowadays, the text continues, it is a day 'when children give presents, flowers, and home-made cards to their mothers'. The term 'home-made' rather than 'hand-made' lends a nice touch of domesticity. A little further down, the text embellishes the story with a further nostalgic tone, reporting that child-servants of yore coming home to see their mothers 'along the country lanes' (presumably from not too far away) 'would pick wild flowers or violets to take to church or give to their mother as a small gift'. This practice was apparently known as 'going-a-mothering'. Although the text states firmly that 'although it's often called Mothers' Day it has no connection with the American festival of that name', the real story is more complicated, and more interwoven with the American event than the BBC claims. The BBC does not purport to be an authority on theological matters, as its reference to 'both Old and New Testament lessons on mid-lent Sunday' attests. Being a Christian concept, the notion of Lent would never arise in the 'Old Testament', itself a term generally avoided due Christian-centric doctrine, with 'Hebrew Scriptures' preferred as a minimum. And yet, the BBC, with its emphasis on the Christian nature of Mothering Sunday, may be close to feeling the pulse of a certain sector of its audience.

The diminishment of Mothering Sunday and its replacement by Mother's Day rankles some older, conservative, and possibly gendered elements of British society. Writing in the conservative-leaning *Telegraph*, under the headline 'The True Origins of Mothering Sunday', religion blogger Christopher Howse notes that:[4]

> Every year, readers write to the *Telegraph* pointing out that the mid Sunday in Lent is not "Mother's Day" but "Mothering Sunday". Many blame America for introducing the former and making it commercial. Blame 'America' as they may, there appears to be little demand in the UK for the celebration of Mothering Sunday in preference to Mother's Day. Whether or not this is indicative of secularization is difficult to say as, like all festivals, this one has a complicated and contested history.

---

[3] <http://www.bbc.co.uk/religion/religions/christianity/holydays/motheringsunday_1.shtml>, last accessed 26.6.15.

[4] <http://www.telegraph.co.uk/news/religion/9918148/The-true-origins-of-Mothering-Sunday.html>, last accessed 26.6.15.

Howse notes that sources vary in their views of its sources, but suggests that most agree that the biblical verse of Galatians 4:26: 'Jerusalem which is above is free; which is Mother of us all' laid the ground for the idea of the 'mother church'. For centuries it was apparently customary for Christians to return home to their original, or 'mother' church or cathedral, on the fourth Sunday in Lent. During periods when children were away from home working in domestic or agricultural servant jobs, this apparently became the day that they returned home to visit their families, taking gifts and flowers to their mothers, with the day being described as 'going a-mothering'.

One of the English women I interviewed reflected on the practice of church attendance in general being linked to the years when working in domestic service was more usual. She told me:

> when you think of the old days when a lot of people went into service and so on, to the big houses, they *had* to come to church on Sunday, they didn't have a choice. Either that or they were going—they had their Sundays off and they had to go home and see their mothers.

On special occasions, so the story goes, the children brought with them a special fruit and marzipan cake baked for the occasion, known as Simnel cake. One website describes this as a 'Traditional British Mothering Sunday Simnel Cake',[5] but few other food sites do, with most referring to it as an Easter Cake. Even the British cookery star Mary Berry, herself a woman of Generation A, recommends that cooks can 'serve it up at your Easter celebration'.[6]

As for the designation of Mothering Sunday more formally, most accounts report that in 1913,[7] Constance Penswick-Smith, a thirty-one-year-old daughter of a Nottinghamshire Church of England vicar, took it upon herself to encourage a revival of Mothering Sunday, founding the Society for the Observance of Mothering Sunday and spending the following twenty-five years working for its widespread adoption. Some sources claim that Constance was inspired by the efforts of an American Pennsylvanian woman, Anna Jarvis, whose mother had died in May 1906. She decided to honour her and began to campaign amongst friends for a Mother's Day to be

---

[5] <http://www.food.com/recipe/traditional-british-mothering-sunday-simnel-cake-214666>, last accessed 26.6.2015.

[6] <http://www.redonline.co.uk/food/recipes/mary-berrys-simnel-cake>, last accessed 26.6.2015.

[7] <https://en.wikipedia.org/wiki/Mothering_Sunday>, last accessed 26.6.2015.

instituted in May. Seven years later, her home state officially designated the second Sunday in May as Mother's Day, and on 9 May 1914 the American president Woodrow Wilson signed a declaration to designate the second Sunday in May as Mother's Day, during which, according to the proclamation, flags should be flown on government buildings and in people's homes 'as a public expression of our love and reverence for the mothers of our country'.[8]

In 2013, the Church of England urged people to celebrate what is described as the 100th anniversary of Mothering Sunday:[9]

> Thanks mainly to Constance's efforts, Mothering Sunday—which has its roots in the pre-Reformation Church—has been widely observed and re-established across the Church of England, and celebrated in wider society.

The extent to which Mothering Sunday became a generally adopted event is disputed, however. Information on a Church of England website operated by the Diocese of Ely strongly suggests that without American influence the occasion would not be celebrated at all.[10] The Diocese of Ely, located in the eastern English county of East Anglia, stressed the contribution of the established American Mother's Day by noting that 'the US Senate and House of Representatives officially dedicated the day to the memory of "the best mother in the world—your mother". It continues the story by reporting that during the Second World War there were nearly half a million Americans stationed in East Anglia as part of the Allied forces campaign against Germany. Most of these men had never been away from home before:

> Away from their families, these young men were surprised to find the English did not have a Mother's Day. They often regarded their English hostess as a kind of foster-mother and each year on the second Sunday in May they did what they would have done for their own mothers—gave her presents and flowers to thank her for her kindness and care. British sons and daughters caught on to the idea and, after the

---

[8] <http://www.archives.gov/global-pages/larger-image.html?i=/historical-docs/doc-content/images/mothers-day-proc-l.jpg&c=/historical-docs/doc-content/images/mothers-day-proc.caption.html>, last accessed 26.6.2015.

[9] <https://www.churchofengland.org/media-centre/news/2013/03/100th-anniversary-of-mothering-sunday.aspx>, last accessed 26.6.2015.

[10] <http://www.ely.anglican.org/about/mothering_sunday.html>, last accessed 26.6.2015.

Americans had returned home at the end of the war, they continued the practice, reverting back to marking it on the fourth Sunday in Lent.

Thus the Americans based in East Anglia helped to revive the centuries-old tradition of paying homage to mothers with a bunch of flowers.

In conclusion, the history of Mothering Sunday is murky and mixed, but if the British people vote with their purses and wallets, the current situation shows a bleak picture for proponents of Mothering Sunday. At the beginning of my study, in February 2012, I undertook a small survey on the availability of Mothering Sunday cards. I chose two shops well known for the selection of greeting cards, Marks & Spencer and WH Smith. In 2012, Marks & Spencer had seventy-seven different varieties of cards in the Mother's Day section, of which two were headed Mothering Sunday, without any explicit religious text. WH Smith had thirty-four cards, including two for Mothering Sunday, without any explicit religious text. I repeated the exercise in 2014 and found similar proportions. Of course, the sample was small and in no way indicative of a process; it did, however, reveal that the proportion of retail space apportioned to Mothering Sunday was tiny in relation to Mother's Day. As retail practices are generally demand-led, this indicates that popular demand for Mothering Sunday is insignificant in size and potential retail value compared to Mothering Sunday.

During the course of my research I attended three Mothering Sunday services at different English churches (one of which occurred in 2011 as I was finalizing the research design process). In each, there were specific prayers said in gratitude for mothers and a sermon preached in honour of mothers and, more broadly, on the theme of mothering and care. I have no longitudinal evidence to show whether sermons extending the idea of a female 'mother' to non-gendered 'care' are more or less frequent than they were. It seemed to be a general rule that during these services there would be some kind of gift, such as a bouquet of daffodils or a little basket of geraniums, handed out to women in the congregation by any children who were present.

Listening to the Generation A women I came to know, I often heard how they talked about their own mothers in terms of their roles in the family's religious upbringing. Their depictions of their mothers as loving, caring people and their own daughters as loving, caring mothers were no different from all the other accounts of how people talked about their mothers in my earlier research on similar and younger generations (see Day 2011 [2013]). The only difference was the role mothers have had in religious socialization. During the time I researched local churches my identity became well known, as many people would talk to me after the services and enquire about my research. One man, in his mid-sixties, told me that he had stopped attending church for many years until returning later in life. He told me about the effect of his mother, a woman of Generation A:

> I was brought up, baptised and confirmed, Church of England. When I was confirmed I had the choice, it was a thing I always felt I was forced to do, go to church. My mother had very strong beliefs so all four of us went to church, same way, baptised, confirmation, then had the choice whether we continued or not and I chose not to.

Given that children are generally confirmed in the Church of England in their early teens, it is interesting to note that he was still living at home when he was allowed to make that choice. This suggests that the ideas of choice, authenticity, and agency were values held and transmitted by Generation A.

THE CLASSED CHURCH 'FAMILY'

Just as nuclear families represent and replicate certain social classes, so too do the organizations to which they belong, including their churches. Class is a contested category and therefore researchers who use such concepts usually try to state clearly how they perceive it. Although disputed as a useful, or even ethically correct category, when the category of class is adopted most widely it refers to a social category operationalized by people as part of a filtering process. Durkheim and Mauss argued more than a century ago that 'The first logical categories were social categories; the first classes of things were classes of men into which these things were integrated' (1963 [1902], 93).

According to academic and clergyman Adrian Stringer (2015), there has never been a systematic study of socio-economic classes and the Church of England, although he notes that several studies provide proximate data and inference about the middle-class nature of Anglicanism: (Towler and Coxon 1979, 212; Davie 2000, 86; Guest 2004). Kynaston (2009, 53) wrote that in the 1950s: 'Women accounted for almost two-thirds of church attendances, with a bias towards the elderly, and a middle class person was at least twice as likely to go to church each Sunday than a working class person.' Stringer (2015) summarizes how social class and organized religion has been studied extensively in the United States, consistently finding that Episcopalians have been disproportionately drawn from the upper echelons of society from the colonial era (Finke and Stark 1997, 156; Roof and McKinney 1987, 110) through to the mid-twentieth century. Stringer cites further studies that continue the link between class and Episcopalians in the twentieth and twenty-first centuries: see, for example: Demerath 1965, 2; McGuire 2002; Smith and Faris 2005; Roberts and Yamane 2012, Davidson and Pyle 2011.

A significant finding about the studies into social class is the connection with families, and with religious transmission. Johnson's (1978) investigations into nineteenth-century Rochester, New York, found that religious congregations were built upon extensive family networks, together with associated networks of friends and colleagues. McCloud (2007) argues that class-related religious culture is transmitted through personal networks, thereby creating a stratification of religion mirroring the stratification of material resources in the wider society. Demerath (1965) analysed Lutherans according to whether they were 'church-like' or 'sect-like'. Those who were church-like not only attended church but also participated in a variety of church-related organizations in the church and parish, unlike the 'sect-like' people, who attended less and participated less, but were more (following Glock and Stark's 1965 typology) experientially, ideologically, and consequentially involved, leading him to conclude that people from different social classes seek different outcomes from religion.

During my fieldwork I spent a lot of time at churches outside the services. On these occasions, often the 'church opening' events or coffee mornings, I talked with many who were not members of the congregation. In Chapter 3 I described the man who came in regularly just to play the piano, for example. He could only do so because he knew someone who attended that church and told him it would be all right. Another coffee morning regular dropped in because she was friends with the woman who organized it. She never attended the services, but enjoyed the opportunity to socialize. These are informal social networks that help populate the space of the church.

In my earlier study about belief and belonging, (Day 2011 [2013]) I explored social class in the context of one of several systems people engage with in order to separate others into groups with whom they may or may not belong. The process by which people claim a social identity is complex, but in that earlier work it became transparent during discussions about who counted as local, or Christian, or English that those distinctions could be understood as strategies to claim and reinforce a sense of collective belonging. Further, I observed that such claiming acts were often the product of specific social interactions, which needed to be understood specifically as they were often tightly secured to a specific time and place. As Barth (1969) described it, identity is formed on the boundary. That particular observation became relevant during the current study about how the women negotiated their and others' places in a kind of social order. Those negotiations were not individualized: as Jenkins (1997) described, identity formation and development involves a dialectical process requiring both an individual sense of belonging to a social group and an awareness that other people, 'outsiders', will also recognize that distinction.

Such negotiations required more agility than that available in standard formulations of social class. In my earlier study I produced social classifications through two means—asking my research participants if they would describe themselves as a member of a certain class, and if so which one, and also by asking them the occupations of their parents. The latter system of class being defined by occupation was fairly widely used at that time: the National Statistics Socio-Economic Classification (NS-SEC) placed people in one of seven main classes according to their occupation and employment status. It did not, however, allow more nuanced wider social and cultural views about the systemization of class.

CLASS AND CAPITAL (B)

During the course of my current study a new classification system was proposed by researchers (Savage et al. 2013) who were analysing the largest survey of social class ever conducted in the UK, the BBC's 2011 Great British Class Survey. The survey sample was initially over-represented by BBC radio listeners, a bias corrected by a supplemental, more representative survey. The theoretical basis for the analysis was situated primarily in the work of Pierre Bourdieu (1984), which argued that different forms of 'capital' confer different social advantages: economic capital, defined as wealth and income; cultural capital, defined as the extent to which people, largely through educational attainment, can appreciate and engage with cultural goods; and social capital, defined as the type and quantity of people's social networks. Savage et al. also noted that ideas about class that rest solely on occupational data fail to recognize the different experiences of women, as argued by feminist critiques (Bradley 1995; Crompton 2008; Skeggs 1997, 2004), which draw attention to how class operates symbolically and culturally to stigmatize and otherwise interpret and represent specific forms of personhood and value.

To summarize, Savage et al. (2013) identified seven new categories: elite; established middle class; technical middle class; new affluent workers; traditional working class; emergent service workers; precariat. It is not possible in my study to make claims about the distribution of those classes across the Anglican Communion, or even across the UK. What was striking, however, was how the nature of congregations mirrored the locale.

For example, the regular members of one congregation I observed at the Queen's Chapel are likely to be members of the elite. Being the Queen and Head of the Church of England it is perhaps not unusual that the Queen should have her own chapels. Yet, being the Church of England, her two main chapels are open to the public for services. The Queen's Chapel is attached to the Palace of St James, in that eponymous neighbourhood best known for exclusive private-member clubs, the Ritz Hotel, and the sorts of restaurants where a meal for two costs at least twice what the average UK family spends on food in a week. While, theoretically, anyone can attend a service at the chapel no matter where they live, during my conversations while waiting outside with those who identified themselves as regular members I often heard them say that they 'didn't have far to come'. That means that, for example, a tourist who visited that church could return home with descriptions of the elegantly dressed, beautifully coiffed women with their equally well-turned out, gracious husbands and claim that British religion was the purview of the upper classes. It is not easy to determine how to arrive at the chapel, as the official website for the Monarchy does not offer directions,[11] and nor is it particularly effusive in its welcome. Following the tab for 'visiting' opens one

---

[11] <http://www.royal.gov.uk/TheRoyalResidences/TheChapelsRoyal/Visiting.aspx>, last accessed 14.6.15.

page with the single sentence: 'The Chapels Royal are not open to the public except for services.'

The website further offers the information that: 'Services are held at 8.30 am and 11.15 am in the Chapel Royal or The Queen's Chapel on Sundays throughout the year, except for August and September. In the Chapel Royal, they are held from the first Sunday in October to Good Friday, inclusive.' There are no directions. It is to be expected that anyone wanting to visit would already know that the chapels are part of St James' Palace, a working royal residence not open to the public. As with so much of the character of the Church of England, it helps to be an insider.

One June morning I visited the Queen's Chapel to attend the Sunday morning 11.15 service, joining the orderly queue that had formed by the time I arrived at around 10.45. An official checked to ensure I was intending to attend the service, which offended me slightly in the same way I had noticed during fieldwork each time someone said something to me that suggested I may not quite 'belong'. The longing for belonging was deep. Most people in the queue outside were smartly, expensively, and conservatively dressed with women wearing skirts or dresses with blazers or jackets, and the men all wearing jacket and tie. In a change from my other church observations, I noticed they were roughly equally split by gender. Once inside, I found myself in a pew next to an elderly couple who immediately engaged me in conversation, asking where I was from and thus immediately establishing themselves as regulars. As we chatted, the woman told me that people used to sit in the same places each week but then they were asked to move around so they could talk to new people. The service was conducted with the Book of Common Prayer, rather than the Alternative Service Book (ASB). I noticed that departure from the norm, where the ASB is more common at late morning services in the Church of England, with the BCP reserved for early mornings or midweeks, in keeping with the tastes of their Generation A regulars. One major, visible difference between the two services is the lack of a 'sharing of the peace' moment in the BCP, when people shake hands with each other and say 'peace be with you'. This seemed, on reflection, in keeping with the more upper class regulars and the attachment, almost literally, to royalty. After all, one does not shake hands with just anyone, and never without wearing gloves. Prayers, described as State prayers, followed a specific hierarchy, beginning with the Queen and continuing through the rest of the royal family. Another unusual element was the lack of women in any formal role, apart from a woman in her thirties who showed us to her seats. The male-dominated effect was particularly noticeable in the small space as twenty-two officials and leaders, including an all-male choir, congregated at the front. As the service ended no one invited us to remain for tea and coffee, as was customary in every other church I had studied for two years in the UK, Canada, and the United States, whether small, large, urban, or rural.

Were my hypothetical tourist to visit churches in financially deprived areas of the country, they would find a more mixed congregation, including a number of those matching the description of 'precariat', as paraphrased here from Savage et al. (2013, 243). The precariat, representing about 15 per cent of the population, are the financially poorest social class, with the lowest social and cultural capital of all classes. They are either unemployed or in semi- and unskilled occupations. Most importantly, as a measure of difference amongst the other social classes, they have high levels of insecurity across all forms of capital. Their lives are lived, as the name suggests, precariously. These are the men and women I often met in the urban churches I studied, sometimes at services, but most often on the church opening days or coffee mornings when they would drop in for a cup of tea, a biscuit, and a chat.

As the contribution of Savage et al.'s analysis resulted in new categories of class that resonated deeply with my current study, so did the earlier work by Max Weber (Weber 1922), who proposed that people would feel varying degrees of attraction to, or affinity with, different types of religion based on a sense of similarities.[12] As I have suggested in earlier work (Day 2005), it is difficult to apply directly to women Weber's theories about why different groups of people are attracted to different kinds of religions, as his analysis is based on men's economic conditions and occupations: the warrior, the peasant, the artisan, the missionary, the tent-maker, the prince, the capitalist, and so on. Other scholars have pointed to similar issues in trying to reconcile such grand theories with women's experience. Most theories about religion, social class included, are largely constructed by men about social contexts dominated by men, where women's voices are subsumed and assumed. As such, theories and definitions tend to

---

[12] The origin of the term 'elective affinity' was not discussed by Weber but appears, according to several authors (see, for example, McKinnon 2010) to derive from a novel by Goethe.

universalize and marginalize women through ignoring anything specific about their experience and constructs (Bowie 2006). This 'gender
blindness' is a distinctive feature of the sociological study of religion,
argued Woodhead (2000, 67–84). She described Weber's idea of the
'iron cage' and Durkheim's concept of 'anomie' as particularly
oriented to men because both assume participation in the public,
paid-for working realm, a realm from which women have traditionally been excluded. This is an important insight for the future of the
church as a social organization, because class and capital not only
confer advantage, they also create barriers: 'class concerns boundaries, those distinctions we make between ourselves and others'
(McCloud 2007, 2). Certain sectors of the Anglican Communion
recognize the salience of the predispositions and skills that help
church members cross boundaries. In her research into how evangelical Anglican leaders think about class, McKenzie (2015) found that
while many leaders were driven by a theological commitment to cross
class boundaries, they often encountered resistance in their own
congregations. Her interviewees 'perceive congregations to be a rare
space in society where sustained cross-class relationships can be
forged and fostered', while also acknowledging 'the significance of
the middle class "habitus" of conservative evangelicalism in frustrating the movement in its quest for more effective engagement with the
working-class' (McKenzie 2015, 84). Many of her interviewees explicitly rejected something called 'the Homogeneous Unit Principle'
developed by McGavran (1980, 227) who argued that it was more
effective to develop congregations that are homogeneous in terms of
class or ethnicity as 'men and women do like to become Christian
without crossing barriers'. Descriptions of this 'principle' can be found
on a website devoted to an important Church of England initiative
known as 'Fresh Expressions'. Here, the proponents describe:[13]

> The homogeneous unit principle is one of the most controversial issues
> in mission thinking. It was originally described by Donald A. McGavran
> in Understanding Church Growth (Revised Edition, Eerdmans, 1990).
> McGavran suggested that for mission and evangelism to be most effect-
> ive, people need to hear the gospel in their language and see it lived within
> their culture. It is positively healthy for churches to appeal to people of a

[13] <https://www.freshexpressions.org.uk/guide/about/principles/diversity/homoge
neous>, last accessed 6.9.15.

similar culture—from youth congregations, to churches for specific ethnic groups to churches for deaf people.

Critics complain that this is a betrayal of the reconciliation which lies at the heart of the gospel. Christ breaks down every dividing wall, making humanity one (Ephesians 2.11–22). Church should reflect this. 'Niche church' panders to a consumerist rather than a kingdom worldview. However, several theological themes support the homogeneous unit principle.

The impact of class on church attendance may also be affected by the gender of the classes being observed. As the Church of England has not recorded such details, any suggested correlation must be tentative. Nevertheless, the extract below from one of my interviews reflects a connection between class and gender.

I come from [. . .] which is a working-class town in the north east- and I can dimly remember a few men who used to come to church but, on the whole, the congregation was female; in Sunday school, in church, yes it was, it was a woman's activity and if my father was ever asked if he went to church, he would say, 'no, no', as if that was a preposterous question, you know, 'the wife goes to church' he would say.

She then compared that early experience in England's north-east to her later life in a more prosperous neighbourhood, describing it as 'sort of very respectable working-class and middle-class. There was no wrong side of the tracks.' She attended there what she described as a prosperous church, and most of the congregation was male.

LAYWOMEN AND THEIR 'OTHER': THE FEMALE PRIEST

I discussed in detail in Chapter 5 the complex relationship Generation A has with its male priests: part son, spiritual leader, and husband. The passion some expressed for the priests they liked conveyed a deep, personal connection. As one woman told me: 'I love him! I love him! I love him! I think I'd marry him! [Laughs].' When I remarked that he, and she, are already married to other people, she continued: 'I'm kidding. We love him. He's just, he's just *such* a good priest.' Being a good priest also meant being good fun, as she described: 'He used to get us doing lots,' she recalled, smiling widely. There were monthly lunches, bingo, quiz nights, and outings in a minibus further afield. I often heard women describing former priests in such ways, as someone who took them places, creating interesting, enjoyable outings.

That such women could view a female priest as an interloper and threat to that relationship is understandable in both emotional and practical matters. In her study described in detail in Chapter 5, Peberdy (1985) describes a Generation A woman saying that she was afraid that a woman priest might not engage sufficiently with the women of the congregation. Given that laywomen carried out most of the labour in the church, it could be a real, tangible threat to have a leader who did not appreciate or respect the laywomen's activities. Brown (1992, 258), comments on how some of those women resisted the movement towards women priests for that reason:

> At one level, moreover—in their reluctance to let go of a particular kind of Christian usefulness, that involving the work of their hands— I suggest that their resistance may indeed be part of the very same impulse that has brought their sisters into the clergy. Both are seeking a more authentic female form of holiness in the church.

That comment resonates with 'Pat', whom I quoted in Chapter 5 (Peberdy 1985, 18) saying that she liked the new deaconess because she 'let us have our say'. Here, Pat is emphasizing the importance of the women's work, the 'jobs' they do and want to do as part of their work in the church. In another parish, an older laywoman described that when she first came to the church there were only two regular communicants: 'She and others busied themselves with fund-raising and gradually support grew.' The newly appointed deaconess also delegated much of the vicar's work to laypeople, resulting in a busier and more friendly congregation.

As for the priests who did not behave in ways the women liked, the women had a way of discouraging their presence. When women raised the examples of such priests, I would ask them how they managed the relationship. Their answers tended to reflect the tactics of a generation raised to be well mannered and deferent to authority: they barely caused a fuss, but just 'sort of ignored him'. Gunderson (1992, 113) described the diary of one priest being replete with detail about men's activities, stressing male conversion, male Bible groups, and leaving women out: 'The women had good reason to wish him gone.' When priests did leave, it was the women who would step in to

keep the congregation stable. One woman told me about the effect of
a priest having to leave suddenly:

> But, and he got into a lot of trouble, female trouble. He disappeared and
> things just went from bad to worse. There wasn't money for synod,
> there was never enough money to pay a minister or to pay an organist.
> I'm just a pianist, but there were times when I had to play the organ too,
> because there was nobody else, I could do hymns and things like that;
> I just played it like a piano.

INCLUSIONS AND EXCLUSIONS

The 'church family' creates a strange, somewhat contradictory insularity in an institution that otherwise professes 'community' and
global outreach. The informal social networks of church members
are seen to be essential: people rarely walk into the Church, whether
for services or Church Watch, without knowing someone. Conceptions of 'community' vary. Some women I talked to expressed it with
a slightly cynical edge to their voices and body language: 'we need to
be seen to be "part of the community"' said one Englishwoman, using
her hands to signal quotation marks around the phrase, while
another, a Canadian woman describing a fund-raising event, noted
that the activity was not just about fund-raising but also: 'it's a
community thing as well as raising money, it's community outreach
or community involvement or whatever you want to call it'.

It is therefore with some caution that writers should use the term
'community' as its definitions vary widely. Hillery (1995) identified
ninety-four different definitions of community, most suggesting 'it
consists of persons in social interaction within a geographic area and
having one or more additional common ties'. The trend in sociology
and anthropology has been to focus attention on processes of identity
formation and expressions arising from difference. As I discussed in
my previous work (Day 2011 [2013], 54), 'community' serves as a
reference group, a real or imagined entity used to distinguish between
one group and others and to provide apparent external validation for
one group's beliefs. The word 'community' often works as a marker to
denote boundaries and claim a cultural identity. Gilroy (1987, 235)
argues that community 'is as much about difference as it is about

similarity and identity'. It is a relational word, he says, laden with different symbols and meanings, most of which serve to create boundaries. Cohen's classic definition (1985, 9) mirrors this by defining community as symbolically constructed as 'a system of values, norms, and moral codes which provides a sense of identity within a bounded whole to its members'.

Just as families may admit new members with different levels of ease, organizations behave in similar ways and find themselves encountering what economists and business writers refer to as 'barriers to entry'. As organizations try to enter new markets, they inevitably find that not everyone can enter new markets with equal ease. Some will already have people inside who can help; others may already have language skills; some may know the technologies used in the new areas; others will have contacts with high-level officials or other leaders. That knowledge, or what Bourdieu (1984) called 'social capital', is important because as quickly as the newcomers acquire skills or networks to facilitate their move inwards, the insiders may create new barriers. Although the Church of England may claim to have a 'presence in every community' and its priests might preach from the pulpit that it is the Christian's duty to love and accept everyone, they also set high barriers to entry for the unskilled, uninitiated, and those lacking the requisite social, religious, and cultural capital. However deliberately or unwittingly, many members of Generation A were active during their lives in maintaining those barriers. Some commentators I talked with during my research repeatedly told me that the women treated the church like their 'club'. That, I concluded, was the wrong analogy: the church is not Generation A's club, it is their home.

Gunderson (1992) traces the development of this historically, exploring the American experience in the late eighteenth and early nineteenth centuries, when home religious life was richly observed with prayers, Bible readings, and other rituals. This began to change, following the division of labour occurring at the time, as women, barred from formal church decision-making processes, turned to building a parish life that reflected and extended their home lives. Gunderson writes (1992, 115–16) that the architecture of churches was not always conducive to these activities, so many had to be reconstructed and extended for kitchens, rehearsal rooms, and Sunday schools 'The church was literally remade into a home that women proceeded to decorate with their handiwork.'

Just as few people would welcome a stranger into their home without checking out who they were, so Generation A considered entrants to their church. It is difficult to summarize accurately the nature of those who were not welcome: it would be unfair, and too crass, to use the obvious distinctions of colour or class. Certainly, the Generation A being studied was made up of women of a time that corresponded to higher degrees of racial prejudice than found now in the general population, and particularly amongst young people. I found little direct evidence of their efforts to directly exclude people of colour because the occasion rarely arose, which in itself may be a form of racism. Direct racism is not always how people are excluded. There are no longer signs in British doorways saying 'no Irish, no dogs', but it is still against the law in the UK for an Irish person to be head of state; the head of state is the monarch, also the head of the Church of England. There are no regulations banning Black people from churches, but Church of England congregations are notoriously white in most areas. While the Church does not keep official statistics about race, as it does not about gender, observations and discussions with colleagues have reinforced my impression about the localized effect. There is also an influence from migration patterns. Kynaston discusses (2009, 270–5) a revival of British fascism and racism that occurred following the arrival of the first large wave of immigrants from Jamaica on the ship, the *Empire Windrush*, on 2 June 1948, carrying 492 black men and one woman, a stowaway. In protest at their arrival, eleven Labour MPs wrote to the Prime Minister (Kynaston 2009, 275):

> an influx of coloured people domiciled here is likely to impair the harmony, strength and cohesion of our public and social life and to cause discord and unhappiness among all concerned.

According to Kynaston's (2009, 176) research, the first people overtly to welcome the immigrants when they arrived in the London suburb of Clapham were members of an Anglican Church, the Church of the Ascension, Balham. They invited the immigrants to a service, followed by a meal in the church hall—prepared and served, I would assume, by women of Generation A. Unfortunately, the Church of England as a whole did not continue that sort of welcome and has a long record of institutional racism (Gordon-Carter, 2003). I will return to questions of racism in the final chapter. For now, it is worth noting that the relationships between the church family, the community, and others that were performed by Generation A were complex and inevitably interrelated with societal shifts as a whole. Theirs was not, typically, a disposition that lent itself to appreciating the kind of postmodernity described by, for example, Bauman (1992, 35), 'subject to their own respective logics and armed with their own facilities of truth-validation'.

Generation A was rarely in the mood for considering meaning-generating agencies beyond those attached to their religious beliefs rooted in a Christian god. Through a process of forming and sustaining relationships through processes of social intimacy, integration, routines, obligation, and rituals, they protected what they understood to be their church family and what it stood for. Although many of their baby-boomer children may have rejected 'ritual' for being staid and boring, it was that permanence that Generation A women wanted. As Muriel, a Canadian woman told me:

MURIEL: The rites, the proper hymns for the proper times, the beautiful anthems: our choir not only sang the hymns, we used to do anthems [. . .]

ABBY: So the liturgy is something that's very traditional.

MURIEL: Yes, yes it's set. That's what a rite is, it's something that's set. We did not do chanting . . .

In the Chapter 8 I will reflect on the social practices of parties and pieties that helped 'family' members internalize and perform habitually a certain set of beliefs and behaviours.

8

More Party than Piety

Church social and fund-raising events have traditionally been the domain of a church's Social Committee, often led by a Generation A laywoman. Sometimes the events are clearly positioned as a means of raising funds, with most of the labour performed and money raised being focused on the immediate church to which people belong. During the fieldwork I observed and also participated in a range of events, including spring and autumn lunches in both churches and in church halls; the Queen's Jubilee parties; concerts; Christmas parties; hymn sings; and fund-raising sales. From those experiences and my analysis, several themes seemed most important: a shift from people to premises; soft labour and hard work; social capital; a self-circulating economy. The events relied on what I call 'soft labour' and produced through regimes of accountability, participation, and a self-circulating economy a strong, interwoven form of belonging. The funds raised were welcomed and the women duly thanked at the appropriate moment in the corresponding week's Sunday service, but on a number of occasions it became clear to me that the money was a by-product of something even more important to the women.

My emotional response to first being asked to join a rota gave me some insight into the feelings produced by social belonging. I was touched by a curious mix of relief, pride, and security: the significance was not in the act of giving time or physical effort, but in being asked. It was assumed I could and would carry out such activities because I could be trusted. I was not wholly 'other', but had shifted into being one of 'them'. Over time, my emotion settled into a taken-for-granted habit, where the obligation to perform a collective duty became routine, and eventually internalized into a mode of behaving that felt 'natural'.

At the end of my project, I presented my broad findings to the congregation with whom I had been most closely connected during my two-year project. It was the conclusion I had reached about the importance of involving members of the congregation, of giving the message that 'everyone had a place', that seemed to resonate most with the audience, many of whom spoke to me afterwards to affirm that insight. The power of being able to perform emplacement through church activities seemed to be understood by Generation A, but this may not be shared by younger generations. For example, a book by Jenkins (1999) is a retrospective account of his emotionally mixed experience some twenty years earlier as a young man living in a small village just outside Cambridge. An 'incomer' (newly established resident, usually of middle class, urban, young background), Jenkins describes himself as a member of the 'egalitarian' faction of the long-established Church of England church, St Mary's. The egalitarians were, he explains, exclusively composed of incomers like himself, in contrast to the long-standing members whom he describes as 'conservative', largely, I would assume, composed of Generation A women and some men of similar age. Jenkins uses his experience to illustrate his idea of two models in the church working in opposition. He describes the egalitarian group as composed of people who were 'on the whole articulate and some are theologically literate' (Jenkins 1999, 67), taking their personal religious commitment very seriously. In contrast, he explained, the conservative group focused mainly on the church itself, rather than a religious life, and continued to raise money through traditional, although increasingly inefficient, methods such as village parties. The egalitarian group preferred a fund-raising route that was more efficient and less labour-intensive or reliant on community activities, namely direct covenanting through one's bank. That practice would ensure timely, electronic payments were made directly to church funds. The conservative element resisted this in preference to the traditional models, Jenkins reported. What he did not explain, or perhaps did not understand, was the extent to which the conservative members understood that is was the activity itself, not simply the financial outcome, that helped form their, and others', religious lives.

While Jenkins' egalitarian group supported Bible meetings, for 'they are interested in matters of theology and spirituality' (Jenkins 1999, 67), the conservative group pursued the traditional business of the congregation, such as acting as sidesmen, churchwardens, organizing the choir, arranging flowers, reading the lessons, and so on. During his description of church politics (Jenkins 1999, 60–9), Jenkins leaves no doubt that there is a serious church split. Words and phrases reinforce the sense of opposition, emphasizing conflict, difference, and hostility. I suggest this serves as a good case example of the heated relationship between Generation A and the next, younger generation. From my own fieldwork and analysis, I would argue that the conservative elements of churches have been unfairly characterized as resisting change and being old-fashioned for the sake of it, when, rather, they may have had a more experienced and thus intuitive grasp of the qualities that really keep a church salient and sustainable. Indeed, one schism I witnessed demonstrated strongly that money was a necessary, but insufficient, resource to support what mattered to them most, the sustainability of their church family. At one church I came to know, the Social Committee became split on the issue of where to host regular church social events. The tradition had always been to have those in the adjacent church hall. Indeed, some church members had stories that wove their personal biographies with the history of the hall. One Generation A English woman told a member who was trying to update historical documents that she could not remember the date the hall was built, until she suddenly recalled that she and her husband 'had our twenty-fifth anniversary celebration in the hall. It was the first event it had—just after it opened.' From her personal history she could date the hall. Church events became important social markers. Another, Canadian, Generation A woman recalled the excitement of being in a church event because it made her feel more grown up, in an era when young women wore 'stockings': 'I was one of the angels with a halo and got to wear white stockings too and I was so thrilled with those.'

And so, when the Social Committee was told by the Church management that the hall was being rented to other people and therefore was no longer available for church events, a crisis loomed. One woman refused to attend church for several weeks, and when she finally did return, she did not take her regular place in a front pew, but stood at the back. I was so taken by the sight of her alone there, I asked if I could take her photograph. She said that would be fine. I checked again, as I wanted to make sure that she understood I was wanting the photo for my research, and might one day want to publish it. Again, she said she would be happy about that. The exchange confirmed for me the kind of resilience and independent thinking of Generation A. They were not shy, timid people, but women who stood up for their strongly held beliefs. In an institution marked so deeply by place-making, her message to her fellow members was obvious, and one she reinforced in conversation with me on several occasions: 'it's the church family I care about', she said. Church hall income, together with income from events such as concerts or plays in the church building, may help pay some bills, but some older members fear such occasions might disrupt the pattern of church belonging. Once again, I was finding different perceptions about what kind of religious life 'counted'. A woman deacon I spoke to during my research said that her role was helping the congregation live practically as a coherent group while the (male) priest busied himself 'with the magic'. This was not said in altogether complimentary tones. Many people with whom I spoke as I carried out research in the churches talked more about the parties than the pieties. Women's activities in such events may indicate both their religiosity and also their desire to belong to such groups, suggested Anna, a Canadian Generation A woman:

> I do know that almost every man in our congregation that I know is deeply, deeply religious. I *cannot* say that for every woman I know in the congregation, I cannot say that. There are many, but, by deeply religious I mean that I can converse with them [*pause*], debate with them on religion and so on whereas women would rather talk about what colour hair we're having this week or whatever. [...] Let's put this another way [*pause*]. It's hard to be a Christian. It's hard to acknowledge to the world that you are a Christian [*pause*]. Yet each man that I know that has come to church has dealt with that and has [*pause*] as I say, is deeply religious. But the women might be there for social reasons sometimes, and these do come and go, they are not as committed to the church as [*pause*] You know, they're not committed through thick and thin.

In his research about people leaving Anglicanism, Brown interviewed people who often described their teenage years and the role of the Church. The social life was a primary draw. For example, Brown (2015, 252) related his conversation with a woman who described how the church was competing with her other activities as a teenager, until a young 'charismatic' priest arrived and started a youth group, which 'made her "happy enough" in her religious connection'.

Generation A women often speak of a time when the church was the social hub of their lives and how this has now become diminished, with fewer regular attendees and less-involved priests. Writing about American church life in the last century (when Generation A's mothers were young), Gunderson (1992, 114) quotes one woman's reminiscences: 'St Luke's was part of our *every*day life'. Men's groups were fraternities, taverns, and political clubs, but women's church activities were the largest form of 'polite' social opportunities available to them. Talking about her church life fifty years ago in Canada, Muriel made a similar point. When I asked her why she thought so many people did not attend church any more, she replied:

> MURIEL: And I don't think they're bad people, at all, no. Well, the society is very different. Many many, years ago, going to church was a social thing too. When the country was being settled, and there weren't a lot of big cities, a lot of activities for people, the church was a social thing, which is why they would have these dinners and these parties and things. That's, that had a lot to do with it.
>
> ABBY: And you think maybe now there's just more social things that people can do—
>
> MURIEL: Of course. Everything, outside the church they can do, yes, yes. Everything fills a basic need and at the time in history that was a basic need and, uh, for some of us it still a need, it's not a *basic* need, but it's a need. Or a habit I guess more than anything. I don't know the answer *quite* to that one. [Laughs]

I observed that the women I came to know have a strong appetite for socializing and all the attendant activities of preparation, decoration, serving, eating and drinking, games, and raffles. It was how they fostered belonging, and gave them a unique position of power.

PEW POWER

Generation A laywomen did not lead from visible positions at the front of the church; they did not need to. They had a specific form of power I called 'pew power' (Day 2014a, 2014c). That is one of the reasons why I predict that this will be the final active Anglican generation. In losing them, the Church will not just be losing numbers, but a specific kind of labour, leadership, and knowledge which has quietly kept churches going. This 'pew power' is different from priestly leadership, but has been, I conclude, instrumental to church life.

'Pew power' was a term I coined originally to describe to a Church of England readership (Day 2014a), the notion of how this particular generation organized, and led much of church life from the pews, rather than from the pulpit. Over the course of research for this book more widely, theorizing the kind of power Generation A embodied and practised became central to understanding how they connected to each other as a generation, how this was implicitly gendered, and what changed to prevent them from socially reproducing that kind of power and their particular practices for future generations.

Mann's (2012) analysis of power, briefly introduced in Chapter 1 in relation to the Anglican Communion, can be applied directly to Generation A. Mann argued that power is not a resource but emerges during the course of needs satisfaction. In this, he says, he agrees with sociologist Giddens (1979, 91) in not theorizing 'power *itself* as a resource. Resources are the media through which power is exercised.' Mann theorized that any history and theory of power was synonymous with a history and theory of human society. His theory of power, therefore, does not rest on ideas of motivations or goals, but rather (Mann 2012, 6) 'the ability to pursue and attain goals through mastery of one's environment'.

His main proposition about power was that societies are constituted of multiple overlapping and intersecting socio-spatial networks of power. He criticized other theories of power for using language that was usually too general, relating to, for example, levels, factors, or dimensions, whereas he wanted to be concrete. He described concrete issues as relating to organization, control, logistics, and communication, all linked to the capacity to organize and control people, materials, and territories. Considering Generation A's activity in this light can be instructive, given that their involvement has been so centrally related to their capacity to be one of the, if not *the*, agent for organizing the people, materials, and areas that have influenced the history and future of the Church. Added to that is Mann's observation that power development is not continuous but grows and declines sporadically. Rather than depict Generation A along the conventional stereotype of dutiful, caring, sometimes-sweet-yet-intimidating old ladies, it would be instructive to construct them more as agents of both their time and making. His description below of 'human beings' seems remarkably apt for Generation A (Mann 2012, 4):

> Human beings are restless, purposive, and rational, striving to increase their enjoyment of the good things of life and capable of choosing and pursuing appropriate means for doing so.

He argued that power should therefore also be analysed in terms of overlapping networks. From this analysis he also notes that societies are messy: all sociologists, from Durkheim, Marx, and Weber invented the idea of ideal types to cope with this. To pursue his theory, he suggests that 'mess' can be better handled analytically as a socio-spatial and organizational model that maps the sources of social power. The kind of social power Generation A embodied and enacted was not, in Mann's (2012, 8) terms, authoritative, but, rather, diffused. The bible, liturgy, priests, bishops, and structures such as the Archbishop's Council or Synod are all examples of the Church's authoritative power, described by Mann as a wilful kind of power that incorporated both commands and conscious obedience. Generation A women obeyed that kind of power but exercised theirs differently. Mann also conceived of power as diffuse, and importantly for Generation A, it is the kind of power that produces similar practices without being explicitly laid out or ordered. The effect of this kind of power is to create a shared understanding that what is being practised is natural, moral, and self-evident. The ways in which Generation A expressed and embodied certain 'solidarities, such as those of class or nation' (Mann 2012, 8) were also examples of diffused power and became one of Generation A's greatest strengths, and, ultimately, weaknesses as those solidarities weakened and became delegitimized amongst their children and wider society.

Foucault's (1997) ideas that power is widely diffused and constituted by knowledge and what is accepted as 'truth' partly resonates with my fieldwork with Generation A. His idea that power is not always negative or overtly coercive is a useful way of thinking about the sort of power the women possessed and acted. Foucault (1997, 194) argued that:

> We must cease once and for all to describe the effects of power in negative terms: it 'excludes', it 'represses', it 'censors', it 'abstracts', it 'masks', it 'conceals'. In fact, power produces; it produces reality; it produces domains of objects and rituals of truth. The individual and the knowledge that may be gained of him belong to this production.

Further, his idea that power is everywhere again helps shift the focus from the obvious representations of power in the pulpit to a more diffuse kind of power in the pew. Ultimately, his analysis of how certain norms and ideas become unquestioningly accepted, internalized, and embodied helped me realize that Generation A's role in producing that kind of power was instrumental in creating a process of belonging. This idea has been discussed throughout this book and summarized in Chapter 9.

What changed for Generation A was not so much how they wanted to exercise their power in the institution, but rather how that institution itself became diminished and de-legitimized in the eyes of others, principally their baby-boomer children. By 'institution' I am referring not to a building or other physical place, but to a formalized ideal to which people subscribe and aspire, whose function is to create and maintain a particular social order, much of which may be invisible and symbolic, and discursive (Giddens 1984). This will include social institutions such as religion, marriage, the family, politics, government, and legal institutions. The women of Generation A shared a sense of loyalty to the idea of institutions more generally, and to Christianity and the Church more particularly.

Generation A operationalized their social power from primarily their adherence to the salience of 'institution', and their recognition that (following Mann 2012) their control was *institutionalized* in the laws and the norms of the social group in which both operate when institutionalization is necessary to achieve routine collective goals. I suggest that their parties were a form of that institutionalization.

PIETY OF PARTIES

One form of pew power I discovered centres on the social calendar. Where there is piety, there's a party, and where there's a party, there are Generation A laywomen providing and serving the food and drink. Like Jesus feeding the five thousand, there always seemed to be a bottle miraculously appearing from a shopping bag to be shared around the table. These days, more is shop-bought than home-made as the women age and have less energy to spend in front of their ovens, but the generosity fuelled by often meagre pensions is abundant. On one special occasion the food was served as a buffet with melon and Parma ham to start, followed by layers of sliced ham, cheese chunks on cocktail sticks, coronation chicken (easy on the curry powder, I was told), sausage rolls, baked potatoes, smoked salmon on brown bread, cold roast beef, green salad with home-made vinaigrette, quiches. For 'pudding' there was cheese, apple pie, and trifle. The space was decorated, and tables set, in themes of the season. As at all the events I attended, there was plenty of talking, a great deal of laughter, always a raffle, and Generation A the last to leave after doing the washing up.

The inclusion of 'coronation chicken' is particularly symbolic for Generation A. It was devised by cookery writer Rosemary Hume for Queen Elizabeth's coronation in 1953, and consists of cold chicken, mayonnaise, and curry powder. The connection between the dish and Generation A must also resonate in the public imagination, as it formed part of the headline for a report on my research in the *Telegraph*.[1]

The social events produced through Generation A labour that was at its best plentiful and enthusiastic and as its worst inefficient and time-wasting. This was evident at one of the first events in which I had been invited to participate. Even the language I use to describe it has been permeated with my happy experience of being involved with the women. 'Invited to participate' was how it felt, as opposed to another possible rendering, such as 'asked to help' or 'given a task'. When I arrived at the church that Saturday I first noticed how many people were crowded into the small kitchen area and adjacent rear portion of the church. It appeared at first to be bordering on chaotic. Eva, who had asked me to come, was supervising the volunteers: one was busy polishing glasses, another two were setting up six large tables, someone else was moving chairs, another was putting table-cloths on the tables (two placed on angles to make a green and white pattern), and two others were polishing cutlery. Surely, I thought, there was no need to have ten people working in a space for what was, after all, a small event for a maximum of, perhaps, fifty people. Not only had I waitressed for years when I was younger, and even owned a restaurant briefly, but I had also spent a few years in the publishing business editing papers and books about business management and leadership. I knew a good deal about time–space optimization, just-in-time logistics, and quality management. If the women's labours were to be judged against standards of rational, bureaucratic work-place behaviours they would, I could see, fail. I began to think about how I could offer advice on streamlining their operation when I was interrupted in my thoughts by Eva. I was asked to put glasses and napkins on the tables: specifically, eight glasses per table, with pink

---

[1] <http://www.telegraph.co.uk/news/religion/12046913/How-the-passing-of-the-coronation-chicken-era-spells-the-end-for-Church-England.html>, last accessed 22.1.2016.

and yellow napkins in each, arranged in the style of a tulip. I froze. How was I to arrange . . . thankfully, another woman spotted my discomfort and hurried over to show me the technique. It wasn't too complicated after all: just open them up, grab them in the middle, pull through, and plonk them in the glass. Suitably trained, I took up my duty and after a few glasses was right in the rhythm of it, relieved not to appear to be incompetent. As I moved with increasing confidence, with what seemed to be, unmistakably, an artistic flair, I could hear, see, and feel the movements all round me of women working.

On another occasion, I noticed the same phenomenon of over-staffing. I had been asked to help out in the kitchen where women were creating plates of food. Each person was slowly and methodic-ally arranging one plate at a time with pâté, pickle, lettuce, peppers, and kale. This could be done more quickly, I mentioned to the woman next to me, if we created a sort of assembly line. She looked at me a little quizzically and said she thought it was working fine as it was. I seemed to be the only one concerned with work efficiency, but it was also the case that I appeared to be the only one without a distinct task. Perhaps, I offered, I could tear the lettuce? Soon, I was fully integrated into the work group, and found myself laughing with them about small, consequential details. Could we really send that plate out without another leaf of purple? Did it look unfinished without a curl of red pepper? A few children were elbowing into the kitchen wanting to help and, suddenly, it all seemed crowded, chaotic, and strangely calm all at once. And that's when I finally realized something important: everyone was happy. They were chatting to each other, laughing, helping with a task here and there, and no one seemed to notice or care that they could have got the job done in half the time with half the people. The same sort of thing happened as we were washing up five deep at a double sink, washing each plate by hand, with others drying.

The flow and physical proximity of bodies reminded me of Durkheim's (1915) insight about the necessity of coming together as a body periodically to re-experience and renew the group's com-mon identity. The purpose was, in his view, to renew that group bonding, a little like the social events Bessie, a Canadian Generation A laywoman described to me:

So I don't know about the other churches, but I can only talk for the Anglican ones here. But, see, years ago the Anglican churches had dances and all sorts of things, and the dances were within their own people, and they were alright, but they're a little bit the other way these days; they don't have dances and those sorts of things, you know.

Even churches in her town that did not have dances had some kind of social events for young people, she said. These were not seen as religious events, but as a type of dating agency where young Christians could meet other young Christians:

> The Anglicans had it one Saturday, the Baptists had it another Saturday, um, the Presbyterians had it another Saturday, and there was another evangelical one; every Saturday night there was something that young people could go to; and a lot of people dated at those churches and people like that, those two brothers at our church, would hire a car and fill it; if they didn't have a car, they'd hire a mini bus and fill it with the kids, you know [. . .] But it was, eh, Christians getting together with Christians. [. . .] Anyway, lots of the other people got married, and it was a good place to date, and a good place to meet people, too.

Now that the dances have stopped, along with the interchurch parties, social events have become more a matter of coffees and teas, she said:

> Maybe some of them do but . . . They have morning tea or afternoon tea but it's not something where everybody gets together.

She seemed to be right. At the events I attended and observed on my travels, the guests were always predominantly regular churchgoers from whichever church was hosting the event. These were not events designed as social work to feed the hungry, but to reward those already part of the family.

FEEDING THE FULL

Often, the church lunches, suppers, teas, and special parties were not publicly advertised. Tickets are often sold inside the church after the services, ensuring only members of the congregation would come. Although described as a 'parish lunch' it was really a church lunch— no flyers were distributed, there was nothing on the notice board outside, and the announcement was only made during the church service. One Generation A English woman was frank about the reasons: if local people saw there was free food, the church family occasion would be spoiled by strangers who were only coming for the food and, on a practical note, how could the women possibly cater for large, unknown numbers? The key point, I suggest, is that these occasions are not 'only' about the food: she was right, they were occasions for the 'family' and not for strangers. Nevertheless, the food was enjoyed on a tangible as well as metaphorical level. Generation A laywomen are like locusts descending on a church buffet. Perhaps it is because many live alone and no longer bother to make themselves special meals, or maybe it is just that the hard physical work they perform every day burns up the calories. In any case, I swiftly learned not to get between those women and the last sausage rolls.

The food rituals of preparation reflect routine, pattern, and symbolic order. They involve more people than strictly necessary and are therefore 'inefficient' compared to commercial practices, but are highly productive means of creating and maintaining church relationships. It is the routine of the regulars that dominates. Labour demarcation reflects expertise, habit, and preference, and it is not easy to break into the long-established teams.

SALES AND THE SELF-CIRCULATING ECONOMY

Two-thirds of the Church of England's annual income is raised by the parishes in many forms, such as fund-raising events, social events, legacies, collections at services, one-off donations, fees from weddings and funerals, letting of church halls, grants from local or national bodies, visitor donations, books, magazines, and pamphlets.[2]

Particularly important are legacies. Members of Generation A were not going to forget their church, even in death, as one woman told me:

> But I was so fond of St [. . .] we had done so much for it, I had made a will and in my will had left everything. Everything I owned. *[Pause]* Which was a big mistake: there were children remember *[laughs]*.

Anna, a Canadian Generation A woman, said that one of the reasons she tithes is that she thinks her money will be used more efficiently than if she gives it to another, secular, charity:

---

[2] <https://www.churchofengland.org/about-us/funding/wherefrom.aspx>, last accessed 22.1.2016.

And I also find that my church needs donation because I still tithe, are maybe get to where it's needed better through the church than some of the other organisations that cost a lot of administration and so on. So I do a lot of my charity through the church. What they do with it is up to them.

The women are well aware of their contribution to the future of the church, and that it was gendered. Muriel, a Canadian woman, told me:

> MURIEL: Yes, and er, we had the Ladies Guild and we had the Anglican women, that did all sorts of things. Er, we made a *lot* of money, put on a *lot* of teas.
> ABBY: So, for the fundraising, was it mainly the women of the church?
> MURIEL: Yes. Of course it was. It was nearly all women, the men well the men, the men in my age group, our age group, a lot of them have gone, had left this world already, or indisposed somehow. Yeah, mostly women.
> ABBY: A lot of work, hard work, physically hard work. And where did the money go? Does the money mainly go to the church or . . . ?
> MURIEL: To Synod, yes.

When I asked one woman where the money being raised would go, she answered briskly: 'Bishops' pensions'. Another woman said:

> and of course there was always a struggle, to to [pause], you know, the little churches all have to pay fees to Synod and they always had trouble getting money for that.

Harsh realities of keeping the church going are understood by Generation A and form a major part of what they consider to be their duties. The notion of a 'self-circulating economy' is here introduced to explain the detailed method of income generation created and sustained by Generation A. They freely supply the labour and materials for sales, parties, and refreshments and then pay to purchase, participate, and consume. Consideration of their 'gifts' illustrate deeply embedded notions of obligation and reciprocity.

I was corrected by a Generation A laywoman for using the term 'jumble sale' when I should have said 'bric-a-brac'. Bric-a-brac refers to ornaments, trinkets, or other similar objects; jumble (or 'rummage' as they say in North America) may include such items, but generally means an unsorted (until the women do their work) pile of books, clothes, kitchen items, and so on. Even the idea of 'ornament' has a Generation A ring to it: younger people today value slimmed-down homes and lack of clutter (hence the popularity of television shows about 'hoarders': these are people depicted as social freaks who won't throw things away). An ornament in this sense could mean everything from a china figurine of a dog, to brooches, clip-on earrings, or a pottery saucer inscribed with 'Welcome to Inverness'.

Generation A laywomen sell items that belonged to Generation A laywomen to other Generation A laywomen. Tables will overflow with them, partly because few people, other than other women such as themselves, will buy such things. The dealers come early to such sales and are gone in moments. It takes a practised eye little time to assess the potential for something that could be sold on eBay or in a second-hand shop for ten times the price the women were asking. And asking is the precisely correct word. At my first sale, I wondered why none of the items on the table were priced: 'Oh, I usually just ask them what they want to pay', the elderly lady explained. The only exception to the general unpopularity of Generation A's fund-raising goods was the bake stall. At the end of one day's event, I asked one woman how the sales had gone: 'The cake stall did really well. Everything sold out by 11 a.m.! We made £200.00.'

The success of church sales will vary by location, particularly given that what is sold invariably reflects the nature of what is given to sell. A small, rural church in a prosperous area of Canada, for example, is well known for its annual day-long fair that attracts people who see the event as a fun family day out. One of the organizers told me:

Well, we work at it all year [...] we set it up so that we have, uh, all these various sales—silent auctions, clothes, books, technological stuff, children's toys, children's clothes, etcetera, etcetera, all these different booths. All outside. And then we have things like hamburgers and hotdogs all day, and, uh, heavenly desserts and tea and uh—and oh by the way we have a bake sale too and book sale and we gather this stuff all year. And we start and we sort it and we work it and whatever and then we do this in the community [...]. Beautiful little church, it's in the country and so there's just one road and we have a half a mile of cars parked along that road [...].

One Saturday morning I was walking past an urban, English Anglican church where an elderly woman was sitting outside the church at a table selling an assortment of jumble: wrapped soaps, costume jewellery, a few paperback crime novels, a box of red candles. Displayed prominently was a leaflet for Christian Aid. I stopped to chat awhile and learned that she was there because the church was open for a few hours and she therefore thought this would be a good opportunity to raise money and also, perhaps, to encourage those who stopped at her table to have a look inside the church. Unfortunately, she continued, few people stopped and even fewer popped inside: 'people are so busy nowadays,' she said, sympathetically. I knew that this was a busy shopping morning in a part of town known for its young, hip population—people inclined to buy high-end botanical hand wash rather than soaps and to browse for e-books on line rather than pick up frayed paperbacks as a bargain. I had participated in enough sales by that point to predict what would happen as her day wore on. The next stage would, typically, involve at least one or two of her friends in the church dropping by and gasping with joy as they picked up to inspect more closely the prettily wrapped soaps which would, inevitably, match their embroidered guest hand-towels in their downstairs cloakroom. They would rummage in their handbags and purses for the correct change and happily hand over £1.50 even though the total was only £1.30. 'Keep the change,' they'd say merrily. At the end of the day, the seller would pack up her unsold items and either take them home to wait for another sale day, or store them in a cupboard of the church. Such activities were satisfying to women who had largely been raised through war and post-war austerity to care about thrift. Elaine told me:

> We don't borrow money like everybody else; that's one big thing. We'll wait until we save up, then we buy what we want. That was the feeling in those days. And because the next generation, if you've got 100 dollars that means you can borrow 200 and buy something else, you know. And that was the feeling people had. But our feeling was, you earned your money; you didn't spend what you didn't have. I think that was a big mark of our generation. And I think most of the people our age still feel like that, you know.

An English woman, Maude, told me a story about a Generation A laywoman friend of hers who prided herself on her knitting. She and another Generation A woman formed a knitting group and spent months creating hats, mittens, teddy bears, bunnies, and so on to be sold in the church sales.

ABBY: I'm guessing. They paid for the wool themselves?

MAUDE: Oh, yes.

ABBY: They thought of it as their contribution.

MAUDE: Of course.

ABBY: And I suspect they didn't sell many items.

MAUDE: Well, no. It doesn't seem many people want those things nowadays.

ABBY: So they took everything home again?

MAUDE: Oh, yes.

ABBY: To be brought out again next year?

MAUDE: Yes, and along with new things they've knitted during the year.

ABBY: I bet they enjoy their knitting group.

MAUDE: They have a wonderful time!

Maude told me about another friend of hers, in her eighties, who always supplies the prizes for the children's games at the church Christmas party and summer fete. She buys them out of her own money, as her 'contribution'. She wraps each item carefully: a chocolate bar, a bag of marbles, a toy car. Sadly, Maude continued, her friend has cancer and is not expected to live many more months: 'So now, of course, she is extra busy wrapping for next year as well in case she's not here.'

All that packing and storing was hard, physical work. As the sale closed down, the tables would be lifted by two women, folded, and put in their rightful place along with folding chairs. I was astonished one day when I turned up to help at a jumble sale to see two women, each in their eighties, lifting large cardboard boxes from an attic storeroom and carrying them down two flights of steep stairs. They repeated this difficult and arduous manoeuvre at least five times that morning and five times later in the afternoon when the sale had ended.

Trust is essential for these cash-based economies as there is little, if any, formal surveillance of what happens to the money on the many occasions when it circulates quickly and immediately during events. Money is put in a saucer on the table, or a bowl in the back of the church: 'I'll put it in the Fair Trade box later,' one woman said about the money donated at a coffee morning. Who does such things, under what authority, and with what system of accountability seemed to be questions no one asked. The consequence of that arrangement is twofold, at least. First, it leaves open opportunities for theft by the women or their helpers or casual visitors. During my fieldwork I only heard about one instance where such a thing had occurred. The immediate response was shock: no one could quite believe it had happened, that their trust had been betrayed. Interestingly, I thought, it did not change the women's behaviour. They recovered quickly and carried on as normal, performing, once again, their roles as survivors and sustainers. The practice also, perhaps more importantly for the long-term sustainability of the church, signalled mutual trust within the church family. Leaving your change on the hall table or your keys on a hook by the door is what one does in a family. To sustain that image everyone needs to join in on the act and behave honourably and openly. The message is clear: we all belong together and respect each other. There are limits and boundaries, however. I was always reminded to put my handbag out of view when I was sitting in the church for an open day, but many people left theirs on their pew when they went forward for Holy Communion. I discussed that act with women and found that they, like me, felt a tortured, self-conscious awareness of their dilemma: should they take their bags with them and be safe, while also clearly signalling that they did not trust their fellow church attenders, or should they take a chance and leave it, showing that they were at ease with each other? That dilemma was never clearly resolved.

Trust is also necessary when giving regular amounts to the church, as Anna, described earlier, did with her tithes, assuming that the church would do whatever it thought best with the money.

SOCIAL EVENTS AND SOCIAL CAPITAL

Women's greater participation in voluntary organizations gives them a wide range of contacts with other women in other voluntary organizations. Their combined knowledge and access to diverse resources allows them to work more efficiently and successfully across a number of projects. A male member of a congregation once described this to me in terms of what happens when someone in the congregation dies. 'As if by magic', he recounted, the women would organize details for the funeral and the refreshments afterwards. The apparently seamless 'magic' ability to organize and materialize complex logistics is possible only through practice and connections. Particularly for groups that operate with limited and diminishing resources, knowing who can help with a certain practical skill, who has an empty garage that can be used for storage, who knows someone with contacts in the entertainment industry can make the difference between, say, a fundraising event happening cost-effectively or at all. This is the kind of social capital referred to by Bourdieu (1985, 248): 'the aggregate of the actual or potential resources which are linked to possession of a durable network of more or less institutionalized relationships of mutual acquaintance or recognition'. In other words, it's who you know.

At one of the funerals I attended, it was clear that the women had organized the food and drink. A buffet of sandwiches, pork pies, and crumbed chicken pieces was laid out, next to the table of wines and juices. The suggestion that this had occurred 'by magic' is a symptom of the tendency to ignore and sometimes make invisible the actual labour and skill behind such practices. The phrase fits into the ways I often saw women being described, where their labour was being masked by such phrases as 'duty' or 'domestic' or 'private',[3] as if the only people who could earn the term 'work' or 'labour' were men. Feminists have pointed out that women's labour is often hidden through concepts such as 'domestic' or 'private' and therefore appears more natural and less significant than male labour in the economy. As Pateman wrote (1983, 157), '[. . .] the dichotomy between the private and public obscures the subjection of women to men within an apparently universal, egalitarian and individualist order'.

Of significant interest for the future of the churches to which Generation A belongs is the variation between the different kinds of capital. One common measurement of social capital is how many different occupations are represented in a person's social network: the higher the number, the greater the social capital. Putnam developed ideas about social capital during the last two decades, explicitly linking social capital to religion and, from there, to women and the well-being of society. He describes (2000, 19) social capital as 'connections among individuals—social networks and the norms of reciprocity and trustworthiness that arise from them'. Putnam viewed these networks both as structural, such as ties of the workplace, neighbourhood and family, and cultural, embodied in social norms.

---

[3] The public and private description, and gender-blind analysis of capital, is explored in detail in the edited collection by Adkins and Skeggs (2005) reassessing Bourdieu through feminist analyses.

He claimed that social capital bestows a general benefit in society through its production via close engagement with others, which in turn creates trust and healthier, happier, richer communities. Churches, he argues, have always been sites for social capital generation and performances of civic duties: 'Faith communities in which people worship together are arguably the single most important repository of social capital in America' (Putnam 2000, 66). He then argues that church attendance is declining, with corresponding decline in other forms of civic engagement.

Because they work in both the church and in the wider area, either as paid or voluntary workers, women are likely to have a higher number and broader range of social contacts than men. Although social capital measured by occupation can be useful in terms of, for example, obtaining a job, measured in other terms of what I call 'soft labour', it may have other important advantages. The women I worked with were often in situations where their social contacts provided a broad range of information that combine to create a unique knowledge base. Through their role in greeting people entering the church for services, serving refreshments to them following services, being involved in voluntary schemes such as church opening, jumble sales, parish lunches, and so on, the women are likely to come into contact and form relationships with a high number of people from different occupations and social classes, and therefore gain greater social capital than many priests whose range of contact may be more limited. Not only do those varied experiences provide knowledge for the women, they also extend the realm in which they operate and feel comfortable—their *habitus*. That extension may help to open routes for others to participate in the life of the church as barriers reduce. Nason-Clark and Holtmann (2015) found that official networks and the conventional hierarchy of male-dominated clergy were not helpful to Christian women suffering from domestic abuse. Instead, it was the informal network of fellow parishioners and people outside the church who offered support.

As Coleman et al. (2016) observed:

> It is this social capital that is easily and readily translated into support to members in need and may account for the heightened availability of support to older members who have often contributed to religious congregations for many years and are thus considered "deserving" recipients of support.
>
> (Schröder-Butterfill 2015; Thelen et al. 2009)

HARD WORK AND SOFT LABOUR

By 'soft labour' I mean labour that is unpaid and performed according to less apparent hierarchal structures, compared to the conventional workplace. I am not, as Hochschild (1983, 167) has also observed, referring to apparently 'soft' skills often characterized as intrinsically feminine or 'natural'. The skills practised by Generation A have been learned, honed and applied through decades of hard work. As Miles (1992, 330) wrote in her study of Episcopal laywomen:

> Historically, the dominant Christian rhetoric defined the place of women in Christian communities as one of privileged subordination. The character traits to which women have been socialized in Christian societies—obedience, humility, submissiveness and attentiveness to others' needs—are privileged, in devotional manuals, sermons, religious art and theological treatises, as central to the 'imitation of Christ' and thus to Christian behaviour.

The type of the labour women perform in that service is often, by laypeople and academics, subsumed into something else or given another term, such as 'duty', 'care', or 'free', all of which displace it as work. Mahmood (2005) describes how the women she studied in Egypt were motivated by duty.[4] A Pakistani-born woman who introduces herself as someone strongly influenced by Critical Marxism, Mahmood ponders a question familiar to many feminists: why would women do that? Mahmood observes a turn to stricter forms of religiosity in the Muslim world, particularly the 'mosque movement'. She introduces her work in the context of a feminist relationship to religion and Islam where, she suggests, many feminists believe that 'women Islamist supporters are pawns in a grand patriarchal plan' (Mahmood 2005, 1). She asks why such a large number of women across the Muslim world actively support a movement that seems inimical to their 'own interests and agendas', especially at a historical moment when these women appear to have more emancipatory possibilities available to them (Mahmood 2005, 2). The concept of 'duty' describes one of the goals of the mosque movement according

---

[4] Before continuing with this example, I want to stress that I am not offering a cross-cultural comparison between 'women in Egypt' and 'women in England': there are far too many potential ways of describing 'woman' to suggest such simplicity.

to principles of '*da'wa*', meaning a call or summons. It is also used as a description for women in the mosque movement where it is understood as a 'religious duty that requires all adult members of the Islamic community to urge fellow Muslims to greater piety, and to teach one another correct Islamic conduct' (Mahmood 2005, 57). Mahmood's analysis of the piety movement moves beyond the role of women and contested versions of feminism, to a central concern about the construction of personhood. It also reminds me that concepts such as duty or 'sacrifice' are not necessarily experienced negatively or as a form of oppression, despite how they might initially seem through my feminist lens (see also Strathern 1984).

Alongside the notion of duty in terms of their labour, there may be other, related ideas such as obligation and commitment, all of which have a specific meaning in the context of a Christian church. In his study of a Swedish church, Stromberg argued (1986, 24) that the congregation is a set of relations that is a symbolic representation of the gospel. There is then produced 'a relationship of commitment occurs when the symbol and the self are, at least momentarily, merged'. Those relationships also directly benefit the person performing them. Brown (1992, 256) refers to the 'spiritualized household' and how the 'work' of domesticity:

> enriches private and public, material and spiritual life. Sunday School programs, church suppers, and moveable feasts held in private homes are all part of practices of commitment to community and communion that help overcome the very real alienation and separation, both voluntary and circumstantial, that our society fosters in countless ways.

The women I spoke with during Church open days, coffee mornings, and other events are acutely aware of their role or, in the words of one of them, Pauline, their 'contribution':

> Yes, it is about obligation, contribution. How can I contribute? That's why I do it. Not because of the church building, I'm not like others who love this building, think it's wonderful. I don't really. It's a big Victorian church, that's it. But it's my contribution.

The way she stressed 'contribution' reminded me about some discussions I had had with others about Generation A's propensity to emphasize the importance of obligation and duty. For people of that generation, duty was taught to them explicitly as they participated in training for Confirmation by memorising the 'catechism', the set of tenets upon which they would be quizzed by the bishop at their confirmation ceremony. Once they had recited the Ten Commandments, the bishop would ask them: 'What dost thou chiefly learn by these Commandments?':

Answer. I learn two things: my duty towards God, and my duty towards my Neighbour.
Question. What is thy duty towards God?
Answer. My duty towards God is to believe in him, to fear him, and to love him, with all my heart, with all my mind, with all my soul, and with all my strength; to worship him, to give him thanks, to put my whole trust in him, to call upon him, to honour his holy Name and his Word, and to serve him truly all the days of my life.
Question. What is thy duty towards thy Neighbour?
Answer. My duty towards my Neighbour is to love him as myself, and to do to all men as I would they should do unto me: To love, honour, and succour my father and mother: To honour and obey the Queen, and all that are put in authority under her: To submit myself to all my governors, teachers, spiritual pastors and masters: To order myself lowly and reverently to all my betters: To hurt nobody by word nor deed: To be true and just in all my dealing: To bear no malice nor hatred in my heart: To keep my hands from picking and stealing, and my tongue from evil-speaking, lying, and slandering: To keep my body in temperance, soberness, and chastity: Not to covet nor desire other men's goods; but to learn and labour truly to get mine own living, and to do my duty in that state of life, unto which it shall please God to call me.

It is reasonable to say that most, if not all, Anglican women of Generation A were confirmed and therefore knew those lines by heart. Duty to God, neighbour, Queen, and country was an explicit, obligatory form of their religiosity. It is also reasonable to say that fewer young people would know such words today as confirmations have declined significantly in the last century. In 1901, 221,000 people were confirmed; by 2012, that figure had dropped by almost 200,000, to just 21,000.[5]

---

[5] <https://churchofengland.org/media/1936517/statistics%20for%20mission%202012.pdf>, last accessed 28.3.2016.

I asked Pauline if she felt that 'duty' was a defining term for her generation, born, as she was, in the mid-1930s. She replied instantly, and forcefully, that it was:

> That's how we were. All of us. People in a big house, always looked after everyone. No one went without. Of course, I can't say that was the way for absolutely everyone, but most people.

Pauline's reference to 'big house' is a familiar term for people from small villages in the UK. It is, according to Collins Dictionary, synonymous with mansion, building, residence, manor, country house, seat, stately home, or manor house. It is where the wealthiest family in the village lived, often because they had an aristocratic background and were, literally, the 'lords of the manor'. Hers was therefore a classed statement that suggested that the village's wealthy family would look after those less fortunate. For some, the class differential might not be seen as a problem, particularly if it appeared to be, in a common-sense way, the way things are rightly ordered, as once expressed in the lyrics of the popular hymn 'All Things Bright and Beautiful', written by the Anglican female poet and hymn-writer Cecil Frances Alexander in 1848. Midway through reflections on birds and mountains is a verse that tells of 'a rich man in his castle, and a poor man at his gate: God made them high and lowly, And ordered their estate'. That verse is now usually omitted when sung, a move that has created some controversy. In 1995 the Catholic Bishop of Leeds, David Konstant, described the hymn as 'wicked' because it 'lay all the blame for social problems at God's door, and takes away the incentive to bring about change on the part of individuals and society, wholly contrary to the Old Testament and Gospel teachings'. He was swiftly rebuked by the Anglican Archbishop of York and the Bradford Cathedral choirmaster, who argued that the hymn was simply a product of its Victorian times, and was only trying to call attention to the natural order decreed by God.[6] Perhaps. Yet again, the divide appeared to be both generational and classed.

---

[6] <http://www.independent.co.uk/news/hymn-not-so-wise-and-wonderful-1599499.html>, last accessed 28.3.2016.

9

The Last Active Generation

This book's objective has been fourfold. First, I have tried, through ethnographic fieldwork, situated historically and socially, to provide a detailed record of a vanishing people. Second, through that process I have offered insights and into why and how the women engage in a particular mode of religious practice. In this chapter, I will summarize my conclusions and move to the third and fourth objectives, to reflect on the consequences of their loss in both religious and secular domains and to revise and introduce theories related to religiosity, women, and generations.

WOMEN OF THEIR TIME AND PLACE: SACRED INSTITUTIONS

Generation A are women of a certain time and place, and it is their contextuality that has shaped their religious lives. Carrying that thought through, it could then be supposed that as the characteristics of wider society changed, the kinds of activities performed by religious people and organizations would also change. Theoretically, I find that convincing. Durkheim and Mauss (1963 [1902] demonstrated how categories of thought arise from society and mirror social concerns, a point made even larger by Douglas (1966, 1973). Durkheim argued (1984 [1933], 168–72) that religion's hold over everyday life decreases as social differentiation increases and moral behaviours and attitudes become more complex.

The generational societal shifts experienced by Generation A have been sweeping and fundamental. As Gell (1992, 9), quoted earlier, said, time is not a pendulum. Time has moved on, away from the period when Generation A women worked and worshipped in a particular way. That way is significantly different from those performed by people who may occasionally attend church or even participate in various religious acts, such as pilgrimage or meditation, those 'episodic forms of faith' as Percy described (2013, 69) that are increasingly being stripped of obvious religious language and meaning.[1] Christenings, one priest told me, are the new weddings. He has observed that couples now may not bother to get married, but celebrate instead their coming together as a family through a large party linked to a baptism or, as the Church prefers to call it as they reach towards the secularized generations, a blessing or naming ceremony.

The popular UK website Net Mums offers advice to parents wanting to mark the birth of their child. Consistently referring to 'christian' or 'christianity' without an upper case 'C', they explain that church attendance may have to feature for a few weeks, and that older women in the family may be able to help with the clothing:[2]

> If you've recently moved or simply want to welcome your child into the christian community (despite not being regular church-goers), you may be expected to attend church for a few weeks before your child is allowed to be christened there [...] Long white or cream christening gowns are often used for traditional christenings. Perhaps you have one in your family that's been passed through the generations or have a clever aunt or gran that will be happy to make one for the event?

Those clever aunts or grans, Generation A women, may indeed have those skills, not because they are old, but because they share a lived religiosity peculiar to that generation. As I explained in Chapter 2, the concept of 'generation' that I am using is an ideal type. With all its internal heterogeneity, the Anglican women of the global North who were born in the 1920s and 1930s share a dramatic period of time, with certain social conditions which produced certain forms of religiosity. My analysis of 'generation' has, therefore, departed significantly from ideas of ageing as the most important influence of religiosity. Some people I talked with suggested that the church might be rescued by a return of the 'lost' generations of their children and grandchildren.

---

[1] For descriptions and analysis of ambivalence and sometimes ironic stances taken towards pilgrimage, see Coleman and Elsner (1998) and Coleman (2013).

[2] <http://www.netmums.com/baby/baby-baby-development/baby-s-first-month/christenings-and-naming-ceremonies>, last accessed 21.7.2016.

With no evidence to support that, despite their wishful thinking, I could not offer them much comfort.[3] Further, I qualify the term with 'active' to delineate further the kind of woman about whom I am speaking. This is not to discount the idea that there is a large 'nominal' population which may, when it suits, define themselves as Christian or even Anglican/Church of England (Day 2011 [2013]), but this is not the population that will sustain the Anglican church, as I am arguing. As Woodhead has shown through surveys,[4] this nominal population is more likely to be estranged from the Church than supporting of it, generally being more liberal than clergy on social issues, and more conservative economically. Further, as Coleman (2015, 226) shows, Anglicanism may persist in various, less visible forms, through, for example, pilgrim sites, hospital chaplaincies, and cathedrals. Collins (2013, 46) describes in detail how spaces and materials associated with hospital chaplaincy are explicitly Anglican, as are the elderly women who arrange flowers there, just as they do in their parish churches.

> At the hospitals in Durham and Middlesbrough, the cross, for example, is portable, and can be removed if the occasion demands. The default setting, however, remains Anglican, with the cross, altar and hymn board prominently sited.

Coleman (2015, 226) argues that:

> Such nooks and crannies are often obscure but they are not only describable as privatized, since they may depend—as in the case of chaplaincies and pilgrimage sites—on the possibly of operating in semi-public contexts, adjacent to the actions and roles of more formal institutions. Furthermore, they are mobile and evanescent, but not placeless as such.

Indeed, they may shift shape and place, but those are not the places nor shapes that meant the most to the church-attending women of Generation A. As I have tried to show in this book, Generation A is a particular, peculiar generation that would not support such hidden, shifting forms of the closely felt and daily practised faith.

Most importantly, I challenge the stereotype of elderly Christian women as worthy, dutiful, carers. Their 'gifts' (see Mauss 1954) of money, labour, time, and emotion were not entirely selfless: they

---

[3] For a decisive and well-argued dismissal of those theories see Brown (2012, 42–6).
[4] <http://faithdebates.org.uk/wp-content/uploads/2014/10/Clergy-survey-Press-Release.pdf>, last accessed 30.5.2016.

received comfort, pleasure, and meaning in equal proportion. My study reveals far more complex personalities, values, and behaviours. Generation A is, I argue, characterized by:

- certain habits and dispositions: in religious terms, particularly a desire for a relationship with a church-based spiritual authority that supports the sacred institutions of their day: church, nation, marriage, and family.

- valuing a kind of authority that is both masculine and 'traditional', embodied in the depiction of their god, their saviour, their priest, and the socially acceptable hierarchies of their day.

- a desire for 'tradition', particularly as understood as a comfort from the past, or what Weber described as a desire and form of respect 'for that which has always been' (Weber 1922, 36).

- holding as sacred ideas and institutions no longer held as sacred by their children and wider society.

- being, above all else, religious women: holy women.

Further, I find that the direct effect of de-Christianization on the women of Generation A has hit them where the heart is. Whether this is felt through, seemingly to the outsider, small details such as the secularization of Mothering Sunday and the decline of the family post-church Sunday lunch, or through changing public norms on issues of family, monarchy, country, and sexuality, the impact has been hardest on the women whose religious lives depended on a traditional Church narrative. In their haste to welcome women priests, and feminist and other forms of new spiritualities, both practitioners and scholars have neglected this, most vulnerable and invisible, group of women.[5] Offen (1988, 136, see also Strathern 1984), describes in her analysis of feminism that historically some feminists have privileged an individualist goal for feminists over a relational:

> By contrast, the individualist feminist tradition of argumentation emphasized more abstract concepts of individual human rights and celebrated

---

[5] As an example, Wingate et al.'s (1998) edited collection on the Anglican communion discusses bishops, dioceses, texts, history, priesthood (mostly male), power (ecclesiastical), theology, electoral rolls, mission, education, and so on, with only one reference to laywomen: a criticism of the Mothers' Union's practices in South Africa. A chapter promisingly titled 'Five years in: where are the women in the Church of England' tells only the story of women priests.

the quest for personal independence (or autonomy) in all aspects of life, while downplaying, deprecating, or dismissing as insignificant all socially defined roles and minimizing discussion of sex-linked qualities or contributions, including childbearing and its attendant responsibilities.

Theories of relationality and the link to belonging have been developed in this book in conversation and sometimes contrast with more commonly accepted versions of a turn to subjectivity and individualization (see also Day 2011 [2013]), and explore how both the needs for individual agency and collective belonging are performed through acts of religiosity, all of which need to be temporally and spatially situated.

Written nearly thirty years ago, Davie's (1994, 2–27) summary of Britain's religious landscape of the late 1980s, paraphrased here, effectively captures the time and place of Generation A's offspring as thirty/forty-something baby-boomers raising the next generation:

The majority of British people persist in believing in God but 'see no need to participate with even minimal regularity in their religious institutions'. Few people have opted out altogether—atheists are rare. The churches attract an audience which is disproportionately elderly, female and conservative. The 'nature of family life, including the traditional codes of morality, are altering rapidly'. Changes in gender roles have 'for better or for worse, penetrated the churches and influenced theological thinking'. An 'influx of immigrants in the post-war period', not all of them from Christian countries, has introduced significant other-faith communities. This represents a trend towards greater religious diversity and has had a 'lasting effect on many aspects of British religious life'. Relationship with belief and practice was different in the past. Significance in age contrast will affect future of religion. Subtle but significant changes in 'mood' since 1945 are generational. The 1960s, for example, produced a more 'relevant' demand on the churches, whereas the dominant mood of the nineties would be more 'new age' or responses to it.

Reviewing her list of descriptions relevant to generational change, it seems obvious that there would be little chance of those generations following in their mothers' and grandmothers' religious footsteps. Little more than a decade after Davie wrote, Heelas et al. (2005) researched the English town of Kendal as representative of the wider population, and concluded that the small population of church-attending Christians would continue to decline and eventually be replaced by an equally small, but fervent, 'spiritual' population. With those studies in mind, it seems inconceivable to suppose that anything would be different from what was forecast.

Taylor (2007, 1) put it succinctly when he described how God is no longer central: 'you can fully engage in politics without ever encountering God [. . .] the few moments of vestigial ritual or prayer barely constitute such an encounter today, but this would have been inescapable in earlier centuries in Christendom'.[6] Taylor's linkage between God and politics is important here because it speaks to Generation A's easy assumption that their religion was *the* religion, *the* Church, of *their* England. For many reasons, including pluralism, globalization, feminism, consumerism, cosmopolitanism, and the media, the 'plausibility structures' weakened dramatically during their lifetime and profoundly affected their children and successive generations' view of the religious and non-religious landscape of choice and loss of deference. Berger and Luckmann's (1966) model depicted how people create a view of reality through a process of externalization, objectification (or habitualization), and institutionalization. They suggested that people confer legitimacy on the institutions they create by imposing 'symbolic universes' to make plausible both social institutions and individual biography. As I have discussed earlier, the most legitimate institutions to Generation A of church, nation, and family have all been diminished in the post-sixties generations.

Further, the source of what is considered legitimate is, I have argued in a previous work, (Day 2011 [2013]), the most important variable in determining a difference between religious and non-religious people. The women I studied were articulate about the importance of their faith in ways that sounded biblically and doctrinally derived—just the sort of faith that younger people may have rejected for exactly that reason. For example, a Generation A laywoman I talked with was clear about what she believed and how she worshipped. When I asked her what her faith meant to her, she replied:

> Well, I'll tell you what my faith means to me. I believe in the Lord Jesus Christ is my saviour, which is an evangelical thing. And I believe that He is in us and we are in Him, that's something that's in the Bible, and it's in our liturgy too, the Anglican liturgy. And I feel, that as a Christian, that we are close to God and the Lord Jesus Christ and we can talk to them.

---

[6] This is one of my few points of agreement with Taylor whose work is, in general, too polemic and theistic to be usefully applied in sociological and anthropological research. See Fraser (2007) for an excellent critique.

As I discussed earlier in this work, a scripturally informed religion was one they valued, and it is an aspect of religiosity that is lessening in significance, at least for mainstream churches such as Anglicanism. Francis and Penny (2015, 68) found through surveying adolescent males in England and Wales, aged between thirteen and fifteen years old, that a 'considerable proportion' classified themselves as unaffiliated to a religion and showed little evidence of Christian belief or a positive association with Christianity. And yet a third 'remain connected with the rites of passage offered by churches' and a high proportion of atheists believed in 'life after death' and reincarnation. Beliefs in an afterlife, as I have argued elsewhere (Day 2011 [2013], 2012b), are likely to be fuelled by a desire for continuing bonds, rather than any doctrine about heaven.

Field commented from his research on the use of the Bible (2014, 520–1) that a turn away from the Bible as a key resource in daily life may be welcomed by some as:

> a move away from fundamentalism, with all its negative overtones, and as a sensible accommodation with modern society. On the other hand, it seems such a profound shift that it is hard to accept that the decline in Bible-centricism is not also a manifestation of a wider process of secularisation. With both its source of authority and means of transmission undermined, it is difficult to see how the long-term decline of Christian faith and practice in contemporary Britain can be reversed.

Engelke's (2013) ethnographic study of the Bible Society, the British organization devoted to promoting the Bible and the prominence of Christianity in public life (itself a convoluted concept which Engelke deftly untangles throughout the book) illustrates the central importance of the Bible to Christians who, simultaneously, are not using it as a literal tool with which to beat people. His interlocutors, like mine, were not didactic, close-minded, crazed street preachers, but people who believed strongly that biblical truths would help people live better, happier lives. The challenge for them, as it was for the churches I visited, was how to convince others, particularly young people, that this was so. The generational issue was as important for the Bible Society as it was for the churches. He writes (2013, 77):

> As with many churches in England, the society was worried about the graying of its constituency. Anglican 'grannies', who were often presented as the key demographic of supporters for Bible Society's work, are generous and loyal, but they are not enough of a base to sustain the Society's future.

Their adherence to the Bible also partly explains why women of this generation were clear about the importance of attending church and mixing with other Christians. I have discussed earlier how they have said to me that they attend church because Christ so commanded. As one woman asked me when we were discussing the importance of attending church: 'I don't even know if you can have communion on your own?' After a few moments' thought she added that she thought there was a passage in scripture 'that says not forsaking the gathering together of people or something like that—it actually says that in the scripture, I think it's somewhere in Romans'.

I would add that they attend church because they understand, possibly without even reading about it, that the core argument advanced by Durkheim (1915) a century ago was right: religious groups need periodic, regular periods of contact and renewal. If the Church body is, in Generation A's view, the body of Christ (1 Corinthians 12:27) it is a body that must remain whole.

RELIGIOUS 'SOCIALIZATION'

The social conditions which produced the form of religion embraced and enjoyed by Generation A have changed, which is why theories of religious socialization need to account for the wider social context and move beyond a narrow view of what it means to be religious (typically counting behaviours such as church attendance or belief in God). On these grounds, the work of Generation A appears perplexing, particularly as they would seem to be wholly responsible for the success or failure of their offsprings' religiosity: 'to this day, the vast majority of Americans inherit their religion from their parents and never change faith' (Davidson and Pyle 2011, 3). They may not change faith, but as studies quoted earlier here (see, in particular, Chapter 2), younger generations are increasingly non-religious. So, what values did Generation A transmit? This work has examined socialization from a wider values standpoint, on the assumption that values, morals, and notions of the 'self' are continually in flux as societies change.

As Miles (1992, 333) pointed out in her study of Episcopal churchwomen, 'there is no pre-existing entity called "the self" that is subsequently appropriated, trained or manipulated to activities that maintain and reproduce society'. Selves are socially constructed. She argues that women are coerced by male-designed institutions such as family (and, I will add, 'religion'), and compulsory heterosexuality.

Hoge et al. (1982, 569, 573) argued that to maintain 'cultural continuity' values must be transmitted intergenerationally, but influences include not only the family but friends, schools, and 'sociohistorical events'. Their study found that the largest generation gap was on morals concerning sexuality: 'The greatest gap is in the area of sexual ethics; and probably its source is in the youth culture of the 1970s, which approves of much sexual freedom.' They found weak parent–child transmission scores and were unconvinced about why— concluding that their data may have been insufficient, with not enough parents participating. Perhaps, I suggest, the weak scores reflected the wider context to which they referred: in a more globalized, plural, arguably 'postmodern' age, the parent–child link is no longer as strong as it once was. Generation A undoubtedly tried their best, but they were up against strong competition.

When I asked Anna, a Generation A laywoman, what she thought about the future, she was pessimistic mainly because she recognized the lack of transmission generationally:

> I think a lot of it's bound up with the schools too, because the last couple of generations haven't had training at school, any religious training, and I think that's partly it. See, what used to happen with some of our friends at home is they would get married, and even if they hadn't been going to church for a few years, as soon as they had kids, they felt that they should have their kids taken them to church. That was their feeling, you know. But I don't think that would their feeling today, because they didn't go themselves. Some of them, their mothers didn't go either.

Further, as I argued earlier in this book, Generation A did successfully transmit values of care, independence, liberty, and authenticity to their children. Mixed with potent ingredients of the cultural, technological, political, religious, and sexual revolutions that took place in the 1960s and 1980s, those values helped create 'baby-boomer and beyond' generations whose caring values translate into behaviours typically performed in non-church spaces by non-religious people: political activism, for example, and campaigns for environmental protection, human rights, sexual and gender equality, to name a few. That the sacred object is different does not mean that the generations following Generation A were not equally dutiful to what they considered to be sacred and legitimate.

CASE EXAMPLE: GIRL GUIDES' MORAL PANIC

An example of how a section of society responded to a change to the Girl Guides may illustrate a generational conflict about what religious girls, and women, ought to be.

When the Girl Guides changed their promise in September 2013, outrage broke out in the media and the Church of England's governing body, the Synod. The original promise for this century-old girls' club was:

> On my honour, I promise that I will do my best:
> To do my duty to God and the King [or Queen] (Or God or my country);
> To help other people at all times;
> To obey the Guide Law.

The new promise omitted 'honour', 'duty', 'to love my God', and 'and my country', to read:

> I promise that I will do my best:
> To be true to myself and develop my beliefs,
> To serve the Queen and my community,
> To help other people and
> To keep the (Brownie) Guide Law.'

Although a secular organization, the Guides has been linked tightly to Anglicanism. The Girl Guides were originally formed in 1910 by Agnes Baden-Powell, sister of Robert Baden-Powell, an army general, who had a few years earlier formed the Scout movement as a training scheme for boys. The Guide Association 'does not subscribe to any particular faith or religion', instead allowing girls to 'explore their beliefs and to take an active part in the religion or faith of her family and community where appropriate'.[7] Baden-Powell clearly had not intended the Scout Association, or indeed the Guide Association, to be solely a Christian one, but felt that religion of any faith 'can and ought to be taught to the boy' (Baden-Powell 2004, 243). Giving a sample timetable, he outlines prayer as a suitable morning activity (Baden-Powell, 2004, 9). Perhaps it was this emphasis on religion, and the fact that the majority of the British public at that time identified strongly with the Church of England, that led to such strong links between the

---

[7] <http://guidingmanual.guk.org.uk/policies/equality_and_diversity.aspx>, last accessed 29.5.15.

Guide Association and the Church that continue between the two until today. Many Guide units meet within church premises, many Guide volunteers come from church congregations, and some Guide units are sponsored by certain churches. The Guide Association forms an 'integral part of the engagement with young people' for the Church of England,[8] to the point it might seem that the Guides Association is really 'one long church parade'.[9] The interwoven, interdependent, non-negotiable dedication to God, King/Queen, and country runs through the institution that Generation A belongs to: the Church of England and, importantly, its head: the monarch. She is, as monarchs have been since Henry VIII, the 'Defender of the Faith'.

The decision to change the promise could be seen as an example of reasonable institutional accommodation in a plural, diverse society, with the aim of opening up the organization to all girls and women potentially interested in joining.[10] The backlash against the change of promise was vociferous, and what was really interesting was the religious tone taken by an apparently secular media. The *Express* declared 'Christian outrage as Girl Guides ditch God',[11] while the *Mail* announced 'An unholy war in the Guides and why we must ALL fight the secular bigots'.[12] Blogger Tim Stanley announced that 'Girl Guides drop God and country from their pledge. Now Satanists and anarchists can go camping, too.'[13] The *Telegraph* quoted the Bishop of Bradford, the Right Reverend Nick Baines, who accused the Guides of 'evacuating the Promise of meaning and filling it with vacuous nonsense' and believed the new changes would 'open the door to little Hitlers'.[14]

[8] <https://www.churchofengland.org/media/1648008/130123keeping%20the%20promise%20brieifing%20paper.docx>, last accessed 2.7.15.
[9] <http://www.independent.co.uk/news/uk/this-britain/how-the-girl-guides-changed-for-the-better-1942867.html>, last accessed 2.7.15.
[10] <https://www.girlguiding.org.uk/news/welcoming_more_members_with_ou.aspx>, last accessed 29.6.15.
[11] <http://www.express.co.uk/news/uk/408854/Christian-outrage-as-Girl-Guides-ditch-God>, last accessed 29.6.15.
[12] <http://www.dailymail.co.uk/debate/article-2401899/MELANIE-PHILLIPS-An-unholy-war-Girl-Guides-ALL-fight-secular-bigots.html>, last accessed 29.6.15.
[13] <http://blogs.telegraph.co.uk/news/timstanley/100222500/girl-guides-drop-god-and-country-from-their-pledge-now-satanists-and-anarchists-can-go-camping-too/>, last accessed 29.5.15.
[14] <http://www.telegraph.co.uk/news/religion/10136374/Girl-Guides-Has-this-woman-broken-a-sacred-promise.html>, last accessed 29.6.15.

Despite some welcoming these changes as 'hugely positive' and suggesting they showed the Guide Association was grasping 'the opportunity to make itself truly inclusive and relevant to the reality of 21st century Britain',[15] others, including religious conservatives within the Church of England, found the changes much harder to accept. Indeed, the change was brought to the General Synod and discussed in relation to how it would affect the church and its role in society. One member feared 'it could be seen as contributing to the further marginalisation of Christianity in this country'.[16] Despite these concerns, and a battle in the press, the Guide Association remained content with the changes, but did provide a compromise to worried Christians, allowing them to 'provide the context of her own belief before making our promise'.[17] The Synod welcomed this approach. The strong feelings expressed towards the changing of the Guides' promise highlights the link between the Church of England and a sense of patriotism and gender. In earlier times, when Generation A was young and many were members themselves, their sacred promise was unequivocal: they promised to do their best, to do their duty, to God, the King (as was when they were teenagers), and the country.

The public reaction in the conservative media geared towards a Generation A readership may reveal a largely unspoken sense of what is held to be sacred. Such a feeling may lie relatively dormant until stoked by an event which prompts a sense of transgression (Lynch 2012). Women, God, the church, and the country are all entangled.

CONSEQUENCES OF LOSING THEIR RELIGION: PREMISES, NOT PEOPLE

Generation A will be the final active generation in the Church of England and, potentially, in wider sections of 'mainstream' Christianity

---

[15] <http://www.theguardian.com/society/2013/jun/18/girl-guides-queen-god-country-promise>, last accessed 29.6.15.

[16] <https://www.churchofengland.org/media/1910046/gs%201943a%20-%20girl%20guides%20promise%20pmm.pdf>, last accessed 29.6.15.

[17] <https://www.girlguiding.org.uk/news/one_promise_for_all.aspx>, last accessed 29.5.15.

that have depended on their labour and their money. The impact of their loss has been neglected mainly because the importance of their routine acts have been underestimated. The Church changed its role as a major social service provider with the advent of the welfare system,[18] but informal social care is a common feature of Generation A's activity, as I have discussed in earlier chapters. Midweek services and Bible studies are almost exclusively attended by Generation A, as are the 'open church' sessions for a few hours on weekdays. The quiet, frequently invisible work of Generation A in keeping churches open and breathing is critical to sustaining their lives and the lives of the church. The steady 'pew power' of Generation A demonstrates the critical role they have in sustaining church communities. The impact on the wider, secular community will potentially be felt as gendered care becomes less practised. Current trends through think tanks such as Respublica present the Church of England as a prime vehicle for social and community care, a proposition undermined by its lack of gendered reality. While church growth projects emphasize attracting young people, the impact of their presence in conducting the invisible, unpaid labour of Generation A is likely to be minimal. In the meantime, the baby-boomers and Generation Xers are missing, leaving a gap.

As I mentioned in Chapter 1, a survey on voluntary labour was commissioned by the think-tank Respublica,[19] created and headed by Phillip Blonde, a former theology lecturer said to be the inspiration for the Conservative Party's vision of the small-government 'Big Society'.[20] One finding was that most common form of voluntary church labour consisted of promoting the church through coffee mornings. I was surprised to see that no further mention of women, or Generation A, was included in the report. At the report's launch event at Lambeth Palace, I put that question to the Respublica panel. Introducing myself as a researcher currently studying older laywomen

---

[18] For a wider, up-to-date discussion on the relationship between the church and welfare state see Bäckström et al. (2011), and for a case study on an Anglican diocese in England see Middlemiss Lé Mon (2009). Several chapters in a collection of work about Grace Davie's contribution to the study of religion also follow the theme of welfare and religion (Day and Lövheim 2015).

[19] <http://www.respublica.org.uk/our-work/publications/holistic-mission-social-action-church-england/>, last accessed 20.4.2015.

[20] <http://www.telegraph.co.uk/news/politics/8131290/Minister-backs-plan-for-massive-state-sell-off-of-assets.html>, last accessed 31.5.2016.

in the Church of England, I asked why the report did not elaborate on that statistic or address the impact of Generation A's demise. There was no answer and the subject swiftly changed. Noting the presence of Archbishop Justin Welby, I resolved to personally ask him that question in the informal reception that was to follow: unfortunately, the opportunity never arose. He explained to the gathering that he had to leave early in order to vote (against) the government bill on same-sex marriage in the House of Lords. Nevertheless, having made my point in the question period, I attended the reception and, wandering amongst the clergy and consultants, I anticipated that someone amongst the two hundred or so people who had heard me would approach me to find out more. In order to test that hypothesis, I did not raise the subject myself and was interested to find that no one else did either. An hour or so later, after briefly sampling the refreshments of indifferent wine and crisps, I left Lambeth feeling irritated on two fronts: first, Generation A was once again being ignored and, second, what were the organizers thinking in not providing a decent buffet at that hour in the evening? 'Wouldn't have happened in "my" church,' I muttered to myself as I stomped angrily down the Archbishop's splendid staircase.

The report and event reinforced for me the main impact of the demise of Generation A. Church officials and their consultants are deluded if they think the Church will be sustained by fund-raising alone. They obviously had never sat through church services observing how congregations could be split over what effect the latest fund-raising effort had on the church 'family'. Bengston et al. (2013) found that successful religious transmission is most effective in religions whose families are embedded in tightly knit religious communities, as is more common with, for example, Mormons, Evangelical Christians, and religious Jews.

Not only may some fund-raising efforts disrupt the 'family', they are organized under the largely untested assumption that funds will be delivered and people will follow. They may not, or at least may not in any numbers that matter. As usual, it was a Generation A woman who brought that point home to me. We were discussing recent fund-raising events, and she relayed a story about how she had invited one of her friends, a widow, to a Robert Burns evening. Although she knew her friend was, in her words, 'a professed atheist', she nevertheless encouraged her on the (to me now-familiar) Generation A logic that there would be good food.

And I said do you *mind* going? She, oh no, I'd love to go to Bobbie Burns Day [. . .] we'll have a drink of wine and some scotch and some haggis. So, I said to her, let's go down to the front so we'll be closer to the food when it comes up and we won't have to, you know, the food is here and the tables are like this, so I said let's go down over here and sit, let's—we were quite early.

When they sat down, they happened to find themselves sitting next to a bishop. This may have caused a few awkward moments, but:

And I said to [. . .] I hate to tell you this but the bishop [. . .] is sitting right beside and she said, oh that's okay. So then she went to get some wine, to get us some wine, and I said to the bishop, I hate to tell you but my friend's a total atheist. And he said, 'I can deal with that'. Well they had a wonderful time, that was the most fun! [*Laughs*]

It was a nice story of community and conviviality. But when I asked if her friend later began to attend services, she looked at me as if I had not been listening: 'No, no, oh God no, no no! She's an atheist.'

The emphasis on fund-raising is one in danger of privileging prem-ises over people and, from a funder's perspective, may become ques-tionable in light of the thin spread today of attenders in relation to churches available. As a standard requirement for funds, the church must explain how they will be benefiting the 'community' (and I can still see, as I described earlier, the woman placing quote marks with her fingers around the word). The style of that engagement reflects the specific demands and definitions of a specific funder. So, for example, in the UK the Heritage Fund demands history events and the Lottery Fund demands social events, variously defined. For some reason, a concert is not 'social' but a knitting or English language class is.

This imposes a rationalist logic on the church, much like the one I tried to impose when I first saw how inefficient were the over-staffed social functions. It is, as Bough suggests, (1990, 126):

a way of thinking which corresponds with the cult of masculinity, a male chauvinism that values physical strength and bravado as an end in itself. This traditional version of masculinity becomes supplemented in the modern capitalist world with the instrumental use of monetary calculations for determining the most effective, most efficient means for realising one's material self-interest.

Writing in the *Guardian*, journalist Harriet Sherwood described how Archbishop Justin Welby was trying to 'defuse Church of England's "demographic time bomb"',[21] amidst critics afraid that the measures would change the character of the church:

> Discord over a radical programme to make the Church of England "fit for purpose" in the 21st century is set to spill into the open this week when the new synod meets at the start of its five-year term. The Reform and Renewal programme was initiated by the archbishop of Canterbury, Justin Welby, and is being enthusiastically driven forward by a cohort of senior figures who share his zeal for modernising and evangelising the church. However, critics fear that traditional values could be lost amid the speed of change, lack of consultation and a new culture of setting goals and targets.

And yet, at £30 per hour for heat, some way must be found to fund large and old buildings if they are not to close down. This leads to another problem I will call the 'liability of loyalty', which I will elaborate on shortly. Church closure occurs for a number of reasons decided by the diocese. The key is finance, and finance is a function of attendance, fund-raising, gifts, legacies, and, not to be forgotten, coffee mornings. Church attendance also comes into the mix, which is why churches become nervous when numbers drop below thirty. The Church of England receives three-quarters (£750 million) from worshippers in the parishes. Around £200 million comes from cash and donations by congregations and visitors. Recalling the activities of Generation A, it is significant that £250 million comes from legacies, special events, bookstalls, fund-raising, parish magazines, and rent from church halls. In the future, the Church of England may increasingly turn to the market: In 2014 the Church Commissioners' total return on its investment was 14.4 per cent.[22]

Amidst debates about the nature of volunteering, and its apparent demise amongst younger generations, a growing preference for 'professionalization' is masked. Rather than reflect on a turn to a more 'individualized' society, most women in the study discussed the growth of business and commerce. Although not expressed in those terms, the emerging picture was one of late modern capitalism where previously local events are overtaken by larger, commercial interests.

---

[21] <http://www.theguardian.com/world/2015/nov/21/justin-welby-church-england-new-synod>, last accessed 15.1.2016.

[22] <https://www.churchofengland.org/about-us/funding.aspx#where>, last accessed 20.6.2016.

Along with all those voluntary activities performed by Generation A came an enriched church life, as described in earlier chapters. This became most obvious to me as a process when I wrestled with what I described not as a crisis of believing but one of be-leaving. In religious terms I was, and remain, 'agnostic', a position I found to be comfortably compatible with many Anglicans.

A CRISIS OF BE-LEAVING: A MODEL EMERGES

My fieldwork was finished. The project was proceeding on schedule. The date had been clearly marked to attend my host church and inform them that I would not be attending any more, apart from a date to be agreed in the future when I would return to share with them my general findings. And so, on that Sunday, I went to service as usual. As it ended I joined the others for tea and was met with a big smile by Emma. She wanted to know what my availability would be for the church opening duty for the next three months. I opened my mouth to tell her that I would not be available, that I was, in fact, leaving, when to my surprise completely different words tumbled out: 'Oh, fairly free, no problem. Maybe gone for a bit in August.' She took out her tiny notebook and wrote that down. I was speechless. I knew I had to create some distance between me and them, and so I decided that I would simply help out on a few days and not actually attend any services. As the next weekend approached I happily anticipated a good lie-in on Sunday morning for a change, followed by a newspaper, and a coffee. That never happened. I was up and getting dressed for church as usual, meanwhile reassuring myself that it was just for the one day, and was no doubt a process of leaving. Of course, there was the lunch later in the month when they would need some help, and didn't someone say she was going on holiday? The others couldn't be left with all that to do themselves, surely . . . and so it went on for a few weeks while I wrestled with ethical and time issues, confiding in two senior colleagues who gave me good advice, until I was struck by the obvious question: how did they do this to me? How was I trapped in a routine I had not wanted, apart from for research reasons? That question forced me to deconstruct the process and create the seven-stage model of belonging that I introduced at the outset and have touched on during the chapters that have followed.

This was when I realized that the people who thought Generation A was resistant to change just because its members were old-fashioned and being difficult were wrong. Generation A was not resisting change; it was resisting loss. The resistance was part of the generation's performance of belonging. What might seem as tedious and repetitive were, in fact, technologies for sustaining belonging, mainly in seven stages, leading from unfamiliarity to intimacy. Generation A organizes and leads from the pews to create belonging through seven effective strategies that bring newcomers and regulars through stages from strangeness to internalization:

1. Recognition: being greeted; remembering names.
2. Intimitization: details of lives recalled and discussed.
3. Integration: being included in events.
4. Routinization: church attendance and participation in events tied to church calendar become regular.
5. Obligation: being given a regular 'job'. As part of a 'rota', knowing activities partly depend on you.
6. Ritualization: becoming a part of key 'holy' events, such as Lenten rituals, Eucharist assistance.
7. Internalization: habits and practices seem 'normal' and part of regular life.

Generation A is not necessarily the easiest to work with. They are firm about what they do and how it should be done. One consequence of Generation A's loss will be felt in the sustainability of the church through the loss of expertise in creating that experience of 'belonging' and the kind of knowledge that can only be passed on through bodily movements.

EMBODIED KNOWLEDGE THROUGH DOING

A Holy Habitus

Calhoun (1993, 77) invites readers to think about tradition, not simply as what may be displaced by modernity, but as a verb referring to the passing on or handing down of information.

> Tradition, then, is a mode of transmission of information, particularly, for present purposes, that crucial to the coordination of action. Following

Bourdieu's account of the habitus, we may note that the information need not be rendered discursive; it may be tacit knowledge, even knowledge embodied in modes of action which agents are unable to bring to linguistic consciousness, like basketball players their hook shots.

If tradition comes from the doing, then it becomes more likely that if the children of Generation A were not with them doing tradition, then the tradition would not be carried on. The women's ways of knowing became their 'tacit knowledge', that being something so ingrained that it became difficult to verbalize. As Polanyi (1966, 4), who coined the term, said, sometimes 'we can know more than we can tell'. Known for their quiet presence more than speeches or pamphlets, Generation A was muted partly by their own predilection and partly through being ignored by younger, perhaps more theologically trained, church members, attuned to a theology that privileged 'the word' over the body (see, for discussion, Keane 2007; Mellor and Shilling 2010).

Current and therefore future generations may lack that expertise and practice through being raised, by Generation A, in post-war austerity and then prosperity. The role Generation A has had in nurturing and socializing the baby-boomers and less religious future generations is often overlooked. Values of interdependence, commitment, respect, and authenticity combined to create visible, perhaps unforeseen, consequences.

The combined effect of smaller, less tightly knit congregations and loss of Generation A's money will lead to more church closures as, Woodhead notes (2012), they become centres of commerce or spaces for other religions, and there is a shift to larger churches and cathedrals. As Agnes told me:

> I think the Anglican Church has lost a lot of its leadership, you know, and they ended up with big churches and no people. I mean, after all, the church is the people and, you know, the bride of Christ is the church, the people, not the building, you know. And especially in [...] there have been money problems, and, er, it's, you know. For instance, we're not going to be paying our minister, we haven't paid any of the ministers.

One advantage for the Church of women priests is that they tend to accept their jobs without payment, and yet even their free labour will not be enough as clergy, like congregations, age and are not replaced. Summing up the problem in an article for the *Church Times*,[23] Woodhead said:

> Put simply, the Church of England is soon going to have to operate with far fewer ministers, both stipendiary and non-stipendiary. Women's ordination has helped a little, but women continue to be disproportionately represented in unpaid, part-time, and low-status jobs in the Church. It is unlikely that this situation can be sustained—even if conscience allowed it.
>
> To put it bluntly, there are no longer enough troupers left to keep the show on the road, and the show will have to change.

LIABILITY OF LOYALTY

In the end, loyalty may work against Generation A. At first it seemed sensible to me for churches to merge with other nearby Anglican churches; surely two or three churches with congregations of thirty people or so would be stronger as one? Church attenders, I soon discovered, are fiercely loyal to their church. Most will not even attend a coffee morning, let alone a major fund-raising event at other churches: these are the competition. With everyone being measured on numbers of attenders, or those who count themselves as part of the 'worshipping community', and on their ability to pay their quota and maintain their church, it is unsurprising that they are not willing to co-operate with others competing in the same, dwindling, market. On one occasion I discussed the experience of church merging with two Generation A women, May and Winifred, who had both been born in the same area, had been baptized at the same church, and had attended all their lives. Their regular church was closed in 1986 and then demolished, which both surprised and saddened them. 'It was a beautiful church,' said May. 'More of a traditional church [than the one, more modern building, they now attend].' The churches managed the dynamic of integration and merger by holding services over two months at the two churches on alternate weeks, so that the congregation could get to know each other. 'It took some time,' said Winifred. Both she and others were

---

[23] <https://www.churchtimes.co.uk/articles/2014/7-february/features/features/not-enough-boots-on-the-ground>, last accessed 1.5.2016.

mainly resistant because they did not like the look of the more modern church. 'It looked low,' she said, 'more like a Methodist church.' That prompted many members of the congregation to seek other churches in more 'traditional' buildings.

Our conversation turned to why they thought numbers overall had dropped in the Church of England. Winifred said she thought it was because the next generations of her children and grandchildren were not interested in coming, although she really did not know why. It seemed that 'young people had so many other things like, if they play football it's on a Sunday morning.' I said I thought those changes were happening in other places as well, and she agreed: 'It's global'. She remembered when the church was 'the social hub of the community. There was always something, Sunday schools, outings . . . '

Her diagnosis of the problem conforms to what I mainly heard from other Generation A women who discussed the future. Young people were busy, and so were their parents, and their families had lost the habit of churchgoing. At no time did I ever hear harsh criticism of them. It was as if Generation A did notice, and did not condemn, the wide array of choices available to people, particularly for increasing their social activities beyond the limited variety offered by the Church.

A sacristan I talked to was worried that no one had come forward to replace her. She takes pride in her work. She has been told that, she tells me, 'we have the best silver in the parish'. But she is also worried. She has been performing the role for, she guesses, nearly twenty years, but so far has been unable to find a replacement. She has been hoping for the past few years that someone might volunteer because it is a big job for her, and the travel alone is nearly an hour's return trip on the bus. But, she explains, nobody else has the time or, maybe, interest. Things have changed, she says: 'it's not as fun these days'. My thoughts about duty quickly melt as she changed the subject to one I had heard from many women at the other churches: the former priest who had involved the congregation in frequent, fun activities both in the church and further afield. When I asked her if she had any idea why younger people are not coming to church these days, she answered that 'Everything's different on a Sunday.' When she was young, she said, the shops were not open on a Sunday so that it would remain quiet as a 'family day'. 'We weren't even allowed to play out,' she said, 'and when we were allowed it was to go to Church in the evening. That was a treat!'

THE FUTURE OF THE CHURCH

My project hypothesis was confirmed: Generation A is unique, and its passing likely signals an inevitable acceleration of the decline of the Church of England and the Anglican Communion of the global North owing to Generation A's not being able to, amidst widespread cultural revolutions, transmit wholly specific church-related dispositions, habits, skills, beliefs, and practices to their baby-boomer children and churches. Counter-intuitively, the church's emphasis on attracting young people is wholly misplaced: it is the 'middle' generation they should have retained. Some impact on the wider, secular community will potentially be felt as gendered care becomes less practised. Generation A is likely to be the last active generation in the Anglican Communion with consequences for church growth and maintenance, and the informal social work within the church, surrounding community, and wider afield. The same Respublica report I referred to earlier placed, after coffee mornings, the second most common voluntary activity as raising funds for Christian charities. One of those is the Mothers' Union, whose most recent annual report drew attention to the challenges of having an ageing support base.

So, what will churches look like in the future? My prediction is that they will be fewer, larger, and increasingly populated by gay men, a demographic least likely to reproduce offspring, religious or otherwise.

Gay Men: The New Old Ladies?

Openly gay men and women featured prominently in many of the UK and North American churches I studied. At one inner city church I was told that the largest funeral in living memory had taken place five years earlier when more than a thousand turned up for the funeral of 'a drag queen'. Buchanan (1992, 311) described churches as becoming smaller but also changing in composition to an older, more female, and 'to a much lesser but nonetheless significant degree gay and lesbian'. Their visible presence is also sometimes problematic for Generation A, who tend to prefer an old-style discretion about one's (homo)sexuality, and for sections of the wider Anglican Communion.

Many churches oppose the idea of women bishops and the recognition of gay relationships. A Sri Lankan priest told me that this issue was one without hope for a resolution. And yet many other aspects of his church's life reflected 'liberal' values of diversity, multiculturalism, and integration. Tamils and Buddhists were a large part of the extended church community. It seemed the Church of Ceylon could absorb the idea of someone loving a different god, but not the same gender.

In contrast, Episcopal churches I visited in Boston and New York showed little evidence of such disputes. At a midweek communion, I attended at a church in New York the urban, professional members of the congregation were largely gay. Gene Robinson of New Hampshire became the first openly gay bishop in 2004. The first woman bishop in the Anglican Communion, Barbara Harris, became Bishop of Massachusetts in 1989: it took the Church of England nearly thirty years to catch up, with Libby Lane ordained as the first female bishop in January 2015.

Keenan noted (2015, 95): 'This is the issue that will not go away, the divisive issue which continues to threaten the binds of the Communion, and the contemporary issue which keeps the Communion in the news.' His research uncovers the somewhat contradictory issue of gay men's attraction to the Church, despite its overtly anti-gay stand. He writes that despite the Church's move towards a stand of 'acceptable homosexuality', it nevertheless (Keenan 2015, 95):

fails to fully engage with experiences of lesbian and gay Christians (particularly those in the clergy), instead Church engagement continues to focus on lesbian and gay Christians as a problem, requiring silence, constraint and assimilation which further marginalizes and excludes.

The faster means of communications available now mean the similarities and differences of the Anglican communion are more audible and visible. Rather than spell the end of the communion, awareness of those differences may provoke an ultimately more constructive conversation, suggest McKinnon and Brittain (2015, 126):

A more positive possibility needs to be considered, at least briefly, and by way of conclusion. Globalization has undoubtedly contributed to the current tensions, making it impossible for church leaders in one part of the world to ignore the very different, but undoubtedly sincere, attempts to live and preach the gospel in very different contexts around the world. Comprehensiveness is much easier—though very much less real—where the different traditions can share the same tent without having to face up to the reality of those differences. The forces of globalization have now shrunk the world to the point where that is no longer possible; perhaps this means that now the Communion can begin to learn how to really live with its differences and disagreements. Seen in this light, it could be that this is not the crisis of the Anglican Communion after all, but the possibility of the Communion—the agony of an Anglican Communion in formation.

Competitive Cathedrals

Attending a conference in a UK cathedral city, I decided to pop into the cathedral for the early 9 a.m. service to gauge attendance. These are my field notes:

Announced at breakfast was off at 0845 to morning prayer where, I said to my colleagues as witnesses, my prediction was that there would be twenty-eight people. Walked in the open door and turned into the nave shocked by beauty of the light coming through rose window above altar, warming the sandstone pillars with a soft pink glow. Sign at end said morning prayer in quire. Thought for a few seconds—what's a quire? Reminded me of conversation with a Jewish colleague a few minutes earlier at breakfast. When I said I was going to the Cathedral he said, 'is it open? Can anyone go?' I had heaved a theatrical sigh and said, 'Do you know nothing of Christian churches? Of course you could go. Anyone can go'.

'But how will I know what to do?', he asked anxiously.

'You won't of course', I replied. 'That's how we keep people out'.

And so, yes, quire . . . I strolled down the nave to where I saw a tall man in black robes standing. 'Are you joining us for morning prayer?' he asked in a friendly voice. I nodded and said yes, I was hoping to (and wondered why I had suddenly adopted a conditional case, as if I was waiting for permission?) He nodded and motioned towards the choir stalls (ah! Quire!) 'We sit in here, where the books are,' he said.

My prediction about numbers was wrong. There were only four of us. After the service I chatted to the elderly women volunteering as guides and found that they had travelled quite a distance to come in, but enjoyed being there for, they said, its beauty.

On another occasion I visited Liverpool Cathedral and was told by our tour guide on the bus, and by the male volunteer who met us at the entrance, that it was big. It seemed everyone wanted to stress how big it was, as if that was something to commend the otherwise,

I thought, rather drab and unexceptional building, particularly in comparison to the Roman Catholic cathedral just up the road. There was a neon artwork above the door by Tracey Emin that said: 'I felt you and I knew you loved me.' It seemed strikingly beautiful but, I gathered from discussion with others and media reports, it was not universally liked. As I wandered around the cathedral talking to volunteers and visitors, I was told by one regular visitor that she liked the Emin piece, but knew that many older people had not at first. I learned that the cathedral had 240 volunteers, mostly over sixty, about half and half men and women. Men and women do different things, I was told: 'men mostly guarding and the ladies doing the flowers. of course'.

Given my proximity to Canterbury Cathedral through my work at the nearby University of Kent, I was able to attend services frequently, including Sundays, and was surprised to find a regular core of people who travelled in from other areas just to attend church on a Sunday. Davie suggested (2012) that cathedrals offer a range of attractions for regular worshippers, such as history and aesthetics, and also the possibility of being more anonymous. If they are doing that, I reflected to one person, that must mean there are fewer people attending the smaller, more local churches. He said he supposed so, but he enjoyed coming for the music and the beauty of the building. At a different cathedral, I raised this point with one of the priests, and he said it was probably true. Until only a few years ago the cathedral respected its place as more of a place of history and ceremony and tried to stay away from behaving like a parish church. But now, he, continued, with falling numbers of regular worshippers everywhere, the cathedral was moving into that territory. I asked him if this meant that with a shrinking market, everyone was doing what they could to survive.

He nodded. 'Gloves off?' I suggested. 'Yes,' he replied. 'Gloves off.'

Sustaining a small parish church with only a few regulars will require a lot of language classes, knitting groups, and concerts.

THEORIES OF POWER AND GENDER REVISITED

Finally, there are two main areas of social theory I will discuss as a result of my research. Power and resistance are key theoretical issues developed here. Generation A represents a form of 'pew power' drawn from daily presence and accountability, rather than institutional hierarchy. And yet, as Lukes (2005) noted about power, their influence in setting agendas and framing discussions has been quietly effective. Their roles in slowing progress towards Synod approval of women priests and bishops is one example.

The systemisation of labour through bureaucratization and rationalization is seen here as critical to sustaining Generation A's power, religiosity, and the life of the church. It is a counter-intuitive claim that rules, regulations, and other forms of bureaucracy benefit those who depend on informal and less recognized forms of power (see Ferguson 1984), and therefore Generation A's informal 'pew power' was quietly effective. Other feminists may disagree, which is exactly my point: it was informal female power within a masculine-dominated structure that appealed to Generation A. An over-emphasis on 'spirituality' and unregulated forms of religiosity in some congregations were resisted for that reason. What counts as power through ritual and labour has been underdeveloped in the literature thus far in emphasizing the public rather than private and preparative. My early work on a women's prayer group (Day 2005) demonstrated how the gendered nature of ritual could be better understood; this current work develops that further.

Interwoven with ideas about power are theories about gender, a topic I summarized in Chapter 2, developed in relation to prayer in Chapter 5, and will return to here. Problematic is the idea being promoted that women are more religious than men, in spite of evidence to the contrary. As reviewed above, the differences only apply when analysed through social surveys that show some differences amongst Christians in Euro-American countries, and even then, the main difference relates to private prayer. I analysed that in Chapter 5 to show that it is women's labour, not religiosity, that explains such a difference.

Every world religion is headed by a man, apart from the Church of England, currently headed by a woman and only because she is the monarch. All Catholic priests and most Protestant ones are men: the possibility of a woman being a priest or a bishop has been tearing the Anglican Communion apart. Most imams and rabbis are men. Monks of every religious persuasion, from Buddhist to Christian, are men; nuns are fewer in number and less institutionally and civically powerful. Saviours and prophets are men. Most gods, and certainly the most powerful, are men. Almost all religious terrorists are men.

Religious rituals are performed by men. Jay (1992) argues that sacrifice is linked to gender in most traditions, securing the lineage of the male as dominant. In Christianity, the male lineage extends from Christ, through his apostle and first pope, Peter, to the present day. Her more general observations about the role of the Eucharist would hold true for the Anglican Communion as well, where the priest does not act as an ordinary man but as a mediator between God and people, reflecting other hierarchies such as God and nature, natural and supernatural.

And yet, within the sociology of religion, there persists a theory at odds with the evidence: women, we are told, are more religious than men. Such counterintuitive, startling conclusions must be based on some kind of evidence, however thin. Not only is there the historical, structural issue of who is allowed to be most powerful: men continue to occupy those positions and will fight hard to retain them. But, there is also the more pervasive, discursive issue: religious power is not only important to men in terms of their sitting in the most powerful positions, but the nature itself of what is considered to be correct religious practice and religious thought is determined by men. Further, theories about gender and religion overwhelmingly theorize women's apparent religiosity without theorizing men's.

Could the main theories about women and religion apply equally to men, and, if not, what kind of theories would be necessary to explain an overwhelmingly male desire for creating and maintaining positions of religious power? One theory that demonstrates how important it is to get the question right is 'risk theory'. I introduced it briefly in Chapter 2 but now, with the benefit of ethnographic research, I will return to it. That theory broadly runs thus: it is riskier to be an atheist than a religious believer; men engage in riskier behaviours than women; men therefore have a higher 'risk preference than women'; that explains why there are more male than female atheists. It is a widely accepted theory thought by some (see, for example, Collett and Lizardo 2009) to be the most compelling explanation of gender differences. Cornwall (2009, 252) summarized the response to it from the perspective of gender scholarship and found it, unsurprisingly, wanting, primarily because is ignored the fact that both risk and religiosity are gendered and not universal constructs.

In the paper that provoked the discussion about risk preference and religiosity, Miller and Hoffmann (1995) begin by saying that studies consistently show that women are more religious than men, described in terms of church attendance, self-identification, frequency of prayer, and Bible study. They say (Miller and Hoffmann 1995, 63–4) that although there is little empirical research to try and explain those results, the two main explanations are that females are socialized into the sorts of behaviours that are also reflected by religions, such as being submissive and obedient, and that they are structurally located in society to bring up children and therefore have more leisure time to bring up children. My experience with Generation A would not corroborate the first explanation: there was little I observed in them that conformed to ideas of submission and passivity. These were, sometimes uncomfortably so, strong, assertive, and forthright women. Many of them had also had professional careers, and while those who had children typically took time off paid work when the children were young, they tended to return to work later in their lives. In neither time period did they have more 'leisure time', as studies by Hochschild and Machung (1990) demonstrate. Women work both inside and outside the home.

The most important flaws with Miller and Hoffman's research are its two main assumptions. The first premise is that it is less risky to believe in God than not; the second is their narrow view of what constitutes 'risk'. Their foundational assumption about God-belief is partly based on the classic 'Pascal's wager' anecdote: there is no risk in wagering that God exists because if he does, the believer gains the benefits and if he does not, then there is no harm done. Believing that God does not exist is riskier because if he does, then the wager goes badly wrong. While Pascal's wager may be an entertaining pastime in playful school debates, it is not taken seriously in social science, anthropology, or in theology. Social scientists know that people do not suddenly wake up one day and decide to become religious, or not, on the basis of a wager. More influential forces, such as socialization, relationships, and cultural context are involved. Anthropologists know that 'belief' is a complex matter and rarely reduced to the propositional, philosophical state assumed by Pascal. In my previous work on belief, for example, (see Day 2011 [2013] and Day 2013f), I found that the importance of relationships, both with human and non-human others, fashioned beliefs which are themselves intellectual, emotional, and embodied. Theologians also assume that belief is more complex, rarely intellectual alone, and often fluctuates with doubt. If one, however, pushes the Miller–Hoffman argument even further, it would have to become evident exactly what sort of God is being discussed. Presumably, a benign, hands-off creator who did not care much about how people lived their daily lives could be blithely ignored, but people who believe in more demanding gods may be at high risk of being punished for failure. Keeping a kosher kitchen or observance of menstrual cycles is a high-risk activity; the penalty for getting those wrong may be, literally, punishment by death.

The second, and more gendered problem is what they mean by 'risk'. Miller and Hoffman assume risk-takers are those who engage in crime, speeding in cars, drug-taking, and dangerous sports. This is because, they explain, criminals must have some awareness that they could be caught, and therefore those who commit crimes have a higher tolerance of risk. That is a psychologically narrow, individualized view of crime that may have pervaded in certain circles but does not reflect a more critical criminology that situates criminals within social structures amongst a variety of social, familial, economic, and political factors that induce criminality. The Miller–Hoffman (1995) errors became compounded a few years later when Miller collaborated with Stark (Miller and Stark 2002) to reinforce the ideas about risk, religion, and gender with a biological explanation. Their claim was that a male preference for risk was fuelled by hormones, particularly testosterone. The argument that testosterone is mainly responsible for male violence, criminality, and other apparently essentially masculine attributes has been widely discredited for at least two decades in favour of more socio-economic explanations.

Further, and possibly most importantly, they ignore the kinds of risks women take more often than men, even when they may claim to be risk averse. Many of the women I met during my research had risked their personal, financial security by giving up jobs when their babies were born. Being economically dependent on another person is a high-risk activity few men perform. The act of childbirth itself is a risky activity and statistically more likely to kill a woman than riding a motorbike. Many other women I met had risked their careers by taking large amounts of time off work to care for elderly relatives. One woman had been in an abusive relationship where her own life had been at risk; as statistics show that an average of seven women every month in the UK are killed by their partners or ex-partners, it seems being in a relationship is far more dangerous for women than men, and yet women continue to take those risks.

Ultimately, the tendency for predominantly male sociologists to pursue the idea that women are universally and ahistorically more religious than men continues a tendency long observed by feminists and politically critical thinkers to cement the idea that women are natural producers of subordinate femininity (Ortner 1995) linked to the 'natural' domestic, 'private' sphere. As Marx and Engels convincingly argued together and separately (Marx and Engels 1948; Engels 1972) by drawing largely on anthropological research of hunter-gatherer societies, the domination of women by men is a class-based phenomenon that allows men to control production and property. They would see religion as just another institution that masks inequalities and strengthens binaries.

Whatever the theory, and it is undoubtedly under construction, it seems certain that successive generations of women in Euro-American countries will continue to be less religious than Generation A. Redfern and Aune (2010) found from their survey of 1,265 women in their twenties and thirties who identified as 'third-wave' feminists that they were less religious and more spiritual than the general population. The authors concluded that this was due to the effects of a more secularized society.

GAZING AT GHOSTS

Towards the end of my research I chatted to the sacristan who had shown me the detail of how to prepare for Holy Communion. She said she has always sat at the back to be able to count the number of communicants for the priest. As she sits there now, she told me, she notices all the empty places of the people who used to sit there: 'They're all dead now.' I could see what she meant. The empty places will remain empty. They would never be filled by the regular church 'family' who knew who sat where and would never move from their own regular spots. Nor would the places be filled with newcomers, as new people don't come. Gazing across the pews at those spaces was like looking at a cemetery with the tombstones inverted. In only the two years I had visited, I could recognize those spaces and recall what the deceased looked like. I understood then what it must be like for her, sitting at the back, week after week, gazing at ghosts.

I also wonder who will be looking out for each other. Recalling my experience described earlier of overhearing people at Morning Prayer saying they would check up on a woman who was absent, I suggest this is one reason for a recent finding that women who attend church more than once a week live longer.[24] A main reason for that, I suggest, is that such regulars are part of a small, tightly bound group who look out for each other: if someone falls one morning stepping out of the bath, she will not be lying there for days slowly dying because another woman will be around her place seeing why she has gone missing. There is some chance that in some churches the priest would recognize such things, but as most priests these days have multiple churches to attend, the occasional missing elderly woman may go unnoticed. As Coleman et al. argued (2016, 588): 'people who are part of religious congregations tend to have larger nonkin networks than those who are not, which in turn increases an older person's potential avenues to support'.

Apart from the empty pew places to remind people of the dead, there will be material objects to remind people of who once belonged. For example, in some churches there are kneelers that were created by Generation A women in the era when worshippers, following the Book of Common Prayer, actually kneeled. I discussed their making with one woman who had been responsible for at least two hundred. I said it must have been difficult work, to stitch the chosen image of, variously, a cross or a landscape, and words of remembrance. She laughed and said no, it wasn't: they came as packs from a supplier and all she had to do was follow the overlaid pattern. Nevertheless, they took time.

In fact, I was thinking about her the other day in a restaurant when I noticed a dessert option of 'sponge pudding'. I recalled when we had gone out for lunch to celebrate her ninety-second birthday, and ordered steamed sponge pudding. When it arrived we both looked at it in horror: thick orange slabs on a plate. She shook her head. A sponge pudding should be light and airy. It went back to the kitchen. Perhaps Generation A's demise is spawning a wave of nostalgia, through baking television shows such as, in the UK, *The Great British Bake-Off*. Mary Berry is a member of Generation A, born in 1935, who judges contestants' results of her demands: lemon drizzle cakes, scones, meringues, and the like all must be cooked to perfection. In one show, the final results were displayed, according to the announcer, 'on the altar of Mary Berry'.

[24] <http://www.huffingtonpost.com/entry/women-who-go-to-church-live-longer-harvard-study-finds_us_573b2ab6e4b060aa781b45e9>, last accessed 27.5.2016.

Newsweek blogger Michelle Goldberg writes about what she sees as a trend towards 'the new domesticity', where some women are trying to recover lost arts of knitting, bread-baking and canning:[25]

> It's easy to mock the twee, hyperlocal, handmade aesthetic that dominates fashionable enclaves in places like Brooklyn and Portland, Oregon. But in her new book, *Homeward Bound: Why Women Are Embracing the New Domesticity*,[26] Emily Matchar makes a convincing argument that it actually represents a generational change in values born of a deep disaffection with the modern workplace, one with real implications for gender equality. Inasmuch as this new domesticity represents a desire to live more sustainably and authentically, it's wholly laudable, if also a bit precious. But a return to home and hearth also has a way of reinforcing traditional gender roles, even if everyone involved says she's only following her heart.

No mention is made amongst the recipes for a return to regular church attendance. As much as Generation A were the producers of coronation chicken and light sponges, their reason for being at church ran deeper, as I have described in this book, to reflect sacred values of church, country, home, and family. I often wondered if they wanted the church to survive beyond them, and I think the answer is a qualified 'yes'—survive, but not at any cost. It would depend on what sort of church. These women were not going to give up their fight for tradition lightly. They were not appeasers; they were not turncoats.

In her chapter on the Church representing an institution related to 'vicarious religion', Davie (2007) argued that even non-attenders sometimes turned to the church for important, often life-related reasons. As Generation A departs and more churches close, this casual, informal relationship between a secular population and a religious space may be disrupted. As one female priest, Deborah, told me: sometimes, non-church attending people 'ring me out of the blue to visit their elderly aunt or sister or mother'. So she goes 'wearing my collar', which seems to help. No one she visits then decides to attend church. She also hosts a lunch club for elderly people, and finds that most who attend are over eighty, but so are the volunteers. She reflects on earlier years when churches remained

---

[25] <http://europe.newsweek.com/urban-mamas-get-crafty-63219?rm=eu>, last accessed 3.4.2016.
[26] Matchar 2013.

open during the week, thanks to the labour of Generation A. This does not occur so much any longer, she says, partly because people recognize the safety issues and partly because there simply are not the older women to do the job. I think about the people I grew to know who were lonely, semi-homeless, or bereaved. Where will they go for a friendly face, a biscuit, and a cup of tea? That unusual social space of nearly unconditional welcome will be shut.

Not all churches will close, but the people inhabiting churches will be fewer and different. Wink and Dillon's (2003) longitudinal study is unique in studying people born in the 1920s through their lives into late adulthood. They found that religious identity is stable over time, but also that religious participation is an important factor for well-being.[27] Wink and Dillon (2003, 922) wrote that:

> religiousness is more closely related to a communal mode of functioning characterized by a focus on participation in a mutual, interpersonal reality, whereas spirituality is more closely associated with an agentic mode of functioning characterized by an emphasis on asserting, protecting and expanding the self [. . .].

As the rate of Generational A demise continues, there will be fewer religious people, and therefore fewer creating a religious 'communal mode of functioning'.

As I finished the project a newspaper item caught my eye because I thought the writer was describing the future Anglican Church:

> what's left is a miscellany of types: the very old, the very loyal, the absolute bricks, the rather lonely, the slightly embarrassed guest and . . . yes, it has to be said, a goodly clutch of ideological obsessives.

Sounded familiar, but in fact it was Matthew Parris on the demise of the Conservative Party as we know it.[28]

It was not an attractive vision. I prefer to imagine a different kind of church congregation, possibly one of gay men enjoying a cappuccino with happy knitters and groups of immigrants learning English. In either case, there will not be a huge societal shift as a result of their passing. That shift has, arguably, already occurred. A survey of Americans

---

[27] Collins et al. (2016) discuss how four Australian parishes reversed decay and decline through adopting more democratic, participative approaches in their congregations. It was, they argued, a top-down, hierarchical, male-dominated model that had suppressed church activity and growth.

[28] *The Times*, 6.7.2013, p. 21.

on their perceptions of religious institutions' role in solving social problems revealed a decreasing number feel the institutions have, or should have, any impact.[29]

There will, nonetheless, be some people who will miss the Generation A laywomen, but they will not be the kinds of people who grab headlines: a few priests sorry that their noon Wednesday communion service has closed for good; an occasional regular gazing sadly at empty pews; a Sleeping Drunk Man who will not find an open door and a cup of tea when he awakes. But they, I suggest, tend not to be amongst those people who 'count'.

[29] <http://www.pewresearch.org/fact-tank/2016/07/18/are-churches-key-to-solving-social-problems-fewer-americans-now-thinkso/?utm_content=buffer8b8ec&utm_medium=social&utm_source=twitter.com&utm_campaign=buffer>, last accessed 31.8.2016.

Bibliography

Adkins, Lisa and Beverley Skeggs. 2005. *Feminism after Bourdieu*. Oxford: Wiley-Blackwell.

Ammerman, Nancy. T. 1997. 'Golden Rule Christianity: Lived Religion in the American Mainstream'. In *Lived Religion in America*, ed. David Hall, 196–216. Princeton, NJ: Princeton University Press.

Ammerman, Nancy T. 2007. *Everyday Religion: Observing Modern Religious Lives*. Oxford and New York: Oxford University Press.

Ammerman, Nancy T. 2014. *Sacred Stories, Spiritual Tribes: Finding Religion in Everyday Life*. New York: Oxford University Press.

Anderson, Benedict. 1991. *Imagined Communities: Reflections on the Origin and Spread of Nationalism*. Revised edn. London and New York: Verso.

Anttonen, Veikko. 2000. 'Sacred'. In *Guide to the Study of Religion*, ed. Willi Braun and Russell T. McCutcheon. London: Cassell, 271–82.

Argyle, Michael and Benjamin Beit-Hallahmi. 1975. 'The Social Psychology of Religion.... and Violence'. *Israeli Annals of Psychiatry and Related Disciplines* 10: 71–7.

Asad, Talal. 1993. *Genealogies of Religion: Discipline and Reasons of Power in Christianity and Islam*. Baltimore, MD: Johns Hopkins University Press.

Asad, Talal. 2003. *Formations of the Secular*. Stanford, CA: Stanford University Press.

Ashworth, Jacinta and Ian Farthing. 2007. *Churchgoing in the UK*. Teddington: Tearfund.

Atkinson, Paul, Amanda Coffey, and Sara Delamont. 2003. *Key Themes in Qualitative Research: Continuities and Change*. Walnut Creek, CA: Alta Mira Press.

Aune, Kristin, Sonya Sharma, and Giselle Vincett (eds.). 2008. *Women and Religion in the West: Challenging Secularization*. Aldershot: Ashgate.

Austin, John L. 1962. *How To Do Things With Words*. Oxford: Clarendon.

Back, Les. 2015. 'Why Everyday Life Matters: Class, Community and Making Life Livable'. *Sociology* 49 (5): 820–36.

Bäckström, Anders and Grace Davie, with Ninna Edgardh and Per Pettersson. 2011. *Welfare and Religion in 21st Century Europe: Volume 2: Gendered, Religious and Social Change*. Farnham: Ashgate.

Baden-Powell, Robert. 2004. *Scouting for Boys*. Oxford: Oxford University Press.

Baker, Joseph. 2008. 'An Investigation of the Sociological Patterns of Prayer: Frequency and Content'. *Sociology of Religion* 69: 169–85.

Ball, Richard A., Francis T. Cullen, and Robert Lilly. 2011. *Criminological Theory: Context and Consequences* (5th edn). Thousand Oaks, CA: Sage.

Bam, Brigalia. 1998. 'All about Eve: Woman of Africa'. In *Anglicanism: A Global Communion*, ed. Andrew Wingate, Kevin Ward, Carrie Pemberton, and Wilson Sitshebo. London: Mowbray, 347–53.

Barth, Fredrik. 1969. *Ethnic Groups and Boundaries*. Bergen: Universitetsforlaget.

Bauman, Zygmunt.1992. *Intimations of Postmodernity*. London: Routledge.

Baumann, Gerd. 1995. 'Managing a Polyethnic Milieu: Kinship and Interaction in a London Suburb'. *Journal of the Royal Anthropological Institute* 1 (4): 725–41.

Bays, Patricia. 2012. *This Anglican Church of Ours*. Kelowna, BC: Wood Lake.

Beaman, Lori G. and Peter Beyer. 2015. 'Researching the Spiritual but not Religious'. In *Social Identities between the Sacred and the Secular*, ed. Abby Day, Giselle Vincett, and Christopher R. Cotter. Aldershot: Ashgate, 127–44.

Beaudoin, Tom. 1998. *Virtual Faith: The Irreverent Spiritual Quest of Generation X*. San Francisco, CA: Jossey-Bass.

Becker, Henck A. 1992. *Dynamics of Cohort and Generations Research*. Utrecht: Thesis Publishers.

Becker, Henck A. and Piet L. J. Hermkens. 1993. *Solidarity of Generations: Demographic, Economic and Social Change and its Consequences*. Utrecht: Thesis Publishers.

Becker, Howard S. 1973. *Outsiders: Studies in the Sociology of Deviance*. New York: Free Press.

Beckford, James. 2003. *Social Theory and Religion*. Cambridge: Cambridge University Press.

Beit-Hallahmi, Benjamin and Michael Argyle. 1997. *The Psychology of Religious Behaviour, Belief and Experience*. London: Routledge.

Bender, Courtney. 2010. *The New Metaphysicals: Spirituality and the American Religious Imagination*. Chicago: University of Chicago Press.

Bengtson, Vernon L. 2001. 'Beyond the Nuclear Family: The Increasing Importance of Multigenerational Bonds'. *Journal of Marriage and Family* 63: 1–16.

Bengtson, Vernon. L., Timothy J. Biblarz, and Robert E. L. Roberts. 2002. *How Families Still Matter: A Longitudinal Study of Youth in Two Generations*. Cambridge: Cambridge University Press.

Bengtson, Vernon with Norella M. Putney and Susan C. Harris. 2013. *Families and Faith. How Religion is Passed Down Across Generations*. New York: Oxford University Press.

Bennett, John, W. 1957. 'From Generation to Generation: Age Groups and Social Structure. S. N. Eisenstadt'. *American Anthropologist* 59 (4): 720–2.

Benson, Michaela and Emma Jackson. 2013. 'Place-Making and Place Maintenance: Practices of Place and Belonging among the Middle Classes'. *Sociology* 47 (4): 793–809.

Berger, Peter and Thomas Luckmann. 1966. *The Social Construction of Reality: A Treatise in the Sociology of Knowledge*. Garden City, NY: Anchor Books.

Bergler, Thomas E. 2012. *The Juvenilization of American Christianity*. Grand Rapids, MI: William B. Eerdmans.

Bielo, James S. 2015. *Anthropology of Religion: The Basics*. Abingdon and New York: Routledge.

Biggs, Simon. 2007. 'Thinking About Generations: Conceptual Positions and Policy Implications'. *Journal of Social Issues* 63 (4): 695–711.

Billig, Michael. 1995. *Banal Nationalism*. London: Sage.

Blackwell, Brenda S., Christine S. Sellers, and Sheila M. Schlaupitz. 2002. 'A Power-Control Theory of Vulnerability to Crime and Adolescent Role Exits-Revisited'. *Canadian Review of Sociology & Anthropology* 39 (2): 199–218.

Bologh, Roslyn W. 1990. *Love or Greatness? Max Weber and Masculine Thinking—A Feminist Inquiry*. London and Boston, MA: Unwin Hyman.

Bourdieu, Pierre. 1984. *Distinction*. London: Routledge.

Bourdieu, Pierre. 1985. 'The Forms of Capital'. In *Handbook of Theory and Research for the Sociology of Education*, ed. John G. Richardson. New York: Greenwood, 241–58.

Bowie, Fiona. 2006. *The Anthropology of Religion*. Oxford: Blackwell.

Bradley, Harriet. 1995. *Fractured Identities: Changing Patterns of Inequality*. Cambridge: Polity Press.

Bradshaw, Matt and Christopher Ellison. 2008. 'Do Genetic Factors Influence Religious Life? Finding From Behavior Genetic Analysis of Twin Siblings'. *Journal for the Scientific Study of Religion* 47 (4): 529–44.

Bradshaw, Matt and Christopher Ellison. 2009. 'The Nature-Nurture Debate is Over and Both Sides Lost! Implications for Understanding Gender Differences in Religiosity'. *Journal for the Scientific Study of Religion* 48 (2): 241–51.

Brewer, John D. 2000. *Ethnography*. Buckingham: Open University Press.

Brierley, Peter. 2000. *The Tide is Running Out*. London: Christian Research.

Brierley, Peter. 2006. *Pulling out of the Nose Dive: A Contemporary Picture of Churchgoing; What the 2005 English Church Census Reveals*. London: Christian Research.

British Social Attitudes: the 25th Report. London: Sage.

Brown, Callum. 2000. *The Death of Christian Britain*. London: Routledge.

Brown, Callum. 2012. *Religion and the Demographic Revolution*. Woodbridge: Boydell Press.

Brown, Callum. 2015. 'How Anglicans Lose Religion: An Oral History of Becoming Secular'. In *Contemporary Issues in the Worldwide Anglican Communion: Powers and Pieties*, ed. Abby Day. Aldershot: Ashgate, 245–66.

Brown, Irene, Q. 1992. 'Women's Works of Devotion: Feasts, Fairs and Festivities'. In *Episcopal Women: Gender, Spirituality, and Commitment in an American Mainline Denomination*, ed. Catherine M. Prelinger. New York: Oxford University Press, 239–62.

Bruce, Steve. 1999. *Choice and Religion: A Critique of Rational Choice Theory*. Oxford: Oxford University Press.

Bruce, Steve. 2002. 'Praying Alone? Church-Going in Britain and the Putnam Thesis'. *Journal of Contemporary Religion* 17 (3): 317–28.

Buch, Elana D. and Karen M. Staller. 2014. 'The Feminist Practice of Ethnography'. In *Feminist Research Practice: A Primer 2nd edition*, ed. Sharlene Nagy Hesse-Biber. Thousand Oaks, CA, London, and New Delhi: Sage Publications, 107–44.

Buchanan, Constance H. 1992. 'The Anthropology of Vitality and Decline: The Episcopal Church in a Changing Society'. In *Episcopal Women: Gender, Spirituality, and Commitment in an American Mainline Denomination*, ed. Catherine M. Prelinger. New York: Oxford University Press, 310–29.

Budgeon, Shelley. 2011. *Third Wave Feminism and the Politics of Gender in Late Modernity*. Basingstoke: Palgrave Macmillan.

Burley, Mikel. 2012. *Contemplating Religious Forms of Life: Wittgenstein and D.Z. Phillips*. New York: Bloomsbury Publishing.

Burnett, Judith. 2003. 'Let Me Entertain You: Researching the "Thirtysomething" Generation'. *Sociological Research Online* 8: 4.

Buss, Allan R. 1974. 'Generational Analysis: Description, Explanation and Theory'. *Journal of Social Issues* 30 (2): 55–72.

Butler, Judith. 1990. *Gender Trouble*. New York: Routledge.

Butler, Judith. 1993. *Bodies That Matter: on the Discursive Limits of 'Sex'*. New York and London: Routledge.

Calhoun, Craig. 1993. 'Habitus, Field, and Capital: The Question of Historical Specificity'. In *Bourdieu: Critical Perspectives*, ed. Craig Calhoun, Edward LiPuma, and Moishe Postone. Cambridge: Polity Press, 61–88.

Cameron, Helen. 2005. *Studying Local Churches: A Handbook*. London: SCM.

Cannell, Fenella. 2005. 'The Christianity of Anthropology'. *Journal of the Royal Anthropological Institute* 11 (2): 191–400.

Cannell, Fenella (ed.). 2007. *The Anthropology of Christianity*. Durham, NC and London: Duke University Press.

Carsten, J. 2004. *After Kinship*. Cambridge: Cambridge University Press.

Carsten, J. (ed.). 2007. *Ghosts of Memory: Essays on Remembrance and Relatedness*. Oxford: Blackwell.

Castells, Manuel. 2012. *Networks of Outrage and Hope: Social Movements in the Internet Age.* Cambridge: Polity.

Chaves, Mark. 1997. *Ordaining Women: Culture and Conflict in Religious Organizations.* Cambridge, MA: Harvard University Press.

Cohen, Anthony P. 1982. *Belonging: Identity and Social Organization in British Rural Cultures.* Manchester: Manchester University Press.

Cohen, Anthony P. 1985. *The Symbolic Construction of Community.* London: Routledge.

Cohen, Stan. 1972. *Folk Devils and Moral Panics: The Creation of the Mods and Rockers.* London: Macgibbon and Kee.

Coleman, Peter G., Elisabeth Schröder-Butterfill, and John H. S. Preadbury. 2016. 'Religion, Spirituality, and Aging'. In *Handbook of Theories of Aging*, 3rd edn, ed. Vern L. Bengtson and Richard A. Settersten, Jr. New York: Springer, 577–98.

Coleman, Simon. 2000. *The Globalisation of Charismatic Christianity: Spreading the Gospel of Prosperity.* Cambridge: Cambridge University Press.

Coleman, Simon. 2013. 'Ritual Remains: Studying Contemporary Pilgrimage'. In *Companion to the Anthropology of Religion*, ed. Janice Boddy and Michael Lambek. Oxford: Wiley-Blackwell, 294–308.

Coleman, Simon. 2015. 'Locating the Church: On Corridors and Shadows in the Study of Anglicanism' In *Contemporary Issues in the Worldwide Anglican Communion: Powers and Pieties*, ed. Abby Day. Farnham: Ashgate, 213–28.

Coleman, Simon and Peter Collins (eds.). 2006. *Locating the Field: Space, Place and Context in Anthropology.* Oxford and New York: Berg.

Coleman, Simon and John Elsner. 1998. 'Performing Pilgrimage: Walsingham and the Ritual Construction of Irony'. In *Ritual, Performance, Media*, ed. Felicia Hughes-Freeland. London: Routledge, 46–65.

Coleman, Simon and Pauline von Hellermann. 2011. 'Introduction: Queries, Collaborations, Calibrations.' In *Multi-sited Ethnography: Problems and Possibilities in the Translocation of Research Methods*, ed. Simon Coleman and Pauline von Hellermann. New York: Routledge, 1–15.

Collett, Jessica L. and Omar Lizardo. 2009. 'A Power-Control Theory of Gender and Religiosity'. *Journal for the Scientific Study of Religion* 48 (2): 213–31.

Collins, James, Helen Collins, and Douglas Ezzy. 2016. *Reinventing Church: Stories of Hope from Four Anglican Parishes.* Northcote: Morning Star Publishing.

Collins, Peter. 2013. 'Acute Ambiguity: Towards a Heterotopology of Hospital Chaplaincy'. In *Social Identities Between the Sacred and the Secular*, ed. Abby Day, Giselle Vincett, and Christopher R. Cotter. Aldershot: Ashgate, 39–60.

Collins, Peter. 2015. 'An Analysis of Hospital Chapel Prayer Requests'. In *A Sociology of Prayer*, ed. Giuseppe Giordan and Linda Woodhead. Farnham and Burlington, VT: Ashgate, 191–212.

Collins-Mayo, Sylvia. 2008. 'Young People's Spirituality and the Meaning of Prayer'. In *Religion and the Individual*, ed. Abby Day. Farnham: Ashgate, 33–45.

Connerton, Paul. 1989. *How Societies Remember*. Cambridge: Cambridge University Press.

Connerton, Paul. 2009. *How Modernity Forgets*. Cambridge and New York: Cambridge University Press.

Cook, Hera. 2004. *The Long Sexual Revolution: English Women, Sex and Contraception 1800–1975*. Oxford: Oxford University Press.

Copen, Casey E. and Merril Silverstein. 2008. 'The Transmission of Religious Beliefs Across Generations: Do Grandparents Matter?'. *Journal of Comparative Family Studies* 38 (4): 59–74.

Cornman, John M. and Eric R. Kingston. 1996. 'Trends, Issues, Perspectives, and Values for the Aging of the Baby Boom Cohorts'. *The Gerontologist* 36 (1): 15–26.

Cornwall, Marie. 2009. 'Reifying Sex Difference Isn't the Answer: Gendering Processes, Risk, and Religiosity'. *Journal For The Scientific Study of Religion* 48 (2): 252–5.

Corsten, Michael. 1999. 'The Time of Generations'. *Time and Society* 8 (2): 249–72.

Coupland, Douglas. 1991. *Generation X: Tales for an Accelerated Culture*. New York, St Martin's Press.

Crompton, Rosemary. 2008. *Class and Stratification*, 3rd edn. Cambridge: Polity Press.

Daly, Mary. 1973. *Beyond God the Father: Toward a Philosophy of Women's Liberation*. Boston, MA: Beacon Press.

Danely, Jason and Caitrin Lynch. 2013. 'Transitions and Transformations: Paradigms, Perspectives, and Possibilities'. In *Transitions and Transformations: Cultural Perspectives on Aging and the Life Course*, ed. Caitrin Lynch and Jason Danely. New York: Berghahn, 3–20.

Davidson, James D. and Ralph E. Pyle. 2011. *Ranking Faiths: Religious Stratification in America*. Plymouth: Rowman and Littlefield.

Davie, Grace. 1990. '"An Ordinary God": The Paradox of Religion in Contemporary Britain'. *The British Journal of Sociology* 41 (3): 395–421.

Davie, Grace. 1994. *Religion in Britain since 1945: Believing without Belonging*. Oxford: Blackwell.

Davie, Grace. 2000. *Religion in Modern Europe: A Memory Mutates*. Oxford: Oxford University Press.

Davie, Grace. 2002. *Europe: The Exceptional Case*. London: Darton, Longman and Todd.

Davie, Grace. 2007. 'Vicarious Religion: A Methodological Challenge'. In *Everyday Religion: Observing Modern Religious Lives*, ed. Nancy T. Ammerman. Oxford and New York: Oxford University Press, 21–36.

Davie, Grace. 2012. 'A Short Afterword: Thinking Spatially About Religion'. *Culture and Religion* 13 (4): 485–9.

Davie, Grace. 2013. *Sociology of Religion*, 2nd edn. Thousand Oaks, CA, London, New Delhi, and Singapore: Sage Publications.

Day, Abby. 2005. 'Doing Theodicy: An Empirical Study of a Women's Prayer Group'. *Journal of Contemporary Religion* 20 (3): 343–56.

Day, Abby. 2006. *Believing in Belonging: A Case Study from Yorkshire*. PhD thesis, Lancaster University, Lancaster.

Day, Abby (ed.). 2008. *Religion and the Individual*. Aldershot: Ashgate.

Day, Abby. 2008. 'Wilfully Disempowered: A Gendered Response to a Fallen World'. *European Journal of Women's Studies* 15 (3): 261–76.

Day, Abby. 2009a. 'Believing in Belonging: An Ethnography of Young People's Constructions of Belief'. *Culture and Religion* 10 (3): 263–78.

Day, Abby. 2009b. 'Researching Belief Without Asking Religious Questions'. *Fieldwork in Religion* 4 (1): 89–106.

Day, Abby. 2010. 'Believing in Belonging: An Exploration of Young People's Social Contexts and Constructions of Belief'. In *Religion and Youth*, ed. Sylvia Collins-Mayo and Pink Dandelion. Aldershot: Ashgate, 97–104.

Day, Abby. 2010. 'Propositions and Performativity: Relocating Belief to the Social'. *Culture and Religion* 11 (1): 9–30.

Day, Abby. 2011 [2013]. *Believing in Belonging: Belief and Social Identity in the Modern World*. Oxford: Oxford University Press.

Day, Abby. 2012a. Comment in 'An Author Meets His Critics: Around Manuel A. Vásquez's More Than Belief: A Materialist Theory of Religion'. *Religion and Society: Advances in Research* 3 (1): 185–202.

Day, Abby. 2012b. 'Extraordinary Relationality: Ancestor Veneration in late Euro-American Society'. *Nordic Journal of Religion and Society* 25 (2): 57–69.

Day, Abby. 2012c. 'Post-Secular Identities: Non-Religious Christians'. In *Scripta Donneriani Aboensis*. Turku: Donner Institute, Åbo University.

Day, Abby. 2013a. 'Euro-American Ethnic and Natal Christians: Believing in Belonging'. In *Social Identities Between the Sacred and the Secular*, ed. Abby Day, Giselle Vincett, and Christopher R. Cotter. Aldershot: Ashgate, 61–74.

Day, Abby. 2013b. 'Everyday Ghosts: a Matter of Believing in Belonging'. In *Ashgate Research Companion to Paranormal Culture*, ed. Sally Munt and Olu Jenzen. Farnham and Burlington, VT: Ashgate, 149–58.

Day, Abby. 2013c. 'Nominal Christian Adherence: Ethnic, Natal, Aspirational'. *Implicit Religion* 15 (4): 427–44.

Day, Abby. 2013d. 'The Problem of Generalizing Generation'. *Religion and Society: Advances in Research* 4 (1): 109–24.

Day, Abby. 2013e. 'Understanding the Work of Women in Religion'. In *The Faith Lives of Girls and Women*, ed. Nicola Slee, Fran Porter, and Anne Phillips. Aldershot: Ashgate, 39–50.

Day, Abby. 2013f. 'Varieties of Belief over Time: Reflections from a Longitudinal Study of Youth and Belief'. *Journal of Contemporary Religion* 28 (2): 277–93.

Day, Abby. 2014a. 'Generation A: The Dwindling Force'. *Church Times*, 2 February.

Day, Abby. 2014b. 'Book Review Symposium: Bruno Latour (translated by Julie Rose), Rejoicing: Or the Torments of Religious Speech'. *Sociology* 48 (2): 408–9.

Day, Abby. 2014c. 'Generation A: The Dwindling Force'. In *How Healthy is the CofE: the Church Times Health Check*, ed. Linda Woodhead, Malcolm Doney, and Dave Walker. London: Canterbury Press, 67–70.

Day, Abby (ed.). 2015a. *Contemporary Issues in the Worldwide Anglican Communion: Powers and Pieties*. Aldershot: Ashgate.

Day, Abby. 2015b. 'The Spirit of "Generation A": Older Laywomen in the Church'. *Modern Believing* 56 (3): 313–23.

Day, Abby. 2017 (forthcoming). 'Doing Qualitative Longitudinal Religious Research'. In *How to Research Religion: Putting Methods Into Practice*, ed. Linda Woodhead. Oxford: Oxford University Press.

Day, Abby and Simon Coleman. 2010. 'Broadening the Boundaries of Belief'. *Culture and Religion* 11 (1) [Special issue].

Day, Abby and Simon Coleman. 2012. 'Secularization'. In *Oxford Bibliographies Online: Anthropology*. New York: Oxford University Press.

Day, Abby and Lois Lee. 2014a. 'Making Sense of Surveys and Censuses: Issues in Religious Self-Identification: Introduction'. *Religion* 44 (3), 345–56.

Day, Abby and Lee, Lois (eds.). 2014b. 'Making Sense of Surveys and Censuses: Issues in Religious Self-Identification'. *Religion* [Special issue].

Day, Abby and Mia Lövheim (eds.). 2015. *Modernities, Memory and Mutations: Grace Davie and the Study of Religion*. Farnham: Ashgate.

Day, Abby and Gordon Lynch (eds.). 2013. 'Belief as Cultural Performance'. *Journal of Contemporary Religion*, 28.2 [Special issue].

Day, Abby and Ben Rogaly. 2014. 'Sacred Communities: Contestations and Connections'. *Journal of Contemporary Religion* 29 (1): 75–88.

Day, Abby, Giselle Vincett, and Christopher R. Cotter (eds.). 2013. *Social Identities Between the Sacred and the Secular*. Aldershot: Ashgate.

Day, Abby and David Voas. 2010. Guiding Paper: 'Recognizing Secular Christians: Toward an Unexcluded Middle in the Study of Religion'. *The Association of Religion Data Archives* <http://www.thearda.com/rrh/papers/guidingpapers.asp>.

Dean, Jonathan. 2010. *Rethinking Contemporary Feminist Politics*. Basingstoke: Palgrave Macmillan.

De Beauvoir, Simone. 1949. *The Second Sex*. London: Vintage.

De Certeau, Michel. 1984. *The Practice of Everyday Life*. Berkeley, Los Angeles, and London: University of California Press.

Della Porta, Donatella and Mario Diani. 2006. *Social Movements: An Introduction*. 2nd edn. Malden, MA: Blackwell.

Demerath III, Nicolas J. 1965. *Social Class in American Protestantism*. Chicago: Rand McNally & Co.

Demerath III, N. J. 2000. 'The Varieties of Sacred Experience: Finding the Sacred in a Secular Grove'. *Journal for the Scientific Study of Religion* 39 (1): 4–12.

Devine, Paula. 2013. 'Men, Women, and Religiosity in Northern Ireland: Testing the Theories'. *Journal of Contemporary Religion* 28 (3): 473–88.

Douglas, Mary. 1966. *Purity and Danger: An Analysis of Pollution and Taboo*. London: Routledge.

Douglas, Mary. 1973. *Natural Symbols: Explorations in Cosmology*. London: Barrie and Jenkins.

Douglas, Mary. 1975. 'Deciphering a Meal'. In *Implicit Meanings*, ed. Mary Douglas. London: Routledge, 249–75.

Douglas, Mary (ed.). 2004 [1970]. *Witchcraft Confessions and Accusations*. London: Routledge.

Durkheim, Emile. 1895 [1938]. *Rules of Sociological Method*, tr. S. A. Solovay and J. H. Mueller. New York: The Free Press.

Durkheim, Emile. 1915. *The Elementary Forms of the Religious Life*. London: George Allen and Unwin.

Durkheim, Emile. 1984 [1933]. *The Division of Labor in Society*. New York: The Free Press.

Durkheim, Emile and Marcel Mauss. 1902 [1963]. *Primitive Classification*. Translated from the French and edited with an introduction by Rodney Needham. London: Cohen.

Eaton, Heather. 2005. *Introducing Ecofeminist Theologies*. Sheffield: Sheffield Academic Press.

Eccles, Janet. 2008. 'Speaking Personally: Women Making Meaning through Subjectivised Belief'. In *Religion and the Individual*, ed. Abby Day. Aldershot: Ashgate, 19–32.

Eccles, Janet. 2012. 'The Religious and Non-Religious Commitments of Older Women in the UK: Towards a New Typology'. *Journal of Contemporary Religion* 27 (3): 469–84.

Edmunds, June and Bryan S. Turner. 2002. *Generations, Culture and Society*. Buckingham: Open University Press.

Eisenstadt, Shmuel N. 1956. *From Generation to Generation: Age Groups and Social Structure*. London: Routledge & Kegan Paul.

Elder, Glen H. Jr. 1974. *Children of the Great Depression: Social Change in Life Experience*. Chicago: Chicago University Press.

Eliade, Mircea. 1959. *The Sacred and the Profane: The Nature of Religion*. San Diego, CA: Harcourt Brace Jovanovich.

Engelke, Matthew. 2013. *God's Agents: Biblical Publicity in Contemporary England*. Berkeley, Los Angeles and London: University of California Press.

Engels, Friedrich. 1972. *The Origin of the Family, Private Property and the State in the Light of the Researches of Lewis H. Morgan*. New York: Lawrence & Wishart.

Erikson, Erik H. 1968. *Identity, Youth, and Crisis*. New York: Norton.

Evans-Pritchard, E. E. 1976 [1937]. *Witchcraft, Oracles, and Magic among the Azande*. Oxford: Clarendon Press.

Eyerman, Ruth and Bryan S. Turner. 1998. 'Outline of a Theory of Generations'. *European Journal of Social Theory* 1 (1): 91–106.

Ferguson, Kathy E. 1984. *The Feminist Case against Bureaucracy*. Philadelphia, PA: Temple University Press.

Fetterman, David. 2010. *Ethnography: Step-by-Step*, 3rd edn. Thousand Oaks, CA, London, New Delhi, and Singapore: Sage Publications.

Field, Clive D. 2014. 'Is the Bible Becoming a Closed Book? British Opinion Poll Evidence'. *Journal of Contemporary Religion* 29 (3): 503–28.

Finke, Roger and Rodney Stark. 1997. *The Churching of America 1776–1990: Winners and Losers in our Religious Economy*. New Brunswick: Rutgers.

Fiorenza, Elisabeth S. (ed.) 1996. *The Power of Naming: A Concilium Reader in Feminist Liberation Theology*. Maryknoll, NY: Orbis Books and London: SCM Press.

Flere, Sergej. 2007. 'Gender and Religious Orientation'. *Social Compass* 54 (2): 239–53.

Flory, Richard W. and Donald E. Miller (eds.). 2000. *GenX Religion*. London and New York: Routledge.

Fortes, Meyer. 1987. 'Ancestor Worship in Africa'. In *Religion, Morality and the Person: Essays on Tallensi Religion*, ed. Jack Goody. Cambridge: Cambridge University Press, 66–83.

Fortier, Anne-Marie. 2000. *Migrant Belongings, Memory, Space, Identity*. Oxford: Berg.

Foucault, Michel. 1987. 'The Ethic of Care for the Self as a Practice of Freedom: An Interview with Michel Foucault on January 20, 1984'. Raúl Fornet-Batancourt, Helmut Becker, Alfredo Gomez Müller, and J. D. Gauthier in *Philosophy & Social Criticism* 12: 112–31.

Foucault, Michel. 1997. *Discipline and Punishment: The Birth of the Prison*, trans. Alan Sheridan. London: Allen Books.

Foucault, Michel, Luther H. Martin, Huck Gutman, and Patrick H. Hutton. 1988. *Technologies of the Self: A Seminar with Michel Foucault*. Amherst, MA: University of Massachusetts Press.

Fox, Kate. 2004. *Watching the English: The Hidden Rules of English Behaviour*. London: Hodder.

Francis, Leslie J. 1997. 'The Psychology of Gender Differences in Religion: A Review of Empirical Research'. *Religion* 27 (1): 81–96.

Francis, Leslie J. and Gemma Penny. 2015. 'Belonging without Practising: Exploring the Religious, Social and Personal Significance of Anglican Identities among Adolescent Males'. In *Contemporary Issues in the Worldwide Anglican Communion: Powers and Pieties*, ed. Abby Day. Farnham: Ashgate, 55–74.

Francis-Dehqani Gulnar, Eleanor. 2004. 'The Gendering of Missionary Imperialism: The Search for an Integrated Methodology'. In *Gender, Religion and Diversity: Cross Cultural Perspectives*, ed. Ursula King and Tina Beattie. London: Continuum, 124–37.

Fraser, Ian. 2007. *Dialectics of the Self: Transcending Charles Taylor*. Exeter: Imprint Academic.

Freese, Jeremy. 2004. 'Risk Preferences and Gender Differences in Religiousness: Evidence from the World Values Survey'. *Review of Religious Research* 46(1): 88–91.

Freese, Jeremy and James D. Montgomery. 2007. 'The Devil Made Her Do It: Evaluating Risk Preference as an Explanation of Sex Differences in Religiousness'. In *Advances in Group Processes: The Social Psychology of Gender*, ed. Shelley J. Correll. Oxford: Elsevier, 187–230.

Friedan, Betty. 1963. *The Feminine Mystique*. New York and London: Norton.

Furseth, Inger. 2005. 'From "Everything Has a Meaning" to "I Want to Believe in Something": Religious Change Between Two Generations of Women in Norway'. *Social Compass* 52 (2): 157–68.

Gell, Alfred. 1992. *The Anthropology of Time: Cultural Constructions of Temporal Maps and Images*. Oxford: Berg.

Gell, Alfred. 1998. *Art and Agency: An Anthropological Theory*. Oxford: Oxford University Press.

Gennep, Arnold van. 1960. *The Rites of Passage*. Chicago: Chicago University Press.

Gershuny, Jonathan. 1983. *Social Innovation and the Division of Labour*. Oxford: Oxford University Press.

Giddens, Anthony. 1979. *Central Problems in Social Theory: Action, Structure, and Contradiction in Social Analysis*. Berkeley: University of California Press.

Giddens, Anthony. 1984. *The Constitution of Society: Outline of the Theory of Structuration*. Cambridge: Polity Press.

Gillespie, Joanna B. 1992. 'Gender and Generations in Congregations'. In *Episcopal Women: Gender, Spirituality, and Commitment in an American Mainline Denomination*, ed. Catherine, M. Prelinger. New York: Oxford University Press, 167–221.

Gilligan, Carol. 1982. *In a Different Voice: Psychological Theory and Women's Development*. Cambridge, MA: Harvard University Press.

Gilroy, Paul. 1987. *There Ain't No Black in the Union Jack*. London: Hutchinson.

Giordan, Giuseppe and William H. Swatos, Jr. 2011. *Religion, Spirituality and Everyday Practice*. Dordrecht and New York: Springer.

Giordan, Giuseppe and Linda Woodhead. 2015. *A Sociology of Prayer*. Farnham and Burlington, VT: Ashgate.

Giordan, Giuseppe and Linda Woodhead. 2015. *A Sociology of Prayer*. Farnham and Burlington, VT: Ashgate.

Glenn, Norval. 1976. 'Cohort Analysts' Futile Quest: Statistical Attempts to Separate Age, Period and Cohort Effects'. *American Sociological Review*, 41: 900–4.

Glock, Charles Y. and Rodney Stark. 1965. *Religion and Society in Tension*. Chicago: Rand McNally.

Gordon-Carter, Glynne. 2003. *The Church of England's Response to Institutional Racism Church of England. Committee for Minority Ethnic Anglican Concerns*. London: Church House.

Greer, Germaine. 1970. *The Female Eunuch*. London: MacGibbon and Kee.

Griffith, Marie R. 1997. *God's Daughters: Evangelical Women and The Power of Submission*. Berkeley: University of California Press.

Gross, Rita M. 2004. 'Where Have We Been? Where Do We Need to Go to? Women's Studies and Gender in Religion and Feminist Theology'. In *Gender, Religion and Diversity: Cross Cultural Perspectives*. London: Continuum, ed. Ursula King and Tina Beattie. London: Continuum, 17–27.

Gubrium, Jaber F. and James A. Holstein (eds.). 2003. *Postmodern Interviewing*. Thousand Oaks, CA, London, and New Delhi: Sage.

Guest, M. 2004. '"Friendship, Fellowship and Acceptance": The Discourse of a Thriving Evangelical Congregation'. In *Congregational Studies in the UK: Christianity in a Post-Christian Context*, ed. Matthew Guest, Karen Tusting, and Linda Woodhead. Farnham: Ashgate, 71–84.

Guibernau, Montserrat. 2013. *Belonging: Solidarity and Division in Modern Societies*. Cambridge: Polity Press.

Gunderson, Joan R. 1992. 'Women and the Parallel Church: A View from Congregations'. In *Episcopal Women: Gender, Spirituality, and Commitment in an American Mainline Denomination*, ed. Catherine M. Prelinger. New York: Oxford University Press, 111–63.

Gupta, Akhil and James Ferguson. 1992. 'Beyond "Culture": Space, Identity, and the Politics of Difference'. *Cultural Anthropology* 7 (1) (February): 6–23.

Hagan, John, John Simpson, and A. R. Gillis. 1987. 'Class in the Household: A Power-Control Theory of Gender and Delinquency'. *American Journal of Sociology* 92 (4): 788–816.

Halbwachs, Maurice. 1992. *On Collective Memory*. Chicago: University of Chicago.

Hall, Peter A. 1999. 'Social Capital in Britain'. *British Journal of Political Science* 29 (3): 417–62.

Hall, Stuart. 1978. *Policing the Crisis: Mugging, the State, and Law and Order.* London: Macmillan.

Hallowell, A. Irving. 1960. 'Ojibwa Ontology, Behavior, and World View'. In *Culture in History: Essays in Honor of Paul Radin*, ed. Stanley Diamond. New York: Columbia University Press, 19–52.

Hammersley, Martyn and Paul Atkinson. 1995. *Ethnography: Principles in Practice.* London: Routledge.

Harrison, Brian. 2010. *Finding a Role: The United Kingdom.* Oxford: Clarendon.

Harvey, Graham. 2013. *Food, Sex and Strangers: Understanding Religion as Everyday Life.* Durham: Acumen.

Heelas, Paul, Linda Woodhead, Benjamin Seel, Bronislaw Szersynski, and Karin Tusting. 2005. *The Spiritual Revolution: Why Religion is Giving Way to Spirituality.* Oxford: Blackwell.

Herberg, Will. 1955. *Protestant-Catholic-Jew.* Garden City, NJ: Anchor.

Hervieu-Leger, Danièle. 2000. *Religion as a Chain of Memory.* Cambridge: Polity Press.

Hesse-Biber Nagy, Sharlene and Patricia Lina Leavy. 2007. *Feminist Research Practice.* Thousand Oaks, CA, London, and New Delhi: Sage Publications.

Hillery, George. 1995. 'Definitions of Community: Areas of Agreement'. *Rural Sociology* 20 (1): 111–22.

Hochschild, Arlie and Anne Machung. 1990. *The Second Shift: Working Parents and the Revolution at Home.* Berkeley and London: University of California Press.

Hochschild, Arlie Russell. 2003 [1983]. *The Managed Heart: Commercialization of Human Feeling.* Berkeley, Los Angeles, and London: University of California Press.

Hoffmann, John. 2009. 'Gender Risk and Religiousness: Can Power Control Provide the Theory'. *Journal for the Scientific Study of Religion* 48 (2): 232–40.

Hoge, Dean R. and Jackson W. Carroll. 1978. 'Determinants of Commitment and Participation in Suburban Protestant Churches'. *Journal for the Scientific Study of Religion* 17 (2): 107–27.

Hoge, Dean R., Gregory H. Petrillo, and Ella I. Smith. 1982. 'Transmission of Religious and Social Values from Parents to Teenage Children'. *Journal of Marriage and the Family* 44 (3): 569–80.

Howe, Neil and William Strauss. 1991. *Generations: The History of America's Future 1584–2069.* New York: William Morrow & Sons.

Howe, Neil and William Strauss. 1993. *Thirteenth Generation: Abort, Retry, Ignore, Fail?* New York: Vintage Books.

Howe, Neil and William Strauss. 2000. *Millennials Rising.* New York: Vintage Books.

Hunt, Stephen. 2014. 'Ordinary Lives and Grand Schemes: An Anthropology of Everyday Religion', *Journal of Contemporary Religion* 29 (1): 158–60.

James, William. 1982 [1903]. *The Varieties of Religious Experience: A Study in Human Nature.* Harmondsworth and New York: Penguin Books.

Jay, Nancy. 1992. *Throughout Generations Forever: Sacrifice, Religion and Paternity.* Chicago: University of Chicago Press.

Jenkins, Richard. 1997. *Rethinking Ethnicity.* London: Sage.

Jenkins, Timothy. 1999. *Religion in English Everyday Life: An Ethnographic Approach.* New York and Oxford: Berghahn Books.

Jeremiah, Anderson H. M. 2015. 'Anglicans in South Asia: Life in the Midst of Religious Marginality'. In *Contemporary Issues in the Worldwide Anglican Communion: Powers and Pieties*, ed. Abby Day. Farnham: Ashgate, 191–212.

Johnson, Paul E. 1978. *A Shopkeeper's Millennium: Society and Revivals in Rochester, New York, 1815–1837.* New York: Hill and Wang.

Keane, Webb. 2007. *Christian Moderns: Freedom and Fetish in the Mission Encounter.* Berkeley and Los Angeles: University of California Press.

Keenan, Michael. 2015. 'Conditional Love? Assimilation and the Construction of "Acceptable Homosexuality" in Anglicanism'. In *Contemporary Issues in the Worldwide Anglican Communion: Powers and Pieties*, ed. Abby Day. Farnham: Ashgate, 95–112.

Keller, Mary. 2004. 'Race and Gendered Perspectives: Towards the Epidermalization of Subjectivity in Religious Studies Theory'. In *Gender, Religion and Diversity: Cross Cultural Perspectives*, ed. Ursula King and Tina Beattie. London: Continuum, 79–97.

King, Ursula and Tina Beattie (eds.). 2004. *Gender, Religion and Diversity: Cross Cultural Perspectives.* London: Continuum.

Klatch, Rebecca E. 1999. *A Generation Divided: The New Left, the New Right and the 1960s.* Berkeley, Los Angeles, and London: University of California Press.

Koopmans, Rauud. 1993. 'The Dynamics of Protest Waves: West Germany 1965 to 1989'. *American Sociological Review* 58: 637–58.

Kynaston, David. 2009. *Family Britain 1951–57.* London: Bloomsbury.

Latour, Bruno. 2005. *Reassembling the Social: An Introduction to Actor-Network-Theory.* Oxford: Oxford University Press.

Laufer, Robert S. and Vern L. Bengston. 1974. 'Generations, Aging and Social Stratification: On the Development of Generational Units'. *Journal of Social Issues* 30 (3): 181–205.

Lawes, Barbara and Louise Vincer. 1998. 'The Mothers Unions of the Future'. In *Anglicanism: A Global Communion*, ed. Andrew Wingate, Kevin Ward, Carrie Pemberton, and Wilson Sitshebo. London: Mowbray, 377–84.

Leach, Edmund. 1971. 'Two Essays Concerning the Symbolic Representation of Time'. In *Rethinking Anthropology*, ed. Edmund Leach. London: The Athlone Press, University of London, 124–36.

Lefebvre, Henri. 1991. *The Production of Space*. Oxford: Oxford University Press.

Lewis, Jane. 1992. 'Gender and the Development of Welfare Regimes'. *Journal of European Social Policy* 2 (3): 159–73.

Lin, Nan. 2001. *Social Capital: A Theory of Social Structure and Action*. New York: Cambridge University Press.

Lin, Nan, Karen S. Cook, and Ronald S. Burt (eds.). 2001. *Social Capital: Theory and Research*. New York: Aldine de Gruyter.

Lindquist, Galina and Simon Coleman. 2008. 'Introduction: Against Belief?'. *Social Analysis* 52 (1): 1–18.

Lipsky, David and Alexander Abrahms. 1994. *Late Boomers*. New York: Times Books.

Livingstone, Elizabeth A. (ed.). 1977. *The Concise Dictionary of the Christian Church*. Oxford: Oxford University Press.

Lukes, Steven. 2005. *Power: A Radical View*. Basingstoke: Palgrave Macmillan.

Lynch, Gordon. 2002. *After Religion: 'Generation X' and the Search for Meaning*. London: Darton, Longman, and Todd Ltd.

Lynch, Gordon. 2007. *The New Spirituality: Progressive Faith in the Twenty-First Century*. London: I.B.Tauris.

Lynch, Gordon. 2012. *The Sacred in the Modern World*. Oxford: Oxford University Press.

McCloud, Sean. 2007. *Divine Hierarchies: Class in American Religion and Religious Studies*. Chapel Hill, NC: The University of North Carolina Press

McGavran, Donald A. 1980. *Understanding Church Growth*. Grand Rapids, MI: Eerdmans.

McGuire, Meredith B. 2008. *Lived Religion: Faith and Practice in Everyday Life*. Oxford and New York: Oxford University Press.

McKenzie, Joanne. 2015. 'A Different Class? Anglican Evangelical Leaders' Perspectives on Social Class'. In *Contemporary Issues in the Worldwide Anglican Communion: Powers and Pieties*, ed. Abby Day. Farnham: Ashgate, 169–90.

McKinnon, Andrew M. 2010. 'Elective Affinities of the Protestant Ethic: Weber and the Chemistry of Capitalism'. *Sociological Theory* 28 (1): 108–26.

McKinnon, Andrew and Christopher Craig Brittain. 2015. 'Anglicans in a Globalizing World: The Contradictions of Communion'. In *Contemporary Issues in the Worldwide Anglican Communion: Powers and Pieties*, ed. Abby Day. Farnham: Ashgate, 113–28.

McKinnon, Susan and Fenella Cannell (eds.). 2013. *Vital Relations: Modernity and the Persistent Life of Kinship*. Santa Fe, NM: School for Advanced Research Press.

McLeod, Hugh. 2007. *The Religious Crisis of the 1960s*. Oxford: Oxford University Press.

Mahedy, William and Bernardi, Janet. 1994. *A Generation Alone*. Downers Grove, IL: InterVarsity Press.

Mahmood, Saba. 2005. *The Politics of Piety: The Islamic Revival and the Feminist Subject*. Princeton, NJ and Oxford: Princeton University Press.

Malinowski, Bronislaw. 1926. *Myth in Primitive Psychology*. London: Norton.

Malinowski, Bronislaw. 1961 [1922]. *Argonauts of the Western Pacific*. New York: E. P. Dutton.

Mann, Michael. 2012. *The Sources of Social Power*. Cambridge and New York: Cambridge University Press.

Mannheim, Karl. 1952. *The Problem of Generations in the Sociology of Knowledge*. London: Routledge.

Manville, Julie. 1997. 'The Gendered Organization of an Australian Anglican Parish'. *Sociology of Religion* 58 (1): 25–38.

Marcus, George E. 1995. 'Ethnography in/of the World System: The Emergence of Multi-Sited Ethnography'. *Annual Review of Anthropology* 24: 95–117.

Markham, Ian, S., James Barney Hawkins IV, Justyn Terry, and Leslie Nuñez Steffensen (eds.). 2013. *Wiley-Blackwell Companion to the Anglican Communion*. Oxford: Wiley-Blackwell.

Martin, Emily. 1991. 'The Egg and the Sperm: How Science Has Constructed a Romance Based on Stereotypical Male-Female Roles'. *Signs* 16 (3): 485–501.

Marx, Karl and Friedrich Engels. 1948. *The Communist Manifesto*. New York, International Publishers.

Mason, Michael, Andrew Singleton, and Ruth Webber. 2007. *The Spirit of Generation Y*. Melbourne: John Garratt.

Mason, Michael C. 2013. 'Making the Sacred Real'. In *Annual Review of the Sociology of Religion*, vol. 4, *Prayer in Religion and Spirituality*, ed. Giuseppe Giordan and Linda Woodhead. Leiden: Brill, 9–26.

Mason, Michael C. 2015. 'For Youth, Prayer is Relationship'. In *A Sociology of Prayer*, ed. Giuseppe Giordan and Linda Woodhead. Farnham and Burlington, VT: Ashgate, 25–48.

Massey, Doreen B. 2005. *For Space*. London, Thousand Oaks, CA, and New Delhi: Sage.

Matthews, Glenna. 1987. *'Just a Housewife', the Rise and Fall of Domesticity in America*. New York and Oxford: Oxford University Press.

Mauss, Marcel. 1935. 'Techniques of the Body'. *Journal de Psychologie Normal et Patholigique*, AnnCe XXXII: 271–93.

Mauss, Marcel. 1954. *The Gift: Forms and Functions of Exchange in Archaic Societies*. Glencoe, IL: Free Press.

Mauss, Marcel. 2003. *On Prayer*. New York: Berghahn Books.

Mellor Philip A. and Chris Shilling. 2010. 'Body Pedagogics and the Religious Habitus: a New Direction for the Sociological Study of Religion'. *Religion* 40: 27–38.

Middlemiss Lé Mon, Martha. 2009. *The In-between Church: A Study of the Church of England's Role in Society through the Prism of Welfare.* Acta Universitatis Upsaliensis, *Studies in Religion and Society* 2. Uppsala: Uppsala University Press.

Miles, Margaret R. 1992. 'Theory, Theology and Episcopal Churchwomen'. In *Episcopal Women: Gender, Spirituality, and Commitment in an American Mainline Denomination*, ed. Caroline M. Prelinger. New York: Oxford University Press, 330–44.

Miller, Alan S. and John Hoffmann. 1995. 'Risk And Religion: An Explanation of Gender Differences in Religiosity'. *Journal for the Scientific Study of Religion* 34 (1): 63–75.

Miller, Alan S. and Rodney Stark. 2002. 'Gender and Religiousness: Can Socialization Explanations Be Saved?'. *American Journal of Sociology* 107 (6): 1399–423.

Miller, Daniel. 2008. *The Comfort of Things.* Cambridge: Polity.

Miller, Eleanor M. and Carrie Yang Costello. 2001. 'The Limits of Biological Determinism'. *American Sociological Review*, 66 (4): 592–8.

Milligan, Christine and Conradson, David (eds.). 2006. *Geographies of Voluntarism: New Spaces of Health, Welfare and Governance.* Bristol: Policy Press.

Mintz, Sidney W. and Christine M. Du Bois. 2002. 'The Anthropology of Food and Eating'. *Annual Review of Anthropology* 31: 99–119.

Mishler, Elliot G. 1991. *Research Interviewing: Context and Narrative.* Cambridge, MA: Harvard University Press.

Mombo, Esther. 1998. 'Resisting Vumilia Theology: The Church and Violence against Women in Kenya'. In *Anglicanism: A Global Communion.* ed. Andrew Wingate, Kevin Ward, Carrie Pemberton, and Wilson Sitshebo. London: Mowbray, 219–24.

Morgan, David (ed.). 2010. *Religion and Material Culture: The Matter of Belief.* New York and London: Routledge.

Mukhopadhyay, Carol C. and Patricia L. Higgins. 1988. 'Anthropological Studies of Women's Status Revisited 1977–1987'. *Annual Review of Anthropology* 17: 461–95.

Nason-Clark, Nancy. 1987. 'Ordaining Women as Priests: Religious vs. Sexist Explanations for Clerical Attitudes'. *Sociology of Religion* 48 (3): 259–73.

Nason-Clark, Nancy and Catherine Holtmann. 2015. 'Naming the Abuse, Establishing Networks and Forging Negotiations: Contemporary Christian Women and the Ugly Subject of Domestic Violence'. In *Contemporary Issues in the Worldwide Anglican Communion: Powers and Pieties*, ed. Abby Day. Farnham: Ashgate, 75–94.

Needham, Rodney. 1972. *Belief, Language and Experience.* Chicago: Chicago University Press.

Neal, Sarah and Karim Murji. 2015. 'Editors' Introduction'. *Sociology* 49: 811–19.

Neitz, Mary Jo. 2004. 'Gender and Culture: Challenges to the Sociology of Religion'. *Sociology of Religion* 65 (4): 391–402.

Nelson, Rob and Jon Cowan. 1994. *Revolution X*. New York: Penguin.

Norris, Pippa and Ronald Inglehart. 2004. *Sacred and Secular: Religion and Politics Worldwide*. Cambridge: Cambridge University Press.

Nunes, Maria José F. Rosaldo. 1996. 'Women's Voices in Latin American Theology'. In *The Power of Naming: A Concilium Reader in Feminist Liberation Theology*, ed. Elisabeth Schüssler Fiorenza. Maryknoll, NY: Orbis Books and London: SCM Press, 14–26.

Nynäs, Peter and Mika T. Lissander. 2015. 'LGBT Activism and Reflexive Religion: a Case Study from Finland in Light of Social Movements Theory'. *Journal of Contemporary Religion* 30 (3): 453–71.

Oakley, Ann. 1981. 'Interviewing Women: A Contradiction in Terms'. In *Doing Feminist Research*, ed. Helen Roberts. London: Routledge & Kegan Paul, 30–61.

Oakley, Ann. 2016. 'Interviewing Women Again: Power, Time and the Gift'. *Sociology* 50: 195–213.

Öberg, Britt-Marie, Anna-Liisa Närvänen, Elisabet Näsman, and Erik Olssen. 2004. *Changing Worlds and the Aging Subject: Dimensions in the Study of Aging*. Aldershot and Burlington, VT: Ashgate.

Oduyoye, Mercy Amba. 1996. 'Poverty and Motherhood'. In *The Power of Naming: A Concilium Reader in Feminist Liberation Theology*, ed. Elisabeth Schüssler Fiorenza. Maryknoll, NY: Orbis Books and London: SCM Press, 124–31.

Offen, Karen. 1988. 'Defining Feminism: A Comparative Historical Approach'. *Signs* 14 (1): 119–57.

Ortner, Sherry B. 1974. 'Is Female to Male as Nature is to Culture?'. In *Woman, Culture, and Society*, ed. M. Z. Rosaldo and L. Lamphere. Stanford, CA: Stanford University Press, 68–87.

Ortner, Sherry B. 1995. 'Resistance and the Problem of Ethnographic Refusal'. *Comparative Studies in Society and History* 37 (1): 173–93.

Otto, Rudolph. 1958. *The Idea of the Holy*. New York: Oxford University Press.

Ozorak, Elizabeth, W. 1996. 'The Power, But Not the Glory: How Women Empower Themselves Through Religion'. *Journal for the Scientific Study of Religion* 35 (1): 17–29.

Palmer, Phyllis. 1991. *Domesticity and Dirt: Housewives and Domestic Servants in the United States, 1920–1945*. Philadelphia, PA: Temple University Press.

Pardun, Carol J. and Kathy B. McKee. 1995. 'Strange Bedfellows: Symbols of Religion and Sexuality on MTV'. *Youth and Society* 26 (4): 438–49.

Parker, Stephen and Tom Lawson (eds.). 2012. *God and War: The Church of England and Armed Conflict in the Twentieth Century*. Farnham and Burlington, VT: Ashgate.

Parkin, Robert and Linda Stone (eds.). 2006. *Kinship and Family: An Anthropological Reader*. Malden, MA and Oxford: Blackwell.

Parry, Jonathan. 1986. 'The Gift, the Indian Gift and the "Indian Gift"'. *Man* (New Series) 21 (3): 453–73.

Peberdy, Alyson. 1985. *A Part of Life*. London: The Movement for the Ordination of Women.

Peiris, Jayasiri. 1998. 'Church in Sri Lanka and Relations With Other Faiths'. In *Anglicanism: A Global Communion*, ed. Andrew Wingate, Kevin Ward, Carrie Pemberton, and Wilson Sitshebo. London: Mowbray, 337–40.

Pemberton, Carrie and Christina Rees. 1998. 'Five Years In: Where are the Women in the Church of England'. In *Anglicanism: A Global Communion*, ed. Andrew Wingate, Kevin Ward, Carrie Pemberton, and Wilson Sitshebo. London: Mowbray, 22–6.

Percy, Martyn. 2013. *Anglicanism: Confidence, Commitment and Communion*. Farnham: Ashgate.

Percy, Martyn. 2015. 'Theological Education and Formation for an Uncommon Occupation'. In *Contemporary Issues in the Worldwide Anglican Communion: Powers and Pieties*, ed. Abby Day. Farnham: Ashgate, 229–43.

Phillips, Dewi Z. 1965. *The Concept of Prayer*. London: Routledge & Kegan Paul.

Picton, Hervé. 2015. *A Short History of the Church of England from the Reformation to the Present Day*. Newcastle upon Tyne: Cambridge Scholars Publishing.

Polanyi, Michael. 1966. *The Tacit Dimension*. Chicago: University of Chicago Press.

Prelinger, Caroline M. (ed.). 1992. *Episcopal Women: Gender, Spirituality, and Commitment in an American Mainline Denomination*. New York: Oxford University Press.

Pui-Lan, Kwok. 1996. 'The Image of the "White Lady": Gender and Race in Christian Mission'. In *The Power of Naming: A Concilium Reader in Feminist Liberation Theology*, ed. Elisabeth Schüssler Fiorenza. Maryknoll, NY: Orbis Books and London: SCM Press, 250–8.

Putnam, Robert D. 2000. *Bowling Alone: The Collapse and Revival of American Community*. New York: Simon & Schuster.

Putnam, Robert D. 2010. *American Grace: How Religion Divides and Unites Us*. New York: Simon & Schuster.

Rake, Katherine. 2001. 'Gender and New Labour's Social Policies'. *Journal of Social Policy* 30 (2): 209–31.

Rakoczy, Susan. 2004. *In Her Name: Women Doing Theology*. Pietermaritzburg: Cluster Publications.

Rao, Krupaveni Prakash and Julie Lipp-Nathaniel. 1998. 'Women within Church and Society in India'. In *Anglicanism: A Global Communion*, ed.

Andrew Wingate, Kevin Ward, Carrie Pemberton, and Wilson Sitshebo. London: Mowbray, 258–63.

Raphael, Melissa. 1996. *Theology and Embodiment: The Post-Patriarchal Reconstruction of Female Sacrality.* Sheffield: Sheffield Academic Press.

Redfern, Catherine and Kristin Aune. 2010. *Reclaiming the F Word: The New Feminist Movement.* London: Zed Books.

Regnerus, Mark D., Christian Smith, and Brad Smith. 2004. 'Social Context in the Development of Adolescent Religiosity'. *Applied Development Science* 8 (1): 27–38.

Ribble, Constance Mary. 1952. *Altar Guild Manual.* Available at: <http://www.acanedio.org/library/altarguildmanual.pdf>, last accessed 8.4.14.

Riesman, David and Mark Benney. 1956. *The Interview in Social Research.* Chicago: University of Chicago Press

Riggs, Anne and Bryan S. Turner. 2000. 'Pie-Eyed Optimists: Baby Boomers the Optimistic Generation?'. *Social Indicators Research* 52 (1): 73–93.

Riley, Matilda White. 1971. 'Social Gerontology and the Age Stratification of Society'. *The Gerontologist* 11 (1): 79–87.

Robbins. Joel. 2013. 'Beyond the Suffering Subject: Toward an Anthropology of the Good'. *Journal of the Royal Anthropological Institute* (New Series) 19: 447–62.

Robinson, Terrie. 2013. 'Women in the Anglican Communion'. In *Wiley-Blackwell Companion to the Anglican Communion,* ed. Ian S. Markham, James Barney Hawkins IV, Justyn Terry, and Leslie Nuñez Steffensen. Oxford: Wiley-Blackwell.

Roberts, Keith A. and David Yamane. 2012. *Religion in Sociological Perspective,* 5th edn. London: Sage

Roof, Wade Clark. 1993. *A Generation of Seekers.* New York: Harper Collins.

Roof, Wade Clark. 1999. *Spiritual Marketplace.* Princeton, NJ: Princeton University Press.

Roof, Wade Clarke and William McKinney. 1987. *American Mainline Religion.* New Brunswick: Rutgers University Press.

Rose, Gillian. 1993. *Feminism and Geography: The Limits of Geographical Knowledge.* Cambridge: Polity Press.

Roth, Louise Marie and Jeffrey C. Kroll. 2007. 'Risky Business: Assessing Risk Preference Explanations for Gender Differences in Religiosity'. *American Sociological Review* 72 (2): 205–20.

Roxburgh, Margaret, J. 1958. *Women's Work in the Church of England, A Consideration of the Last Hundred Years.* London: n.p.

Ruel, Malcolm. 1982. 'Christians as Believers'. In *Religious Organization and Religious Experience,* ed. J. Davis. Asa Monograph 21. London and New York: Academic Press, 9–32.

Ruether, Rosemary Radford. 1993 [1983]. *Sexism and God-Talk: Toward a Feminist Theology.* Boston, MA: Beacon Press.

Ruether, Rosemary Radford and Rosemary Skinner Keller (eds.). 1986. *Women and Religion in America*. San Francisco, CA: Harper & Row.

Rushkoff, Douglas. 1994. *The GenX Reader*. New York: Ballantine.

Ryder, Normon. 1965. 'The Cohort as a Concept in the Study of Social Change'. *American Sociological Review* 30 (6): 843–61.

Santer, Henriette. 1996. 'Stereotyping the Sexes in Society and in the Church'. In *The Power of Naming: A Concilium Reader in Feminist Liberation Theology*, ed. Elisabeth Schüssler Fiorenza. Maryknoll, NY: Orbis Books and London: SCM Press, 139–49.

Savage, Mike, Fiona Devine, Niall Cunningham, Mark Taylor, Yaojun Li, Johs Hjellbrekke, Brigitte Le Roux, Sam Friedman, and Andrew Miles. 2013. 'A New Model of Social Class: Findings from the BBC's Great British Class Survey Experiment'. *Sociology* 47 (2): 21–5.

Savage, Sara, Sylvia Collins-Mayo, Bob Mayo, and Graham Cray. 2006. *Making Sense of Generation Y: The Worldview of 15–25-Year-Olds*. London: Church House Publishing.

Schielke, Samuli and Liza Debevec (eds.). 2012. *Ordinary Lives and Grand Schemes: An Anthropology of Everyday Religion*. EASA (European Association of Social Anthropologists) Series 18. New York and Oxford: Berghahn Books.

Schneider, David. 1980. *American Kinship: A Cultural Account*. Chicago: Chicago University Press.

Schwadel, Philip. 2008. 'Poor Teenagers' Religion'. *Sociology of Religion* 69 (2): 125–49.

Skeggs, Beverley. 1997. *Formations of Class and Gender: Becoming Respectable*. London: Sage.

Skeggs, Beverley. 2004. *Class, Self, Culture*. London: Routledge.

Smith, Christian and Melina Lundquist Denton. 2005. *Soul Searching: The Religious and Spiritual Lives of American Teenagers*. Oxford: Oxford University Press.

Smith, Christian and Robert Faris. 2005. 'Socioeconomic Inequality in the American Religious System: An Update and Assessment'. *Journal for the Scientific Study of Religion* 44 (1): 95–104.

Stark, Rodney. 1999. 'Micro Foundations of Religion: A Revised Theory'. *Sociological Theory* 17 (3): 264–89.

Stark, Rodney. 2002. 'Physiology and Faith: Addressing the "Universal" Gender Difference in Religious Commitment'. *Journal for the Scientific Study of Religion* 41 (3): 495–507.

Stark, Rodney and Roger Finke. 2000. *Acts of Faith: Explaining the Human Side of Religion*. Berkeley: University of California Press.

Strathern, Marilyn. 1984. 'Domesticity and the Denigration of Women'. In *Rethinking Women's Roles: Perspectives From the Pacific*, ed. Denise O'Brien and Sharon W. Tiffany. Berkeley: University of California Press, 13–31.

Stringer, Adrian. 2015. 'Addressing the Problem of Socio-Economic-Classification'. In *Contemporary Issues in the Worldwide Anglican Communion: Powers and Pieties*, ed. Abby Day. Farnham: Ashgate, 149–68.

Stringer, Martin D. 2008. *Contemporary Western Ethnography and the Definition of Religion*. London: Continuum.

Stromberg, Peter G. 1986. *Symbols of Community: The Cultural System of a Swedish Church*. Tucson, AZ: University of Arizona Press.

Stromberg, Peter G. 2008. *Language and Self-Transformation: A Study of the Christian Conversion Narrative*. Cambridge: Cambridge University Press.

Sullins, Donald, Paul. 2006. 'Gender and Religion: Deconstructing Universality, Constructing Complexity'. *American Journal of Sociology* 112 (3): 838–80.

Swartz, Oswald. 1998. 'New Wine, Old Wineskins: Possibilities for a Rural Diocese in a Changing Society'. In *Anglicanism: A Global Communion*, ed. Andrew Wingate, Kevin Ward, Carrie Pemberton, and Wilson Sitshebo. New York: Church Publishing and London: Mowbray, 182–8.

Sykes, Stephen and John Booty (eds.). 1988. *The Study of Anglicanism*. London: SPCK/Fortress.

Taylor, Charles. 2007. *A Secular Age*. Cambridge, MA: Belknap Press of Harvard University.

Te Paa, Jenny Plane. 2008. 'Anglican Identity and Theological Formation in Aotearoa New Zealand'. *Journal of Anglican Studies* 6 (1): 49–58.

Thrasher, Frederic Milton. 1927. *The Gang*. Chicago: Phoenix Books.

Tilley, James, and Anthony Heath. 2007. 'The Decline of British National Pride'. *The British Journal of Sociology* 58 (4): 661–78.

Trisk, Janet and Luke Pato. 2008. 'Theological Education and Anglican Identity in South Africa'. *Journal of Anglican Studies* 6 (1): 59–68.

Trouillot, Michel-Rolph. 1991. 'Anthropology and the Savage Slot: The Poetics and Politics of Otherness'. In *Recapturing Anthropology: Working in the Present*, ed. R. G. Fox. Santa Fe, NM: School of American Research Press, 17–24.

Trouillot, Michel-Rolph. 2003. *Global Transformations: Anthropology and the Modern World*. New York: Palgrave Macmillan.

Trzebiatowska, Marta and Steve Bruce. 2012. *Why Are Women More Religious Than Men?* Oxford: Oxford University Press.

Turner, Victor. 1969. *The Ritual Process: Structure and Anti-Structure*. New York: Aldine Publishers.

Turner, Victor. 1977. 'Symbols in African Ritual'. In *Symbolic Anthropology: A Reader in the Study of Symbols and Meanings*, ed. J. L. Dolgin, D. S. Kemnitzer, and D. M. Schneider. New York: Columbia University Press, 183–94.

Voas, David and Alasdair Crockett. 2005. 'Religion in Britain: Neither Believing nor Belonging'. *Sociology* 39 (1): 11–28.

Voas, David and Laura Watt. 2014. 'Numerical Change in Church Attendance: National, Local and Individual Factors'. *The Church Growth Research Programme Report on Strands 1 and 2, Church of England*, <http://www.churchgrowthresearch.org.uk/progress_findings_reports> last accessed 8.9.16.

Walby, Sylvia. 1990. *Theorizing Patriarchy*. Oxford: Blackwell.

Walter, Tony and Grace Davie. 1998. 'The Religiosity of Women in the Modern West'. *The British Journal of Sociology* 49 (4): 640–60.

Wassmann, Jurg. 1995. 'The Final Requiem for the Omniscient Informant? An Interdisciplinary Approach to Everyday Cognition'. *Culture and Psychology* 1 (2): 167–201.

Weber, Max. 1922. *The Sociology of Religion*. Boston, MA: Beacon Press.

West, Candace and Don H. Zimmerman. 1987. 'Doing Gender'. *Gender and Society* 1 (2): 125–51.

White, Harrison C. 1992. *Identity and Control: A Structural Theory of Social Action*. Princeton, NJ: Princeton University Press.

Wild, Emma. 1998. 'Working with Women in the Congo'. In *Anglicanism: A Global Communion*, ed. Andrew Wingate, Kevin Ward, Carrie Pemberton, and Wilson Sitshebo. London: Mowbray, 281–6.

Williams, Raymond. 1961. *The Long Revolution*. Harmondsworth: Penguin.

Williams, Raymond and Michael Orrom. 1954. *The Restructuring of American Religion: Society and Faith since World War II*. Princeton, NJ: Princeton University Press.

Wilson, Bryan. 1966. *Religion in Secular Society*. London: C.A. Watts & Co. Ltd.

Wingate, Andrew, Kevin Ward, Carrie Pemberton, and Wilson Sitshebo (eds.). 1998. *Anglicanism: A Global Communion*. London: Mowbray.

Wink, Paul and Michele Dillon. 2003. 'Religiousness, Spirituality, and Psychosocial Functioning in Late Adulthood: Findings From a Longitudinal Study'. *Psychology and Aging* 18 (4): 916–24.

Wood, Josephine Smith. 1915. *A Manual for Altar Guilds with Suggestions for the Care of the Altar and Altar Linen*. New York: Edwin S. Gorham (Project Canterbury).

Woodhead, Linda. 2000. 'Feminism and the Sociology of Religion: From Gender-Blindness to Gendered Difference'. In *The Blackwell Companion to Sociology of Religion*, ed. Richard Fenn. Oxford: Blackwell, 67–84.

Woodhead, Linda. 2007. 'Gender Differences in Religious Practice and Significance'. In *The Sage Handbook of the Sociology of Religion*, ed. James Beckford and Nicolas J. Demerath III. Los Angeles, CA: Sage, 550–70.

Woodhead, Linda. 2008. 'Gendering Secularization Theory'. *Social Compass* 55 (2): 187–93.

Woodhead, Linda. 2012. 'Introduction'. In *Religion and Change in Modern Britain*, ed. Linda Woodhead and Rebecca Catto. London: Routledge, 1–33.

Woodhead, Linda. 2012. 'Spirituality and Christianity: The Unfolding of a Tangled Relationship'. In *Religion, Spirituality and Everyday Practice*, ed. Giuseppe Giordan and William H. Swatos, Jr. Dordrecht and New York: Springer, 3–21.

Wuthnow, Robert. 1994. *Sharing the Journey: Support Groups and America's New Quest for Community*. New York: Free Press.

Wuthnow, Robert. 1998. *The Restructuring of American Religion: Society and Faith Since World War II*. Princeton, NJ: Princeton University Press.

Yin, Robert K. 2003. *Case Study Research Design and Methods*. Thousand Oaks, CA and London: Sage.

Index

single mothers, marginalisation of 44
sitting in same place 117–18, 149, 160
Smith, Christian 137, 146
social activism 106
social and fund-raising events 158–62
  advertising 168–9
  belonging 158, 161–2
  closure of churches 196
  dances 167–8
  efficiency 159, 166–7, 169, 195
  egalitarians 159–60
  family of the church 169, 174, 195
  food, making and bringing 165–9,
    194–5, 212
  future of the church 202
  halls, holding events in church 160–1
  identity 167–8
  location of events 160–1
  loss of Generation A, consequences
    of 194–5
  loyalty, liability of 200
  over-staffing 166–7, 195
  piety of parties 165–8
  place-making 160–1
  self-circulating economy and
    sales 158, 169–74
  social capital 158, 174–6
  Social Committees 158, 160
  social life, importance of 161–2
  social markers 160
  soft labour 158, 176, 177–80
  spirituality 159
  Sunday services, thanks during 158
  theology 159
  time-wasting 166–7
  United States 44–5, 161–2
  young people, events for 168
social capital
  civic engagement 85
  community, definition of 155
  contacts 174–6
  knowledge 176
  occupations, representation of
    different 175
  social and fund-raising events 158,
    174–6
  social class 148, 150
  soft labour 176
  United States 85, 176
social care *see* carers, women as;
    social work
social class 139, 145–52

attendance at church 145–6, 152
barriers, creation of 151
belief 146–7
belonging 146–7, 149
capital 147–52
conservative evangelicalism 151
culture 147–8
duty and obligation 180
family and community 139,
    145–52, 156
gender 145–6, 149–52
generations 34
Homogenous Unit Principle 151–2
middle-class 28, 145–6
missionary work 43
occupation, defined by 147–8, 150
precariats 56–7, 148, 150
Queen's Chapel and Chapel Royal, St
    James' Palace, attendance
    at 148–50
sect-like people 146
social capital 148, 150
social identity, formation of 147
subordinate femininity, women as
    natural producers of 210
surveys 147–8
transmission of religion 146
United States 146
upper classes 146, 148–9
working class 28, 146, 148, 151–2
social construction
  gender 25, 37, 105, 107, 207
  identity 147
  personhood and time 32–3
  religiosity 207
  self 188–9
social life 17–18, 28, 35, 155–6,
    161–2
social markers 160
social media 35
social movements 106–7
social networks *see also* social capital
  informal networks 146, 154, 176, 211
  insularity 106
  kin relationships 137–8, 146
  overlapping networks 8–9, 163–4
  pew power 163–4
  socio-spatial networks of
    power 163–4
social shifts 7, 157, 181–2 *see also*
    cultural shifts of 1960s
social theory 7, 105–6